AS TEXAS GOES . . .

ALSO BY GAIL COLLINS

When Everything Changed:
The Amazing Journey of American Women from 1960 to the Present

America's Women:
Four Hundred Years of Dolls, Drudges, Helpmates, and Heroines

Scorpion Tongues: Gossip, Celebrity, and American Politics

The Millennium Book (with Dan Collins)

William Henry Harrison

AS TEXAS GOES . . .

HOW THE LONE STAR STATE
HIJACKED THE AMERICAN AGENDA

GAIL COLLINS

Jefferson Madison
Regional Library
Charlottesville, Virginia

LIVERIGHT PUBLISHING CORPORATION

A Division of W. W. Norton & Company

New York • London

Copyright © 2012 by Gail Collins

For information about permission to reproduce selections from this book,
write to Permissions, Liveright Publishing Corporation,
a division of W. W. Norton & Company, Inc.,
500 Fifth Avenue, New York, NY 10110

For information about special discounts for bulk purchases, please contact
W. W. Norton Special Sales at specialsales@wwnorton.com or 800-233-4830

Manufacturing by RR Donnelley, Harrisonburg, VA
Book design by Chris Welch
Production manager: Anna Oler

Library of Congress Cataloging-in-Publication Data

Collins, Gail.
As Texas goes— : how the Lone Star State hijacked the American agenda /
Gail Collins. — 1st ed.
p. cm.
Includes bibliographical references and index.
ISBN 978-0-87140-407-7 (hardcover : alk. paper)
1. Texas—Politics and government—1951– 2. Texas—Social policy.
3. Texas—Economic policy. I. Title.
JK4816.C67 2012
320.60973—dc23

2012007794

Liveright Publishing Corporation
500 Fifth Avenue, New York, N.Y. 10110
www.wwnorton.com

W. W. Norton & Company Ltd.
Castle House, 75/76 Wells Street, London W1T 3QT

1 2 3 4 5 6 7 8 9 0

For Gary, Mary Ann, and Patricia

Contents

AS TEXAS GOES . . .

Prologue

My fascination with Texas began rather suddenly. It was the spring of 2009—you will remember, that was the season when the political right was failing to adjust to the idea of a President Obama. And there was Governor Rick Perry at a Tea Party rally in Austin, publicly toying with the idea that his state might consider seceding.

It was quite a moment. Perry was standing behind a podium with a "Don't Mess With Texas" banner, wearing jeans, his trademark boots, and looking pretty damned ticked off. "Texas has yet to learn submission to any oppression, come from what source it may," he said, quoting the state's great founding father, Sam Houston. When Houston made that remark, he was definitely attempting to break away from the country to which Texas was then attached.

"We didn't like oppression then, we don't like oppression now!" Perry roared to the cheering crowd, some of whom were waving "Secede!" signs. It did sure sound like an Alamo kind of crisis. Their backs were to the wall!

And, important point: this was just a rally about the stimulus package.

It was perhaps the first time the rest of the country had taken notice of the fact that twenty-first-century Texans did not necessarily consider the idea of breaking away to become a separate nation as, um, nuts. We non-Texans were somewhat taken aback. How long had this been going on? Was it something we said?

"We've got a great union," Perry assured reporters after the rally ended. "There's absolutely no reason to dissolve it. But if Washington continues to thumb their noses at the American people, you know, who knows what might come of that?"

Does this sound like a serious commitment to you? Try to imagine a husband telling his wife that he saw absolutely no reason to get a divorce—but if she continued to fail to live up to expectations, who knows what might come of that?

You had to pay attention. Not necessarily to Perry himself, who of course went on to become one of the worst candidates for president in all of American history. But the rally, with its combination of egomania (We're the best!) and paranoia (Don't mess with Texas!), was a near-perfect reflection of the Tea Party's war cry in national politics.

That's not an accident. The more I looked at Texas, which seemed to be having an anti-Obama rally every time a cow mooed, the more important it seemed. Without anyone much noting it, Texas had taken a starring role in the twenty-first-century national political discussion. For one thing, it had the hottest economy—which the rest of us were told we'd better emulate unless we wanted all the local employers to pack up and move to Plano. The reason Perry imagined he could be president was the way Texas had created job growth by hewing to the low-tax-low-regulation ethic that the political right believes should be the model for the entire country. (The model had certain flaws, such as the assumption that every state could scrimp on higher education and just build a large professional class by importing people who went to college in other states. We'll get to that later.)

Then a friend sent me a headline from a Texas news report: "Man Allegedly Beat Woman with Frozen Armadillo." I was totally hooked.

So I started thinking a lot about Texas. Looking back over the last quarter century or so, I was stunned by how much of the national agenda it had produced, for good or ill.

Texas banking laws set the stage for the savings and loan crisis in the 1980s. The 2008 economic meltdown was the product of a financial deregulation that was the work of many hands, but most particularly the paws of Texas senator Phil Gramm. Our energy policy is the way it is in large part because Texas politicians and Texas special interests like it that way. (If the polar ice caps melt, it's not going to be Utah's fault.) Schools from Portland, Oregon, to Portland, Maine, have been remade, reorganized, and sometimes totally upended under a federal law based on Texas education reform. For several generations, our kids have been reading textbooks written with an eye to Texas sensibilities. Texas presidents have led the country into every land war the United States has been involved in since Vietnam.

Texas *runs everything.* Why, then, is it so cranky? Is it because of its long string of well-funded but terrible presidential contenders? True, being the home state of Rick Perry, the "oops" candidate, had to be embarrassing. On the other hand, thanks to the Bushes, there's been a Texan president or vice president for twenty of the last thirty-two years, so the lack of White House access hardly seems like an appropriate subject for sulking. Is it the weather? The state of Washington has terrible weather, and you don't see people there threatening to secede.

The crankiness is actually a source of Texas's political power. The state has a remarkable ability to be two contradictory things at once. As we'll see later, it's a fast-growing, increasingly urban place whose citizens have nevertheless managed to maintain the conviction that they're living in the wide open spaces. And its politicians are skilled at bragging about the wonderful Texas economy and lifestyle while wailing and rending their garments over their helplessness in the hands of the federal Death Star in Washington. You need that sense of victimhood because it creates energy and unity. You can't build a Tea Party on good news.

Another reason the Texas influence on the US is outsized is that the place is just so damned big. The country has other hugely influential large states, like California and New York, but they're not on an upswing. California has more people, but it's hit a bad patch and it's struggling. New York is the media capital and it has Wall Street, but its population is flat. Texas just keeps growing, by leaps and bounds. (Think jackrabbit. It's a good metaphor. A really, really large jackrabbit.)

The huge Texas population—up 4.3 million in a decade—has an enormous impact on the country all by itself. We've got a super-big state with a young citizenry and a very high birth rate. You have to figure that by 2050, the entire United States will have a distinctly Texas cast. The state's ability to rear, educate, and pre-pare all the little Texans to take their place in the national economy is going to be an excellent predictor of how well the whole country will be faring down the line.

We will get into that later, but—spoiler alert—the odds of success would be better if Texas had more control of the teenage birth rate. Did I ever tell you about the time Rick Perry defended abstinence-only sex education by saying that he knew from his own personal experience that abstinence worked? No? Well, I will. Soon.

We're not used to thinking of Texas as a driving force in Ameri-can affairs, but there you are. Even when Democrats held the White House in recent decades, Texans seemed to be holding the reins—reins that were being used mainly to hog-tie the chief executive. Bill Clinton had to deal with two Texans—House majority leader Dick Armey and whip Tom DeLay—whose lasting contribution to American history was mainly the thwarting of the Clinton agenda, particularly health care reform. Barack Obama has been ham-strung by the power of the Tea Party Republicans, whose first big coming-out parties were organized by Armey and whose ideology sprang, as much as from any place coherent, from the thinking of Texas congressman Ron Paul.

In this book, I want to try to show you how Texas has driven the national agenda, and then what it means to have Texas as the Republican model for the entire American economy. But first, in the next few chapters I want to introduce you to Texas and its political history which, no matter how you slice it, is pretty amazing.

You'd imagine a place with a motto like "Don't Mess with Texas" would be a small, scrappy state. But Texas is a *huge*, scrappy state. What could be more unnerving? And really, there's never a dull moment. Take the frozen armadillo situation. I couldn't resist looking into it, and at one point in my research I ran into an officer of wildlife enforcement who assured me that it was illegal to sell a live armadillo in Texas. "Dead armadillos you can sell parts of them," he added. "Make a curio of a little armadillo on his back drinking a bottle of beer."

How could you not want to know more about a state like that, particularly when it appears to have been setting the entire national agenda for decades, while continually howling about how the federal government is pushing it around?

And the people are great. I can attest that I had a wonderful time with everyone I met while I was wandering around, trying to figure out how Texas inspired a national education law which the politicians in Texas now denounce on an almost hourly basis, or why a state that would get more economic benefit than anybody from the health care reform law is so determined to repeal the health care reform law.

Anyhow, that's how I became obsessed with Texas. To paraphrase the old saw about elections and Maine, it really does seem as if these days, as Texas goes, so goes the nation. Whether we like it or not.

PART ONE
TEXAS

GETTING TO KNOW YOU

1

Remember the Alamo

"Sort of a cultural identity thing"

T his is the Republic of Texas seal. On every elevator you can find that seal, and every original doorknob," says the tour guide in the state capitol in Austin. It's a sweaty summer weekday, and the place is crawling with families—a multicultural mix of somber little kids, parents, and seniors, all wielding their cameras at the lofty dome, which rises precisely 14.64 feet higher than the one in Washington DC. At this moment, we are peering from the third floor down into the rotunda, where the big symbol of the Republic of Texas (1836–45) is celebrated in the terrazzo floor.

"There are a couple of other states that have been republics," the guide continues. He is a young man with amazingly long sideburns and a habit of saying "pretty cool." "Vermont was a republic—for like *seven days*."

Actually, fourteen years, although Vermont doesn't dwell on it.

Our little group is mulling the design on the rotunda floor, and someone on the tour wants to know about the five smaller seals surrounding the big symbol of the long-gone republic.

"This is the famous six flags—sort of a cultural identity thing," says the guide.

Besides its nine glorious years of independence, Texas brags that it has been, in its history, a part of France, Spain, Mexico, and the Confederacy, not to mention the United States of America. There is a famous amusement park in Arlington, Texas, that celebrates this six-flags concept. France is sort of a stretch (we are talking about one deeply unsuccessful settlement somewhere near Louisiana), but it's the small, off-center placement of the American flag in the design on the rotunda floor that's seriously unsettling. It's as if Texas's nine years of independence was the center of its story, while its role as part of the United States is a colorful afterthought, like the brief flirtation with the French.

If we want to understand what Texas means to the rest of the country, first we have to understand a little about what Texas means to Texans. The memory that it was once an independent country, and the conviction that it could be again, any time it wants to, weighs heavily in the state mentality. "We are very proud of our Texas history," Rick Perry said in the wake of the secession dustup. "People discuss and debate the issues of can we break ourselves into five states, can we secede, a lot of interesting things that I'm sure Oklahoma and Pennsylvania would love to be able to say about their states, but the fact is, they can't. Because they're not Texas."

The governor's certainty that the rest of us are mooning around wishing we could have secession discussions is sort of touching, in a terrifying kind of way. But he is right that Texans do enjoy having lively exchanges about their state's history. I was once at a dinner party in Austin where I listened to an intense debate about whether Davy Crockett had died fighting at the Alamo, or had been captured and executed later, and I must say I enjoyed that conversation very much. Texas cannot, however, secede. They tried it once, and Abraham Lincoln did not have a positive reaction.

It is true that when the state was annexed the door was left open to dividing itself into five pieces. (If you want to be paranoid, just imagine a Congress with ten senators from Texas.)

The idea that Texans actually want to secede from the union is, no matter what Perry has said, another myth. A Rasmussen poll in 2009 found that only 18 percent of the respondents said they favored breaking away. That's still a tidy number—when you're talking 18 percent in Texas you're talking way over 4 million people. But there is virtually nothing, no matter how crazy, that you can't get about 18 percent of Americans to support if they're in a bad enough mood. In the spring of 2011, 17 percent of likely Republican primary voters said they thought it would be a good idea to nominate Donald Trump for president.

The secession talk is actually just another way of complaining about the federal government. But people in Texas do have a self-consciousness about being *Texan* that you don't generally find elsewhere. "Texans, more so than any other state's citizens, feel something special about their state," Governor Bill Clements once claimed in a letter begging novelist James Michener to write a book about the state's "powerful leaders and rugged individuals whose foresight knew no boundaries." (Remarkably, Michener complied, and brought forth an appropriately mammoth 1,000-plus-page tome of historical fiction, inventively titled *Texas.*)

From an early age, Texas children learn that being Texan makes them special. They study their state's history as part of their fourth- and seventh-grade curriculum. In most public schools, they pledge allegiance to the Texas flag at the start of every day. So does the state legislature. Texas Independence Day, which celebrates the adoption of the declaration of independence from Mexico, is an official state holiday. "Texas! Texas! Texas!" Governor Perry used to yell at his rallies, before they briefly took on a presidential tone. You do not often hear governors yelling "Nebraska! Nebraska! Nebraska!" or "North Dakota! North Dakota!"

I come from Ohio, a fine state which once prided itself on being an incubator of presidents. In fact, when I was in high school I won a patriotic speech contest and was rewarded with the high honor of reciting my composition in front of the tomb of William Henry Harrison. But the speech was about how great it was to be an American, not an Ohioan. And at the time I only had a dim notion that Harrison was the ninth president, since we didn't study Ohio history in school. We certainly didn't pledge allegiance to the Ohio flag—Ohio didn't have a pledge back then, and we wouldn't have recognized the state flag if you'd dropped it on our heads. And try envisioning a bunch of Cincinnatians or Clevelanders running around in "Don't Mess with Ohio" sweatshirts.

"So there's going to be a crisis boiling point"

Pictures of the presidents of the republic and former governors of the state wind around rotunda walls in the state capitol—the newest at the bottom, so that every time there's a replacement, the whole passel has to move. When Rick Perry leaves office, he'll be the fifty-second picture, and all the others will scoot over to make room. Everybody is there: Sam Houston, who's all over the place, actually, and Anson Jones, the final president of the republic, who was so upset at not being given a Senate seat when Texas joined the Union that he went batty and shot himself in the head. And there's the deeply obscure Governor George Wood (1847–49), who is best remembered for never wearing socks.

Farther along, there's Jim Hogg (1891–95), the sometimes-populist who is remembered today mainly for naming his daughter Ima, and James "Pa" Ferguson, whose second term began in 1917 and was somewhat marred by his impeachment. Ferguson's wife, Miriam, universally known to the public as "Ma," is on the wall twice, having taken up the family banner and gotten elected to two nonconsecutive terms, 1925–27 and 1933–35. She's also got a bust down in the rotunda. Following in her husband's footsteps, Ma made a habit of pardoning prisoners at a clip of about 100 a month. Whether you believe this was in return for bribes or to relieve jail overcrowding is an excellent test of the natural optimism of your character.

Then there's W. Lee "Pappy" O'Daniel (1939–41), a flour salesman turned politician who won the hearts of the voters with renditions of songs of his own composition, such as "The Boy Who Never Gets Too Big to Comb His Mother's Hair." And, of course, there are late arrivals like Ann Richards (1991–95), the second woman and last Democrat to serve as governor, and her successor, George W. Bush.

"There are only seven spaces left," says the guide, looking down at the portraits. "So there's going to be a crisis boiling point."

For some reason, this reminded me of the legend of St. Malachy and the 112 popes. Back in the Dark Ages, Malachy allegedly wrote a list of all the future popes, each of them described by a phrase that captured his special identity. If you believe that he actually did this, and that the list was not the work of a forger from a later era, you would also believe that we are down to the last pope before "Peter the Roman," during whose reign the world will come to an end. (Believing this also requires that you believe Malachy had some good reason for tagging the current pope, Benedict XVI, with the phrase "glory of the olive.")

Despite our guide's pessimism, authorities at the state capitol seem confident they can make room for a lot more governors. But sooner or later the last slot in the dome will be filled—and will that mean the end is near for Texas? That it'll break into five average-sized states? That the Last Governor will take the oath, then cackle wildly and announce he doesn't really believe in God, thus undermining the state constitution, which contains a clause prohibiting atheists from holding elective office? There are a lot of ways for the world as we know it to come to an end, but in Texas's case whatever happened would undoubtedly be action-packed.

"Shaping the history of North America and the world"

Even if Texas were not powerful enough to set the country's course on everything from energy to education, and to create the terms of our public debate on everything from jobs to prayers before football games, the rest of the country would still give it way more attention than one-fiftieth of the union deserves. American movies and television shows are set in locales all over the nation, but the ones about Texas clearly had to be there and only there—*Red River* and *Giant* and *The Last Picture Show,* and on TV everything from the beloved and recently departed *Friday Night Lights* to that thing about people from Texas who bid on abandoned storage lockers. (In the penultimate scene of *Friday Night Lights,* some of the main characters sit drinking beer under the sky and toasting "Texas forever." It's been quite a while, but I do not remember Mary Tyler Moore going off the air with a salute to Minnesota.) In the 1980s we obsessed over the first series of *Dallas,* when 350 million people around the world tuned in to see who shot J. R. and everyone had very specific images of what it would be like to go to the Oil Barons Ball. Going even further back to the early days of television, the networks had a ton of adventure series featuring Texas heroes, including *Tales of the Texas Rangers, The Adventures of Jim Bowie,* and a show about Judge Roy Bean, "the law west of the Pecos." It's been more than fifty years since Judge Roy Bean was a television feature, but people still come to Pecos, Texas, looking for his courthouse, which in reality was a long distance away in Langtry. Pecos, which has fallen on hard times since the wells dried up, accommodates them anyway, with a replica.

Above all there was David Crockett—who I am going to call Davy, since that's the way all non-historians have known him since Walt Disney rechristened him for his miniseries. Davy was born on a mountaintop in Tennessee, but died in Texas at the battle of the Alamo. (Or as a prisoner of war after the battle of the Alamo; let's not take sides in that fight.) The Alamo sits right at the center of the Texas imagination, as well as in the center of the city of San Antonio, where it attracts more than 2.5 million visitors a year. It's hard to find a Texan who didn't make the pilgrimage before puberty. Even on the hottest days, the place is packed with families examining Sam Houston's shaving mug or sitting in the courtyard listening to a short talk on the creation of the Republic of Texas. ("It's important to understand these events," a young lecturer urged the small but attentive audience on the day I visited. "They're not only important in shaping the history of Texas, but in shaping the history of North America and the world.")

The turnout is particularly impressive because, to be brutally honest, there isn't all that much to see at the Alamo. Part of the old mission church and a small segment of the barracks have been preserved, but the only fully realized section is the gift shop. Those seeking more information are invited to a little room where a History Channel version of the story is constantly replayed on a large and elderly TV set, flanked by a painting of the Death of Travis on one side and Clara Driscoll, a leader of the Daughters of the Republic of Texas preservation movement, on the other.

"We had a terrible black sheep"

"The Alamo is not a museum. It is a shrine to the 189 men who died here. The Alamo *is a shrine*," says Karen Thompson, the president general of the Daughters of the Republic of Texas. She has large, wide eyes, grey hair, and a forceful voice. We are sitting in a small collection of offices where the DRT engages in the business of preserving the shrine for the edification of the world. The Daughters have been running the Alamo since the beginning of the twentieth century, but lately there have been several dustups over their performance, and proposals that the state should take control of the shrine-keeping duties. Which drives Thompson completely crazy, given all the trouble her organization has gone to over the years. "In 1910 there was no money. You didn't have a lot of tourists," she says, recounting the way the original DRT guardians of the Alamo made hand-drawn postcards and sold them to help support the place. "They had their gardeners come to tend the grounds."

To become a member of the Daughters of the Republic of Texas, you have to prove conclusively that one of your ancestors lived in Texas before statehood, in 1846. Being able to trace your family back that far is the equivalent of having a relative who came over on the *Mayflower*—or possibly better, since the Texas settlers were far more colorful. A number of them, in fact, appear to have been flat-out deranged. "We had a terrible black sheep involved in the war of 1836. We don't talk about him," said Frank Cahoon, a Midland realtor and former Republican state representative. He is a thin, chipper man with wispy grey hair, sitting in a downtown office that's decorated with African artifacts and the skull of a Texas woman who lived about 2,000 years ago, and whose bones were blown back onto the surface of the shifting west Texas sand.

"He was from North Carolina," Cahoon says, getting back to his ancestor, of whom he actually seems to be rather proud. "He was impeached by the North Carolina legislature. Gone to Texas."

"Gone to Texas" or "GTT" was what you were supposed to write on your fence or front door when you left your old, unsuccessful life in the States and took off for a new start in what was then a section of Mexico being colonized under the leadership of Stephen Austin. Frequently, people were GTT for reasons more exciting than crop failure or debt. Cahoon delicately skipped over the fact that the ancestor in question, Robert Potter, also represented North Carolina in Congress until he was forced to resign for castrating two men he believed were being overly familiar with his wife. Later, he was expelled from the state legislature for cheating at cards. All of which suggests that perhaps we should pay more attention to the history of North Carolina. However, GTT gave Potter a new start, and he made his name as the founder of the Texas navy.

"VICTORY OR DEATH"

The center of the legend of the Alamo is the moment when the commander, William B. Travis, tells the defenders that the choice is death, flight, or surrender, then draws a line in the sand and asks everyone who is prepared to stay with him and die to step across. All but one man, the legend says, stoutly walked over the line and joined Travis in his heroic stand. (Louis "Moses" Rose, a French soldier of fortune, was the one who decided that he'd prefer to live to fight another day. Rose had served under Napoleon during the invasion of Russia and probably had had enough of doomed enterprises.)

Historians now doubt the line incident ever happened, but nothing about the Alamo is for sure. Generations of scholars have pored over every scrap of evidence as if they were the Dead Sea Scrolls. Did Sam Houston want the Alamo abandoned as a hopeless and actually pretty useless cause? (Yeah, probably.) Could the men have gotten out if they wanted to? (Ditto.) Did they really believe they were going to die, or were they still hoping for a rescue? What the hell happened to Davy Crockett? All that's for sure is that your reaction to the Alamo story says quite a bit about your general worldview.

"The Alamo is a great monument to heroism. It's not a great monument to intelligence," opined James Haley, a biographer of Houston.

"They had a reason to be there. They just ran out of luck," said Stephen Harrigan, the author of *The Gates of the Alamo*. He added, "I don't think they made a decision to die there. Who does that?"

"The Alamo is a blank slate," said Jan Jarboe Russell, a San Antonio writer and biographer of Lyndon Johnson's wife, Lady Bird. If Russell could fill in that slate herself, the Alamo would be remembered as an old Spanish mission that was "a place of community and life" rather than its later incarnation as "a symbol of Anglo males who wanted to die to be heroes."

The Alamo's ability to stand for different things to different people is particularly true when it comes to the story of William Travis, who became the sole commander when Jim Bowie got too sick to get out of bed. Travis was an émigré from Alabama, where he had abandoned a pregnant wife and baby son. "Most of the colonists thought he was a stuffed shirt and really full of himself," said Haley. Whether or not Travis drew that line in the sand, he did definitely send out a letter at the beginning of the siege that became central to Texas's sense of how one goes about standing up for one's principles. "I have sustained a continual Bombardment & cannonade for 24 hours & have not lost a man," he wrote in an appeal for aid. "The enemy has demanded a surrender at discretion, otherwise, the garrison are to be put to the sword, if the fort is taken —I have answered the demand with a cannon shot, & our flag still waves proudly from the walls — *I shall never surrender or retreat.*" He signed his missive VICTORY OR DEATH."

"I cannot read Travis's letter and not cry," says Karen Thompson of the DRT. "And I've read it a thousand times."

So the Mexican army came, all the Americans died, and today William Travis lives on in legend. In Texas, schools are named after him, and office buildings, at least one lake, a historic fort, and the entire county where the state capital is located. His portrait is on a huge oil storage tank in Houston. George W. Bush, when he was running for president, sent a copy of Travis's letter to the American Ryder Cup team, which was in danger of losing the biannual golf tournament between the United States and Europe. The Americans rallied and Justin Leonard, a team member from Texas, sank a 45-foot putt that saved the day.

Victory or death on the putting green.

Travis strikes me as an excellent example of everything you wouldn't want in a commander, particularly if you were one of the guys being commanded. Davy Crockett should have whacked him over the head and gotten the men out of the fort. If they wanted to be heroes, there was still Houston and his army, desperate for reinforcements. I asked Thompson to put herself in the place of one of the defenders' wives, sitting at home waiting for some help with the crops while Travis was maximizing the chances of having her husband die for the cause. "Oh, I'd have been pissed! I'd be—what are you *doing*? I'd be a very angry wife," she admitted.

But Thompson always goes back to Travis's side. "If you take it from the military standpoint, when Houston says 'I don't think that's the spot,' I can certainly understand that," she said. "Except Travis wasn't that kind of person. He's not your ordinary person. Some people are different. They're the leaders—the Mandelas of the world."

William Travis and Nelson Mandela are not two people that I would personally put on the same page, but then I'm from Ohio.

The idea of the defiant Texan, standing up for principles so deeply felt that they must be defended at all costs, regardless of how sensible the battle, lives on today. In 2011, the *Houston Chronicle* referred to a state senator as "donning the patriotic trappings of a Patrick Henry—or maybe a William Barret Travis" while making a dramatic speech about the death of his pet piece of legislation. That was Dan Patrick, who in his non-legislative life is a radio talk show host once known for painting his face blue in honor of the Houston Oilers. The bill for which he was endorsing Alamo-levels of defiance was known as the "anti-groping bill." It would have given Texas authorities the power to arrest any federal airport personnel who touched a passenger's "private" areas during airplane security checks.

Victory or death at the x-ray machine.

In late December of 2011, after the US Senate came to a bipartisan agreement to extend a payroll tax cut for two months, the House Republicans unexpectedly rebelled, demanding that Speaker John Boehner fight to the (political) death on behalf of either their plan for a longer-term cut balanced by stringent spending reductions or nothing at all. The political fallout was disastrous. Everyone from Senator John McCain to the *Wall Street Journal* demanded that the Republicans in the lower chamber get with the program. In a few days, Boehner caved.

"House Republicans felt like they were reenacting the Alamo, with no reinforcements and our friends shooting at us," said Texas Republican Kevin Brady, one of the House deputy whips. The issue of how many months to extend a tax cut isn't less earthshaking than winning a golf tournament, but it was a little peculiar that Brady seemed to be comparing the Senate Republicans to the Mexican army. Brady's office did not respond to my queries, except to send me his full statement, in which he insisted that he wanted to "fight on."

"To the devil with your glorious history!"

Texas politics currently boasts a number of women given to that same overheated, self-dramatizing style. There is, for one, Debbie Riddle, a Republican state representative from a district outside Houston, who worried publicly about female terrorists sneaking across the border to give birth to what opponents quickly dubbed "terror babies" who would use their citizenship as a tool in the war against America. During a committee hearing Riddle once demanded: "Where did this idea come from that everybody deserves free education, free medical care, free whatever? It comes from Moscow, from Russia. It comes straight out of the pit of hell."

So it's not as if the hyperventilating is only coming from the male side of things. However, looking back over Texas history, the female sector does seem, overall, to have exhibited more practical sense. Perhaps that was because they had more to put up with—there was a famous saying that Texas was "heaven for men and dogs but hell for women and oxen." Robert Potter, the ancestor we met earlier, broke up with his first wife after the unfortunate series of castrations. He married again in Texas, and when he died his second wife discovered that in his will he had left their home to another woman. Her memoirs were turned into a novel, *Love is a Wild Assault.*

One of the first women to play a notable role in the war for independence was Pamela Mann, whose oxen Sam Houston had commandeered to drag artillery in the lead-up to the Battle of San

Jacinto. "She had . . . a very large knife on her saddle. She turned around to the oxen and jumpt down with the knife & cut the raw hide tug that the chane was tied with . . . nobody said a word," reported a witness. "She jumped on her horse with whip in hand & away she went in a lope with her oxen."

Even without Pamela's livestock, the Texans ultimately won a decisive victory at San Jacinto, on the farm of Peggy McCormick, who demanded that the rotting corpses of the more than 600 slain Mexicans be taken away and buried.

"Madam, your land will be famed in history," Houston declaimed proudly.

"To the devil with your glorious history! Take off your stinking Mexicans!" she snarled.

This isn't a whole lot of evidence, but I'm working under the theory that if a woman had been in charge of the defense of the Alamo, she'd have figured out how to evacuate. This is perhaps why you see so few women with their portraits painted on the side of oil refinery tanks.

"She's got an airport terminal"

So what we have here is a state that celebrates excess, particularly excess in the pursuit of personal independence or a personal code of justice. This can sometimes be a marvelous thing. Think of Lyndon Johnson battering through Congress with the Civil Rights Act, all the while knowing that he was destroying the power of the Democratic Party in the South. Or Sam Houston. Houston might not have wanted to waste Texan lives defending the Alamo, but he committed political suicide himself when, as a senator during the lead-up to the Civil War, he fought to keep Texas in the Union. Turned out of office, Houston paraded through Washington in a leopardskin waistcoat, telling the world that come what may, he would not change his spots.

The Texas capitol is full of his pictures and busts. "They called him the Raven," says our guide, pointing to a portrait of Houston in the state senate chamber. "That was his warrior's name. So. Pretty cool."

Houston did indeed live for a long time with the Indians, taking an Indian wife and attempting to defend Indian rights throughout his career. On the other hand, he abandoned the wife. And the Indians also called him the Drunkard. A man of many parts, Sam Houston.

Pointing to another portrait and leaping ahead a century or so, the guide says, "That's Barbara Jordan. Not only are schools named after her, she's got an airport terminal."

Jordan, who died in 1996, was only the third black woman to become a lawyer in all of Texas history. She was the first black state senator since the Reconstruction era, and she became nationally famous during the Watergate hearings, when, as a member of the House Judiciary Committee, she declared that despite the fact that the Founding Fathers had not included *her* people when they wrote "We the people" at the start of the Constitution, her faith in that document "is whole, it is complete, it is total. I am not going to sit here and be an idle spectator to the diminution, the subversion, the destruction of the Constitution."

Molly Ivins watched the state legislators who had served in Austin with Jordan—a few of whom had privately referred to her as "that nigger bitch"—sitting mesmerized in front of the TV set. "As she lit into Richard Nixon, they cheered and hoo-rahed and pounded their beer bottles on the tables as though they were watching U. T. pound hell out of Notre Dame in the Cotton Bowl," Ivins wrote.

By the time she became famous, Jordan was used to being the only black woman in one venue after another, so if she's looking down on the Texas capitol, she's probably not surprised to be the only black woman hanging on the walls. Like most state capitols, Texas's is not replete with portraits of females of any ethnicity, although there are "Ma" Fergusons all around the place, and of course the one of Ann Richards, the second and last woman to be elected governor of Texas. Outside the building, there is a generic tribute to the women pioneers, and a little way toward downtown, on Congress Avenue, you have Angelina Eberly, the heroine of the Texas Archives War of 1842. Eberly's moment in history occurred after Houston, still smarting over his enemies' victory in getting the capital moved out of the city named for him, hatched a plot to reverse things. In the dark of the night, workers arrived in Austin with a wagon and began removing the state's papers. They had not counted on Mrs. Eberly, a boardinghouse owner, who saw what was going on and ran to the town square, where she fired the cannon that was standing there. A mob gathered, retrieved the papers, and put them in the Eberly boardinghouse for safekeeping. Her statue, by the cartoonist Pat Oliphant, is seven feet tall and has the heroine of the Archives War standing by her cannon looking fierce and formidable, and actually a little bit naked around the top, ready for battle.

And that's the traditional Texas spirit, at its best when there's an enemy to rise up against. Outsized and brave. And frequently somewhat lunatic.

2

Empty Places

"But it's an urban state!"

To understand Texas's role in our current national politics, you have to start with the great, historic American division between the people who live in crowded places and the people who live in empty places.

Think about it: if your home turf is crowded, you will need rules to protect you from all sorts of intrusive behavior—noisy neighbors, factories that spew out pollution, dogs that poop on the sidewalk. Basically, you want a buffer between your family and the rest of the world. That buffer would be government. Go regulation!

But if you live in an empty place, government may look a lot different. What's the point? It's just going to tax you or get in your way. If a robber breaks into your house, it could take hours for law enforcement to arrive; carrying a gun is more practical. Government can't help you and it has no business telling you what you can do with your property. Who could you hurt? There's nobody else in sight. You're on your own and you like it that way.

There are a few problems with the empty-world vision. Environmentalists are going to want to know whether you're expressing your right to private property by dumping pesticides into the aquifer or killing off the last pair of blue-pelted ferrets on the planet.

26

And there are actually quite a few things the empty-place residents expect to get from government as their rightful due. Finally, even though you'd never know it by looking at the composition of the US Senate, the number of people who are actually living in empty places is pretty small. They don't call them empty for nothing.

The current Tea Party strain in the Republican party is all about the empty-place ethos. And Texas is the natural leader, because it's managed to hold tight to its historic alone-on-the-prairie world-view while growing by leaps and bounds.

"Ask my students," says Tom Dunlap, a professor at Texas A & M. "They all associate themselves with the country. They're living a myth. They think of Texas as open wide—but 80 percent of the people in Texas live in one of the major metropolitan areas."

"People still think of this as the frontier," says Martin Melosi, the director of the Institute of Public History at the University of Houston. "But it's an urban state!"

Describing their state, Texans don't generally say "empty," although there are exceptions. (Rick Perry, who grew up in the very small west Texas town of Paint Creek, said his dad called their neighborhood "the big empty.") It's more likely you'll hear them call their state "open"—whether they are liberals stressing multi-cultural hospitality or conservatives talking about the anti-union right-to-work laws. But however you slice it, Texas believes people deserve plenty of elbow room. Its politics has always been based on an empty-place ideology. And the more crowded it gets, the more intense the feeling becomes.

"If you've got a car, you can carry a gun"

Texas is so big that the entire population of the planet would fit in it if everybody in Texas lived as close together as New Yorkers. Which they don't intend to do. But you get the idea—very large place. Texans seem to think very little of jumping in the car and driving 300 miles to see a football game, or taking a job four or five hours away with the understanding that they'll commute back home for weekends. This tends to confirm the feeling of empty-placeness, even if the trip is between San Antonio and Fort Worth.

No matter where they live, Texans believe they only need to get behind the wheel to leave civilization behind. "We just like to pour concrete and get in our pickup trucks and drive. That's what we do," laughed Lois Kolkhorst, a Republican state representative who successfully sponsored a law to raise the maximum speed limit to 85 mph.

Nobody can tell me what to do in my own car. Empty-place politics does tend to lap over into motor vehicle laws. For instance, in 2011 Governor Perry vetoed a bill that would have outlawed texting while driving. The practice of sending text messages while theoretically steering a car was "reckless and irresponsible," Perry said, but he was opposed to "a government effort to micromanage the behavior of adults."

Rather than wasting time discussing the possible feelings of nontexting drivers about this position, we will take this opportunity to mention that Perry once named his boots Freedom and Liberty.

In the same spirit, the governor in 2007 signed a "traveling rule" making it clear that Texans have a right to carry concealed weapons in their cars whether they have a permit or not. It is also legal to carry a concealed weapon without a permit if you're *on the way* to your car. The bottom line, a Dallas police officer told the *Dallas Observer*, is "If you've got a car, you can carry a gun."

Guns laws are a close-to-perfect reflection of the empty-versus-crowded mind-set. If you're on your own, you might feel more secure if you have a weapon to protect yourself against the bad guys. But if you live in a place where police are easy to summon, and where a lot of strangers may be bumping up against you in the course of a day, you would probably feel safer if only the cops are packing heat. (Before we go any further, let me say that this discussion does not have anything to do with hunting. Or keeping a gun in the house in case of intruders. Most Americans, be they empty-place or crowded-place dwellers, think it is fine for people to have rifles for hunting if that's what they like to do. And they also approve of the gun-in-the-home thing although honestly, it's not all that great an idea.)

The Texas creed is that the more people carrying concealed weapons the better, even in what would seem to be the most wildly inappropriate situations. The legendary former lieutenant governor Bob Bullock, who was intensely attached to both alcohol and firearms, once drunkenly pulled a gun on a waiter, pressing the barrel to the man's head and cocking the hammer. Nobody appeared to hold it against him.

Real-world experience suggests that a passel of law-abiding citizens carrying concealed weapons at their local shopping center will not react fast enough to stop one armed and crazy person from shooting a child, several senior citizens, a judge, and the local member of Congress. But arguing about this is pretty fruitless. While there are a number of dedicated people who are spending their lives trying to talk empty-place states into more prudent gun laws, I have personally given up that battle. If you're a Texan who feels disturbed by the fact that it's legal for virtually anyone with a car to keep a loaded Uzi with a fifty-round ammunition magazine under the front seat, I sympathize. But you'll probably have to adapt or move someplace else.

Our primary question, though, is what Texas does to the rest of us. And the gun thing doesn't stop at the border. Consider sales. California has the most stringent gun laws in the country, and it makes a huge effort to restrict sales in ways that keep weapons from getting into the hands of criminals. Texas doesn't, and in 2010 law enforcement officials tracked 368 weapons used to commit crimes in California back to gun dealers in Texas. In the same year, ninety-three Texas guns were used in crimes far away in New York. And nearly 15,000 guns sold in Texas wound up being used in crimes in Mexico, which is not part of the United States but certainly doesn't need the extra firepower.

When it comes to guns, Texas loses its obsession with states' rights. Most of its congressional delegation supports a "national concealed carry" law that would force states to honor concealed weapons permits granted anywhere in the country. That would pose a terrible problem for a place like New York, which has been very successful in controlling crime by controlling guns. It's very hard to get a concealed weapon permit in New York, and New Yorkers like it that way. Allowing people from states that hand out permits like bingo cards to walk around with pistols under their coats "would be a disaster," said police commissioner Ray Kelly. But advocates of the bill are indifferent to the issue of local control. "Studies show that carrying concealed weapons reduces violent crime rates by deterring would-be assailants and by allowing law-abiding citizens to defend themselves," claimed House Judiciary chairman Lamar Smith of Texas, when his committee approved the bill in 2011.

"States' Rights! States' Rights! States' Rights!"

Guns aside, Texas has been obsessed with states' rights forever. It began, at least in mythology, with that pre-independence period when Mexico ran the land, and sometimes ran it very badly. (On the other hand, Mexico did allow American settlers to come into its territory, granted them large tracts of free land, and showed a certain amount of patience when the newcomers engaged in smuggling and ignored all the immigration laws. But we're looking at things from the Texas side now.) Then after the Civil War, outsiders representing the federal government rigged elections, restricted freedom of the press, and deprived former Confederate soldiers of the right to vote. So, like the other former rebels, Texas returned to the Union with a near-paranoia about the dangers of Washington overreach. (On the other hand, once the outsiders were gone, the white Texans rigged elections, imposed vicious segregation laws, and deprived African Americans of their vote with a vengeance, just as an earlier generation of newly independent Texans had thumped down on the peaceful Mexican American settlers in their midst.)

To this day, the state is organized so that no one in government will have much power and no one in private business will be under much control. The state house and senate meet once every two years, for 140 days, unless the governor decides to call an emergency session. Given the specificity of the constitution, it's impossible to do much of anything without the cumbersome process of amending it. (The Texas constitution is now the second longest in the country. At last count it had been amended 467 times.) The legislators receive $7,200 a year for their service. This, too, is in the constitution, along with the proper method of purchasing stationery and the rule that atheists cannot hold elective office.

The legislators' salary is not the lowest rate in the nation—Alabama only pays its representatives $10 a day, which is certainly a model to look toward if your goal is turning your state into another Alabama. But no other large state has such a low salary. And given the amount of travel involved, and the fact that state legislators really do spend a great deal of time working on constituents' problems, responding to calls for emergency special sessions, and running for reelection, it hardly seems like a job for an average middle-class citizen. "The Lege," says Professor Christopher King of the University of Texas at Austin, using the familiar Texas nickname. "We pay these guys the princely sum of $7,200 a year. The lobbyists write the bills. It really is driven by 'bidness,' as we say." (The lobbyists far outnumber the legislators, and at way better salaries. Texans for Public Justice, a nonprofit that tracks campaign finance and lobbying expenditures, said that in the legislative year of 2009, special interests spent $344 million on lobbying contracts. Given that the legislature has thirty-one senators and 150 representatives, that averages out to nearly $2 million per lawmaker.)

The Texas governor has historically been weak as well. Many people give Rick Perry—who has been governor since 2000—

credit for creating a new model of a powerful chief executive, which seems to be built around the principle of never going away. Yet Perry does not appear to be feeling empowered, because he is so overwhelmed by the oppressive forces of Washington. "Texans know how to run Texas," he told the crowd at that Tea Party rally. "States' rights! States' rights! States' rights!" (Perry has a habit of saying the same thing over and over in a loud voice. Perhaps it comes from his days as a yell leader at Texas A & M.)

All the top Texas politicians, including Perry, are stupendously proud of Texas's population boom and job growth, but it's important to note—although almost nobody ever does so—that the state would probably still be a mainly poor, rural economy if it weren't for massive federal aid. No one who has read Robert Caro's biography of Lyndon Johnson can forget the description of the farmers in the Texas hill country during the New Deal setting out the best food their families could afford for the workers who were going to "bring the lights"—and the sense of amazement and euphoria when the lights actually went on. For Texas to become something more than an underdeveloped supplier of raw materials to the rest of the country, it needed a network of highways and power grids. Electrifying remote rural areas was not something that private enterprise was going to find profitable. It took the federal government to make it happen, and taxpayers from other states to provide the money.

Now that Texas is sort-of booming, it's no longer a big winner in the transfer of payments which the federal government makes between wealthy states and poor ones. It tends to break about even, although it still leads the country in farm subsidies, raking in $24.4 billion from 1995 to 2010. One of the beneficiaries used to be Rick Perry, cotton farmer. But that was then.

"Smoker and dog OK"

The law of the empty places is that neighbors help neighbors. A barn needs raising, the community rallies around. A disaster strikes, they're there. "Remember Jessica McClure?" offered a Texan with whom I was discussing the state's culture. That was "Baby Jessica," the eighteen-month-old who tumbled into a well in the family backyard in Midland and got stuck 22 feet underground. It was back in 1987, and volunteers rushed to the scene, working heroically around the clock for two and a half days to rescue her. There was a happy ending and a TV movie. Texans had every right to be proud of the story, although truly, I would trust Americans to rise to a child-trapped-in-a-well crisis anywhere.

A more remarkable example was the way Houston responded in 2005 when Hurricane Katrina decimated Louisiana. Mayor Bill White promised the city would open its arms, and it did—to an estimated 200,000 refugees. The Astrodome "radiated security and services," reported the *New York Times*, thanks to an estimated 60,000 local volunteers who did everything from mop floors to hand out drinks and snacks. Thousands of doctors and nurses from the area's vast array of medical institutions lent their services. Houston residents took refugees into their homes—the *Times* reported a sign at the Astrodome posted by a local lawyer, offering to take "1 wheelchair + 1 attendant, smoker and dog OK."

However, once the barn is raised or the child is rescued, the empty-state presumption is that the family will get back to business and take care of itself. (A year after Katrina, when about 150,000 displaced Louisianans remained in Houston, a local congressman, John Culberson, announced that "The time has long since passed for these folks to go home.") Texas has always shown a stupendous lack of enthusiasm for ongoing social services. It ranks second from the bottom in the percent of low-income people covered by Medicaid, dead last in state spending on mental health, fifth from the bottom in the maximum grant for temporary assistance to a

family of three with no income ($250 a month) and last in the
average monthly benefit for poor mothers on the Women, Infants,
and Children Program. But all that is Texas's business—unless you
look at low-income Texans as low-income Americans. Or maybe
as neighbors.

"It's a developer's dream"

More than 60 percent of Texans live in a central triangle that takes
in Austin, Houston, Dallas, Fort Worth, and San Antonio, all of
which are among the twenty largest cities in America. But many
of them still feel that they're perched at the far edge of civilization.
"They talk about that triangle all the time," says Representative
Kolkhorst, of 85 mph speed limit fame. "But that triangle's *large*."

And with really big gaps between the settlements. "I can go ten
minutes from now and be out on the open plain," said Chris Steinbach, who works in Austin as Kolkhorst's chief of staff.

Houston is so huge that the regional planners cannot find any-
place to meet that doesn't require some of the members to drive
more than 75 miles. It goes on *forever*. But its size feeds into the
empty-place mentality because it's not an urban bigness with everything mashed together. There's something here, something there,
but you'll still see a large open tract of land between this shopping
area and that neighborhood, between that block of houses and the
apartment building . . . over there. It creates the impression that
you're just a stone's throw from the open plains, even if you're actually five minutes from downtown.

Houston has no zoning because—well, zoning smacks of telling
people what to do with their property. In some neighborhoods,
the no-zoning ethos has created a patchwork of homes and stores,
backyard car repair businesses and only minimally disguised bor-
dellos, all flung in a mash that creates a throbbing energy, particularly for passersby who do not actually have to live next to a tire
recapping shop or palm reader. (A Houston planner who looked

askance at Austin suburban sprawl because "they're raping and pillaging those hills" added that his city had no sins to be forgiven because in Houston "see, over here we don't have anything to rape and pillage.") Of course none of the anything-goes ethos applies if people have enough money. There are deed covenants, historic preservation laws, and even tiny "gallstone cities" with their own government and rules scattered around the Houston map. In River Oaks, the swankiest of the swanky residential areas, there does not seem to be any danger of a gas station plopping itself down in the middle of the block. "I knew a guy in River Oaks who was going to attach a basketball hoop to his garage for his kids, and his neighbors sued him," said John Mixon, a professor at the University of Houston Law Center.

"IT'S A DEVELOPER'S dream—flat, treeless prairie," says Stephen Klineberg, a professor of sociology at Rice University. He and David Crossley, the president of Houston Tomorrow, are tooling down the city's endless highways, past the city's endless strip malls, heading toward the endless suburbs.

"It all starts with land speculation. Then they try to get elected officials to promise to build a road. They never want to see transit," says Crossley, who is an ardent champion of the city's light rail service, an extremely pleasant but still very limited 7.5-mile line of small trains connecting the city's medical center and Reliant Stadium to downtown. It has a surprising number of city advocates, but it is far from universally popular. "Light rail is not mass transit," sniffs former mayor Bob Lanier, a champion of the developers. "It's little bitty transit."

People like Crossley hate unchecked exurban growth, particularly government-enabled unchecked exurban growth. He'd like to see less investment in highways built to fulfill developers' dreams. He figures the lack of new roads would force development inward, to fill all the many gaping holes in Houston's central city.

Klineberg, who regularly surveys the attitudes of city residents, says a substantial minority of Houstonites would like to live in a place where they could walk to the store, or even to work. But as desirable as this might seem, it's totally contrary to the empty-place ethos. And discouraging suburban sprawl is, if not unAmerican, definitely unTexan. "Let people live where they want to live!" growls Bill Hobby, the former lieutenant governor and one of the few remaining beloved Texas Democrats.

Most people who live in other parts of the country wouldn't love the idea of do-what-you-will development, at least not if it meant the possibility that a massage parlor would suddenly pop up next door. But Texas does have one lesson the rest of us can't ignore. Housing there is easy to build, and therefore very cheap. "Houston's the only place in the world that if the demand were there they could put 60,000 lots on the ground next year, mainly because there's no red tape," said Ronald Welch of the University of Houston.

You are probably waiting to hear the downside, and there are several. For all its energy, Houston proper is a stupendously ugly city, and many of the suburbs have a mind-numbing sameness. "If you paint your door a different color, they'll take away your house," claims Crossley.

But again, those are issues for Texans to deal with. If it works for them, God bless. For the rest of us, the big concern would be things like air pollution and global warming. Guess which state is the largest emitter of carbon dioxide?

"Family capital of the free world"

Texas's empty-place ethos has deep roots, but it also very definitely has its limits in the real world. For an example, let's take a little trip to Midland. There are few places in Texas that embrace the anti-government concept more enthusiastically than Midland, the oil patch city where George W. Bush grew up and where you can still take a tour of his childhood home and marvel that there was a time really not all that long ago when middle-class families with a handful of children got by with one very small bathroom.

Midland had fewer than 30,000 citizens then. Now it has more than 110,000, and a history of painful booms and busts. During the big oil boom of the 1970s, the entrepreneurs of the moment celebrated their hopes for the future by throwing up a ton of big, square glass office buildings that obliterated whatever there was of actual life signs in the downtown. The crash of the 1980s left those buildings vacant, and even though Midland has come back, big time, in recent years, oil industry captains have discovered that they don't actually need to *live* there to run their local operations. As a result, nests for short-term occupancy—hotel rooms and apartments—are almost impossible to come by, while the big glass blocks continue to be half empty and the downtown resembles a set in one of those zombie movies where the kids emerge from a night in the basement to discover that there's no other warm-blooded entity in sight. There is only one coffee shop in the entire Midland downtown and mayor Wes Perry is worried about its financial prospects.

"We're struggling," he says, unable to avoid beaming even while delivering not-great news. "We're having meetings to say we want Midland downtown to be more *vibrant*. That's the word we use. We have a lot of young people moving back. They want to have fun places to go downtown."

Where do young Midlanders go now when they want a night of entertainment? Perry looked hopefully at a young aide, who looked back, startled.

"Church?" the aide proposed. (The churches do indeed abound. However, I've run into a few jaded expatriates who offered different answers, which ran along the line of "doing drugs in the basement rec room.")

Midland may not have achieved *vibrant*, but it has definitely embraced the Texas vision of limited government. "I always describe Midland as an independent, family capital of the free world. We don't look to the government for help," said the mayor. Perry himself is a conservationist who turns off the water when he's brushing his teeth or soaping his hair in the shower. But he's the last person who would attempt to impose his environmental lifestyle on other Texans. When it became necessary to restrict water use during Texas's 2011 killer drought, the mayor announced that the limits on lawn-watering and car-washing were requests, not laws or ticketing mandates. "We don't respond really well to, 'Okay, the government says you've got to do this, and by God you're going to do it or we're going to string you up,'" he told Kate Galbraith of the *Texas Tribune* in April of 2011.

By that summer, there were laws and tickets. The people of Midland might not have liked being told what to do, but they really hated watching their neighbors break the rationing rules and get away with it. They demanded a crackdown.

"It was really interesting," said Perry. "That's the way it went."

The next time you hear a politician extolling the idea of life without rules, remember Midland. Libertarianism looks a little different when your lawn is turning brown.

"Don't tell me what to do with my land or my cattle"

Despite the fact that it doesn't necessarily work in the real world, the sense that every man (or, presumably, woman) should simply be *let alone* permeates Texas culture. "It's the whole 'Don't tell me what to do with my land or my cattle' phenomenon," says Tom Smith, the executive director of Public Citizen Texas, who has spent over twenty years trying to convince his fellow state residents that global warming is real.

About the cattle: Texas thinks of itself as the land of the cowboy, and it is the top producer of beef in America. But even in Marfa, a small west Texas town surrounded by high desert and ranchland, the appearance of an actual spur-wearing cowboy on the streets is cause for note. "We see them in town buying feed or sometimes meeting for breakfast at Alice's Café," reported Tom Michael of Marfa Public Radio as he listed recent sightings. In very few parts of Texas do you experience a significant portion of cowboys per capita. Nevertheless, when Houston has its annual livestock show and rodeo, you would think that the entire metropolis was made up of cowhands—cowhands with a real affinity for fringe.

For a theoretically hard-bitten state, Texas does love the imaginary. Drive down Highway 67 in west Texas, in the high desert country between little Marfa and the border city of Presidio, and you will pass an official road sign announcing "Shafter Ghost Town." It's near the road sign that announces a rock shaped like an elephant and the one pointing out a ridge that looks like Abraham Lincoln's profile. (Ridges that resemble Lincoln's profile are pretty much like star clusters that resemble the Big Dipper. Almost anything works if you stare at it long enough.) The ghost town does indeed have an abandoned look, if you discount the big TV reception dish and a handwritten sign pointing out where to make deliveries to the Rio Grande Mining Company. Actually, Shafter is the home of a few dozen exurbanites reveling in the scenery and a functioning silver mine. But it's the thought that counts.

You are what you will in Texas. Millions of hopeful emigrants have Gone To Texas, fantasizing about what they would make of themselves there, and some of them found it as wonderful as they had hoped. "I am rejoiced at my fate," wrote Davy Crockett, who thought he might be able to reestablish his foundering political career in exchange for service in the settlers' fight with Mexico. Whoops.

SO THAT'S THE first key to Texas's outsized influence on the rest of the country: it's the keeper of the empty-places flame. There are kindred souls all over America, who also want to be free spirits of the open range, some of them living in rather crowded places, like Miami or Las Vegas. And God bless. Really, live and let live. The problem comes when the folks yelling "States' rights!" start to infringe on the rights of people outside their territory, or threaten the future well-being of the nation as a whole.

The empty-places worldview is part of the philosophy of the Tea Party, which makes it part of the crazy-ticked-off nature of the nation's political debate. But it could also be a key to cooling the madness down. The great thing about seeing politics in terms of empty versus crowded is that you can appreciate the way differences arise from reasonable responses to perceived reality. You may feel the other side is wrong/living in the past/getting carried away. But it's not necessary to think of politics as a battle between good and evil. Between the heavenly hosts and the demon spawn of Beelzebub. Between the defenders of the Founding Fathers' dream and the tribunes of European socialism who huddle in dank basements plotting to make Americans pathetic dependents on government largesse.

You get the idea.

3

It's My Party

"Never underestimate the situation"

Ever since the Civil War, Texas has been a passionately one-party state. Different parties, but it's the passion that counts.

Looking at the story in the least flattering way possible, you could say that the Texas voting majority has very consistently gone wherever the African Americans are not. After Reconstruction, when the Republicans were identified as the champion of the ex-slaves, Texas became completely Democratic. After the Democrats passed the Civil Rights Act of 1964, the state began galloping toward the GOP. This is a familiar story in the American South, but most of modern Texas thinks of itself as part of the West. Really, it's western. Just ask. Being a western state is part of the Texas identity, along with the Alamo and the conviction that the weather will cool off as soon as the sun goes down.

These days, Texas Republicans have both US Senate seats and twenty-three of the thirty-two seats in the House. Democrats haven't won a statewide race since 1994, and there are many, many statewide races to be not won. If you count statewide judicial contests, Democrats have gone zero for ninety-one since 1996. The Republicans also totally control the state legislature. In the 2011 session they had a 101–49 edge in the House. Since 101 members constitute a quorum, the *Texas Observer* noted, "that meant the House could still function even if all the Democrats never showed up." Which was probably what the Democrats felt like doing on many a day.

As you might expect, these switches in power did not happen calmly. In 1874, E. J. Davis, the final Reconstruction-era Republican governor, refused to leave the capitol when he lost reelection to Democrat Richard Coke. Davis holed up at his desk while his militia tried to hold off Coke's men, who were allegedly singing "The Yellow Rose of Texas" while they stormed the building. (Let us stop here to note that the original "Yellow Rose of Texas" was a mixed-race indentured servant named Emily West, who supposedly helped the Texans win the Battle of San Jacinto by seducing the Mexican general at a crucial moment. This part of her story is somewhat iffy. However, if true, it would reinforce my theory that the practical part of the Texas colonial experience was mainly female.)

Anyhow, former governor Davis held out until it became apparent that President Grant was not going to intervene and declare the election invalid. He then gave up the armed resistance, but he still refused to hand over the office keys.

Much, much later, in 2003, when the Texas Republicans were nailing down their permanent majority by remapping the congressional districts for the second time in two years, Democratic state legislators escaped across the Oklahoma border to camp out in a Holiday Inn and deny their opponents a quorum. "We got on a bus. We didn't know where we were going," recalled Joaquín Castro of San Antonio, who was a freshman state representative at the time. Castro asked one of his more veteran colleagues what clothes he should take. "Oh, just some shorts and tennis shoes," the older man shrugged. It was not, in the end, the outfit Castro would have chosen to be wearing when the bus was greeted by a mob of media on the Oklahoma end of the trip. "I learned a lesson—never underestimate the situation," Castro said.

As a drama, the Oklahoma holdout wasn't exactly the Yellow Rose of Texas, but the Republicans' leader, Representative Tom DeLay, did turn some heads when he asked the Department of Homeland Security to help him search for the plane of one of the missing members.

"I woke to find I was going to be the only one"

In between the Democrats' storming of the state capitol and their last-ditch flight to Oklahoma, Texans spent more than a century making all their real political choices in the Democratic primaries. (For most of that period, we are talking only about white voters. A 1923 Texas law, getting right to the point, said "in no event shall a Negro be eligible to participate in a Democratic primary in the State of Texas.") The Democratic populists fought the Democratic plutocrats, the Democratic New Deal loyalists fought the Democratic Roosevelt-haters, and the Democratic liberals fought the Democratic conservatives. Mainly, the conservatives won. Meanwhile, the Republicans donated money to the national party and got invited to dinners at the White House.

Frank Cahoon, the descendant of that interesting Robert Potter—the Texas navy founder who castrated his wife's admirers—had the bad luck to be chairman of the committee tasked with finding a Republican candidate for state representative in the oil-pumping city of Midland in 1964, the year Lyndon Johnson was preparing to sweep to victory in the presidential race. Cahoon wound up being stuck with the job himself when his last hope dropped out on the day the nomination papers had to be filed. He won the election and became the entire Republican caucus in the 150-member house. "That was the Goldwater year," he recalled. "I woke to find I was going to be the only one."

Serving as the lone Republican was not as bad as you might imagine. "John Connally was the governor and he was very conservative," Cahoon said. "A big part of the Democrats were very conservative." The liberal Democrats treated him well, too: "They thought my uniqueness was fun." The liberals, in fact, were pretty much in the same boat as Cahoon was, power-wise. "The conservatives were in control and the liberals had difficulty passing anything. They knew they were going to be outvoted so they thought they might as well have a good time." This was the era of Charlie Wilson, a hard-partying lawmaker so colorful that legend has it he once tried to drive his car up a flagpole while on a toot. Wilson later went on to Congress, where the rest of us will remember him as the guy who helped get the United States involved in Afghanistan.

By Cahoon's era, the Texas legislature had developed a tradition of bipartisanship, in which Democrats actually went so far as to appoint Republicans—when there were Republicans—to chair committees. It was nice, but not actually all that surprising. When one party is pretty confident it's going to be running things for the foreseeable future, it tends to become rather benevolent about the hapless minority. "We made lifetime friends," Cahoon said.

Nobody joining the Texas legislature now seems to be expecting to make lifetime friends in the opposition party. "People ask if I miss it," said Bill Ratliff, a much-respected retired Republican state senator who once served as acting lieutenant governor. "I miss the way it was when I served. I guess I *could* be in the legislature now, but it wouldn't be any fun."

"And I didn't drive any girl off a bridge"

The Texas legislature is overwhelmingly Republican now, with a strong Tea Party cast. The tradition of allowing members of the minority party to chair committees continues, although Senator Rodney Ellis, a Houston Democrat, says the committees the Democrats get are seldom major spokes in the legislative wheel. (Ellis, who Ratliff appointed to run the Finance Committee back when the Republicans first held the senate majority, is now head of the somewhat less critical Government Organization Committee.) "This session was a real damper on bipartisanship," he said in 2011.

"They passed the budget with a parliamentary maneuver. They passed the voter ID bill with a parliamentary maneuver." The senate had long abided by a consensus-building (and sometimes progress-halting) rule that required two-thirds of the body to vote in favor of bringing up any bill, including the budget. At the end of the last session, one Republican leader told the *Houston Chronicle* that the rule had been "destroyed."

The great and steady march toward the GOP really took off in 1978 when Bill Clements, a wealthy oilman, became the first Republican governor since Reconstruction. Clements won after an action-packed campaign that was highlighted by a dinner party at the Amarillo Industrial Exposition, when he threw a rubber chicken at his Democratic opponent, attorney general John Hill. The chicken landed in another diner's plate, but Clements had made his point: he intended to hang the deeply unpopular President Jimmy Carter around Hill's neck the way farm folk hung dead poultry around the necks of chicken-killing dogs. It turned out to be an extremely successful—and extremely Texan—method of connecting the state Democrats to the increasingly liberal national party in voters' minds.

Clements's victory, with all its powerful poultry symbolism, was even more impressive because he was not a guy who coasted on personal charm. When an oil rig he owned suffered a blowout, dumping 3.3 million barrels of oil into the Gulf of Mexico, then-Governor Clements suggested that the state just wait for "a big hurricane to take care of the problem." When the *Wall Street Journal* unfavorably compared his refusal to admit mistakes to the way the late president Kennedy had taken responsibility for the Bay of Pigs, Clements verbally rounded up the entire Kennedy clan and snarled, "Well, I don't have any Bay of Pigs. And I didn't drive any girl off a bridge either."

The last Democrat ever to be elected governor in Texas was Ann Richards in 1990, after an astonishingly awful primary in which one opponent, Jim Mattox, turned on her during a televised debate and said, "Ann, you look awfully sober tonight. If you're not off the wagon after what you've been through the last couple of weeks, then you're cured." Non-Texans knew Richards mainly from her career-making keynote speech at the 1988 Democratic national convention, when she brought down the house with lines like "Poor George, he can't help it—he was born with a silver foot in his mouth." They probably presumed that the sassy Richards, a recovering alcoholic who knew plenty about the dark side of her state's politics, took her opponents' dirt with a shrug and a jibe. But she was thrown by the awfulness of the campaign, and she could not quite control her fractious campaign staff. "Everyone wanted to let Ann be Ann. But they had different Anns," she told a friend. Fortunately for the Democrats, once Richards made it through the primary, she was blessed with a Republican opponent who refused to shake her hand after a debate, and described rape as being like bad weather—"If it's inevitable, you might as well lay back and enjoy it." Somewhere between that and his casual acknowledgment that despite rather spectacular wealth he had not paid any taxes one year, Richards managed to squeak out a victory.

(No matter who's running for what, Texas politics frequently tends toward the knee-in-the-groin variety that the entire country now seems to be adopting. When Perry announced his presidential run, a Ron Paul supporter took out a full-page ad in an Austin alternative weekly asking "Have You Ever Had Sex With Rick Perry?")

Anyhow, that was the Democrats' last hurrah. In 1994, after Richards lost to George W. Bush, Lieutenant Governor Bob Bullock, who referred to Richards and her staff as "hairy-legged lesbians," was the only Democrat left standing. Bullock retired four years later, and that was that.

When Democrats tell this story, they include multiple conspiracy theories about Republican dirty tricks, but really, nothing could have stopped the political migration. It was happening all over the South, although of course in Texas it was happening on a much bigger scale. The majority of voters simply thought more like Republicans, and the old loyalties of the Civil War had finally died off. Ambitious conservative Democrats who had their finger to the wind went racing for the door. Former governor Connally, who had been wounded in the motorcade when John Kennedy was assassinated, became a Democrat for Nixon and then a flat-out Republican. When the final transition occurred, Bullock, outraged at this political disloyalty, said Connally "ain't never done nothin' but get shot in Dallas." (Later, Bullock endorsed George W. Bush for governor when Bush was running against the father of Bullock's two godsons.)

That was just the beginning of the stampede. Democratic congressman Phil Gramm resigned from his seat in 1983, changed parties, and won as a Republican in the special election to replace himself. "It's the last copter out of 'Nam, and you'd better get on it," he warned his colleagues. A Democratic state representative named Rick Perry was among those who were listening.

"But they were such violent Republicans"

During its Democratic phase Texas, like other Southern states, acquired its clout by sending savvy politicians to Washington and then keeping them there for decades, while they built up seniority. In Congress, Texans munched away at the top of the food chain, as committee chairs and sometimes Speaker of the House (John Nance Garner, Sam Rayburn, Jim Wright) or Senate majority leader (Lyndon Johnson). But they had trouble with the national stage. Texas Democrats were members of a party that was much more liberal than the state they represented, and people in that sort of situation generally do their best work behind the scenes. The most they could hope for was the vice presidency, a job that Garner, who held the post under Franklin Roosevelt, described as not being worth a quart of warm spit. (Or a pitcher or a bucket. This is a famous quote with obscure origins.) Neither Garner nor Johnson, when he held the post, was given anything much to do.

And of course no one expected Johnson to wind up stepping in for a president who was nine years his junior.

Before we go any further, we need to address the mystery of Lyndon Johnson, the president who passed more liberal, transformational domestic legislation than anyone in American history except FDR: Medicare, the Civil Rights Act, a ton of sweeping environmental laws, and the War on Poverty. How did all that come out of Texas? (The war in Vietnam is easier to explain. "Lyndon Johnson was obsessed with the Alamo. It's creepy," said Jan Jarboe Russell, the biographer of Lady Bird.)

But about all that domestic legislation: Johnson came from the Texas hill country outside of Austin, a place with a strong populist tradition going back to the old People's Party of the late nineteenth century, a national movement of small farmers, working men, and blacks. The Texas version foundered on the black part, but not before it put a special stamp on the politics of Johnson's part of Texas, which continued to yearn for a government that would help raise people up. The hill country, and Lyndon Johnson, would be ready and waiting when Franklin Roosevelt came along. "His first slogan was 'Roosevelt, Roosevelt, Roosevelt. 100 percent for Roosevelt,'" said Johnson's great biographer, Robert Caro.

Johnson's mammoth ambition led him into alliances with the Texas business oligarchy that would pay for all his major campaigns. "He gave them what they wanted, which was contracts," Caro said. "He gave them these immense contracts and they financed his campaigns and the campaigns of people he wanted them to finance." As a senator, Johnson swung right to accommodate the conservative-to-reactionary Texas forces outside his own district. "But then when he becomes president he changes completely," said Caro.

The politician who, as a young man, had once taught impoverished Mexican American children and swore "if I ever had a chance to help those underprivileged kids I was going to do it," actually did it. And as long as Johnson was around, he kept the Texas Democrats together, through the sheer force of his overwhelming personality and the great expectations of gain from Washington that his growing powers promised. "Johnson was a very unusual human being," said Caro.

But after LBJ was gone from power in 1969, and the Civil Rights Act he had championed was infuriating a generation of segregationist Texans, the conservative part of the Democratic Party broke off and ran for the other side. When they got there, they turned out to be far righter of wing than many folks had appreciated. When Caro started working on his Johnson books, he went to Texas to talk to some of the people who had known the late president. "I think I went down the first time in 1977," Caro said. "I was sort of astonished, because the people who had backed Johnson, like John Connally and George Brown, they were by this time Republicans. But they were such violent Republicans."

"DeLay took things to a much more poisonous level"

The Texas right wing had been a slightly uncomfortable, inside-player power in the Democratic Party. But once it switched sides, it fit right in. The new Texas Republicans were ready to help turn the rest of the GOP into something more aggressive, more radically conservative, a party ready to do battle for the empty-place ethos with the fighting spirit of the Alamo. Picture William Travis as head of the House Rules Committee.

It's not as if the old Texas Democratic flame has died out. San Antonio still worships the memory of liberal icon Henry Gonzalez. Houston has elected a gay Democrat as mayor. To some, Austin may look like Berkeley with low unemployment and country music. But statewide, Texas politics has become a mixture of Tea Party populism and big-business conservatism that fits in perfectly with the national Republican tide.

There are several reasons why the state got this political tone so fast. For one thing, although money talks loudly in all American politics, it really yells in Texas. The campaign finance laws basically allow any individual to give any amount to anyone, as long as he or she reports it. And Texas has always had more than its fair share of very wealthy people who want to make their opinions felt. Its early history as a semifeudal economy dominated by the cattle barons, oil barons, and mining barons set the pace. Campaigns in Texas tend to be very expensive because it is so big—more than twenty distinct media markets, far more than any other state. Also, voting participation is generally terrible. (In 2010, Maine had the highest turnout in the nation at 56 percent of the eligible population. Texas was dead last at 33 percent.) The record is likely to get worse in the future, thanks to a new voter identification law that is pretty clearly designed to discourage poor people from going to the polls.

In a one-party state with low turnout and high campaign costs, power flows disproportionately to anyone with the money to organize and advertise. The people with that kind of cash in Texas tend to be extremely conservative. The combined effect of all this is to give the state a relatively united, high-volume voice in national affairs—the voice of the state's wealth oligarchy, and the wide open spaces.

The biggest barrier to Texas's national political influence has been the rest of the country's suspicion of Texas politicians. Modern history is littered with disastrous Texas presidential candidacies, from John Connally—who proved that money really isn't everything— to Rick Perry, who demonstrated that good hair won't get you all that far, either. Other than Lyndon Johnson, who came to office via the Kennedy assassination, the Texans who made it to the White House were people who were born somewhere else. The perfect bridge candidate was George H. W. Bush, a Texas oilman with roots in Connecticut and Kennebunkport, Maine. "H. W. was not a Texan," said Jim Marston, the director of the Environmental Defense Fund's Texas office. "We don't use 'summer' as a verb."

H. W. had settled with his family in Midland, in that pleasant but extremely modest house where he and Barbara raised their young family, which today still bears testimony to the fact that their oldest son was once both a Boy Scout and a charter member of the Roy Rogers Riders Club. (That was about as close to horses as W. was ever going to get.) A defender of business interests, especially when the business was oil, H. W. was otherwise not actually all that conservative by current standards. As president, he signed a major new civil rights law for the disabled and the Clean Air Act, which his son would ignore as governor and then later undermine when he reached the White House himself. H. W. actually raised taxes. When he got into a war—and it was admittedly a war in which American oil interests had great, um, interests—he brought all of America's allies on board, and he ended it without trying to topple his main enemy, the farthest thing possible from the Alamo spirit.

Bush's middle-of-the-roadness failed to get him a second term. But Congress was changing in ways the empty-place wing of the Texas party was finding much to its liking. Really, things could not have been much better unless Newt Gingrich, the new House Speaker, had been from Amarillo instead of Carrollton, Georgia. Texans found Gingrich's aim—to create a new Republican majority that was united in right-wing ideology—totally appealing. And the man who would be his majority leader when he came into power was a Texan, Dick Armey, who helped Gingrich write the Contract With America, and who would later be a key organizer of the Tea Party movement. Then there was Tom DeLay, the hardcharging exterminator from the Houston suburb of Sugar Land, who had first decided to run for office when the Environmental Protection Agency banned his favorite product for eliminating fire ants. DeLay inserted himself into the leadership and became whip, the number three House leader. In DeLay's case, he was a number three with special interests in partisan fighting and obsessive fundraising. "DeLay took things to a different and much more poisonous level," said Norman Ornstein, a resident scholar at the conservative American Enterprise Institute.

Armey and DeLay, who succeeded him as House majority leader in 2003, were not a team. In fact, Armey once referred to the DeLay camp, with its incessant focus on hot-button social issues, as "those nitwits who took over after we left." Armey was a libertarian who prided himself on his credentials as an economist, while DeLay was part of the social right who would eventually come to pride himself on cha-cha-cha-ing on *Dancing with the Stars*. But they had a similar antipathy toward government. DeLay was once asked whether there were any government regulations worth keeping, and responded, "None that I can think of."

DeLay oversaw the K Street Project, an effort to reserve all the good lobbying jobs in Washington for Republicans and to punish any special interest group that dared to employ Democrats. Meanwhile, the minority party was elbowed out of any role in the House. Under DeLay, committees began to draft legislation in meetings closed to Democrats, and the product of their work was pushed onto the floor with straight party-line votes. The Democrats had ignored the Republicans in a more polite way when they were in charge, partly because they felt confident of their power and partly because so many Democratic members were conservative. Now the split between the parties was clearer and the domination more brutal.

And their agenda was totally clear. Lower taxes. Less government. Phil Gramm moved up to the Senate and became a principal architect of financial deregulation. Armey led the Republicans' successful fight against the Clinton health care plan.

Meanwhile, back in Texas, George W. Bush had become governor with the help of consultant Karl Rove, who would become almost as influential a player in Texas—and then national—politics as the men whose victories he engineered. (It would be Rove who recruited Rick Perry to run for agricultural commissioner, and put him over the top in a last-minute ad blitz that tied the populist liberal incumbent, Jim Hightower, to the twin sins of flag-burning and shaking hands with Jesse Jackson. ("He was innocent of the former and guilty of the latter," wrote a trio of political journalists in their Rove biography, *Boy Genius*.)

The first President Bush was an easterner who learned to talk Texan—or at least, to talk like a founder of Zapata Petroleum Corporation. ("I am delighted to be here with you this evening, because after listening to George Bush all these years, I figured you needed to know what a real Texas accent sounds like," Ann Richards told the Democratic National Convention in 1988.) His oldest son was, like his father, born in New England. But W. nevertheless grew up as a real Texan, albeit one who was shipped off to school in the East to rub off some of the western edges. As governor, George W. was eager to get along with legislators of both parties and enthusiastic about improving education, particularly for poor and minority children. He was also extremely conservative, especially when it came to the empty-places priority of keeping government small and underfunded. He was a fiend for privatization—the Rove biographers reported in *Boy Genius* that Bush told one state legislator that he dreamed of privatizing the University of Texas. Previewing another cause he'd champion as president, Governor Bush pressed to give faith-based organizations a bigger role in providing social services. (Texans, after all, could get a child out of a well without government help.) He also pushed through a big tax cut that blew the state surplus and left Texas sitting with a monster deficit, while its architect went to Washington to do exactly the same thing to the country. Once in the White House, Bush II also gave us a huge federal education bill that would remake America's public schools in the image of the ones in Texas, an energy bill that was drawn up by the energy interests, and two wars.

Perhaps it's a coincidence that Texas presidents keep getting us into conflicts abroad. To be fair, American involvement in Vietnam started before Lyndon Johnson came into power and ratcheted things up. The first Gulf War under H. W. was a limited engagement. You could argue that the fact that W. got us into Iraq and Afghanistan had more to do with W. than with the grand Texas love affair with dramatic gestures. And maybe it's beside the point that people called Afghanistan "Charlie Wilson's war" after the Texas congressman who was so deeply gung-ho to get America involved in the Afghani guerrilla war against the Soviet Union.

Just sayin'.

By the Obama era, Tom DeLay was a political wreck, appealing a three-year sentence for money laundering and licking his wounds after being forced to retreat from *Dancing with the Stars* due to stress fractures in both feet and a bad samba performance. (We bid a temporary adieu to DeLay in his immortal words from the final TV appearance: "What's a little pain when we can party?") But Dick Armey had never been more ready to roll. He became head of FreedomWorks, which turned the town hall meetings that members of Congress traditionally hold during summer recess into raucous protests against Obama's health care reform. Then he and the FreedomWorks organizers staged the Tea Party's big coming-out party, the Taxpayer March on Washington, in the fall of 2009. "Armey and FreedomWorks have been the invisible hand behind much of the recent conservativism in this country," Republican political consultant Mark McKinnon told the *New York Times*.

Texas Congressman Ron Paul, another libertarian, became the closest thing the Tea Party had to an intellectual guide. Paul, who ran as a presidential candidate in 2008 and 2012, differed from other high-profile Republicans in his adamant opposition to an activist American foreign policy. He called for a return to the gold standard and a federal government that was small to the point of itsy-bitsy. He was a perfect empty-places politician—critics might argue that his ideas, if implemented, could turn the entire country into one large empty place. But Paul's anti-war, anti-drug war, and general anti-authoritarian message won him a devoted following, particularly among young people.

It was the new political flavor, one that was nearly as hostile to traditional mainstream Republicanism as it was to the Democrats, although of course when it came to things to complain about, the Democrats and Barack Obama got top billing. "Nearly every important office in Washington DC today is occupied by someone with an aggressive dislike for our heritage, our freedom, our history, and our Constitution," Armey told his crowds.

It really was a declaration of political war. No surrender! No retreat! What could be more Texas?

PART TWO
HOW TEXAS CHANGED THE NATION

4

Financial Deregulation—
the Texas Angle

"In a Gramm administration,
we will keep the cake"

Becoming a Republican worked very well for Phil Gramm, who not only won the 1983 special election to replace Democrat Phil Gramm in the House, but then moved on up to the Senate two years later. Waving his PhD in economics everywhere he went, Gramm got himself appointed to the Senate Budget Committee and became both a kind of economic guru to some conservatives and a recipient of mammoth campaign contributions from wealthy Texans. In February of 1995, armed with his huge bag of cash, he announced his candidacy for president of the United States.

Almost instantly, the Gramm luck ran out. As a presidential candidate, he was awful. We've already taken note of the state's talent for producing deeply unsuccessful White House contenders. (Outside of Lyndon Johnson's post–Kennedy-assassination victory in 1964, the only native-born Texan ever elected president was Dwight Eisenhower, who moved to Kansas when he was two.) But even by that standard, Gramm's presidential run was pretty dismal. In the end he won all of ten delegates, at an average cost of $2.1 million apiece.

One of the many terrible things about candidate Gramm was his campaign stump speech, in which he told his audience, "What we have to share with a hungry world is not our cake but the recipe that we use to bake that cake." (Finally, we had a public figure even less sympathetic than Marie Antoinette, who at least never suggested that the state let the starving poor eat the recipes.)

"That recipe is private property, free enterprise, and individual freedom," Gramm would continue. He is a tall, balding man with a rather long neck that he would stick forward as he peered at the crowd with his tiny little eyes. The general effect was of a turtle, wearing glasses and a really good suit.

"In a Gramm administration, we will keep the cake and share the recipe!" the candidate concluded triumphantly, often to deafening silence from his listeners. Nobody really got the part about the cake. The audiences may have been wondering whether the hungry nations had enough sugar and eggs and butter to follow the cookbook.

Gramm is important to this story because he represents what happened when the empty-places philosophy turned toward financial regulation—be it of savings and loan associations, commercial banks, energy markets, or all those inexplicable investments we have come to think of under the fits-all term of "swaps." A former economics professor at Texas A & M, Gramm was in love with the vision of endless financial prairies where Americans could enjoy the blessings of a free market, roaming unfettered by federal regulation like happy mustangs on the range. "When I am on Wall Street and I realize that that's the very nerve center of American capitalism and I realize what capitalism has done for the working people of America, to me that's a holy place," he said in 2000 after a visit to New York.

"The worst in the nation and that's saying something"

Gramm became a key player in setting the national agenda on financial deregulation. But this story started earlier, back in the 1970s, when Texas began applying the principles of the wide open economic spaces to its state-chartered savings and loan associations. The S & Ls—which we can never mention without pointing out that Jimmy Stewart ran one in *It's a Wonderful Life*— had traditionally taken in deposits for a modest fixed rate and then lent out mortgage loans for slightly more. That hardly allowed for much elbow room, let alone free range-roaming. So the state decided to let them loan more money with fewer assets to back up the loans. It also permitted the S & Ls, which had formerly been all about home ownership, to lend money on commercial properties.

The results were spectacular—profits soared—and then spectacularly disastrous. Texas S & L owners—some of them crooked, some of them just inept—loaned money at very high interest rates to people with no capacity, and sometimes no intention, to repay. They invested in stuff that was wildly speculative at best, and at worst, total theft. One historic state thrift spent depositors' money to send its president and his friends on a luxury tour of France under the theory that it was research for a high-end restaurant the thrift planned to open in Dallas. A collective of crooked Texas S & Ls shuffled their bad loans around, creating paper profits for the edification of the accountants.

Meanwhile, the Reagan administration was trying to figure out what to do with the federally chartered S & Ls, which were floundering in a world of double-digit inflation. They had already been effectively permitted to set their own interest rates, and by 1981 were paying depositors an average of 11.53 percent. But they were only taking in 10.02 percent from all those mortgage loans. The Federal Home Loan Bank Board, which regulated the S & Ls, went looking for a new economic model that would allow them to get their income and outgo back in balance. At the time, state-chartered thrifts in Texas, which were less regulated than the federal S & Ls, were thriving. When it came to profits, "Texas was at the top of the charts," said Bill Black, who worked for the Bank Board in the 1980s and had a ringside seat for the chaos that was to come.

Of course, Black added, that was "because more of its savings and loans engaged in accounting fraud than anywhere else."

The Bank Board team wrote up a bill, which became the basis of the Garn–St. Germain Act, pretty much deregulating the S & Ls. If Black is right about the inspiration, they wanted to go where Texas had gone—without, of course, the still-unnoticed fraud.

In fact, the feds went even further, in hopes that if they gave the S & Ls enough leeway, they could grow their way out of their huge losses. That created what Black called "a race to the bottom" when it came to control and oversight. First out of the box was California, which attempted to lure business back to the state by making its charters even more permissive than those of the feds. Texas upped the ante, deregulating its already pretty well deregulated thrifts even further.

Black was head of litigation at the Bank Board and then deputy director of the Federal Savings and Loan Insurance Corporation, the agency that was on the hook for compensating depositors when an S & L went under. He came to have a painfully detailed knowledge of the Texas S & L scene, with its cowboy-culture rules and skimpy oversight. "Its state regulatory system was the worst in the nation and that's saying something," he concluded.

The most infamous of the Texas S & Ls was Vernon Savings and Loan, which the regulators fondly referred to as "Vermin." It lives on in history for the theory that using S & L funds to hire a prostitute to entertain a bank regulator wasn't a bribe if the regulator was unable to rise to the occasion. (The lawyer for the thrift's former president made that argument at his trial.) But for a time, Vernon was, on-paper-by-its-own-accounting, the most profitable S & L in America. Its owner, Don Dixon, was a real estate developer who discovered innumerable advantages in the Texas thrift business. One was that acquiring Vernon cost him no actual money—like all the crooked insiders in this game, he paid for his investments with borrowed funds from other insiders, who kept the Ponzi chain going until the string ran out. Among the disadvantages was that running Vernon Savings and Loan involved working in Vernon, a humble city north of Wichita Falls that was, until its moment of infamy, best known as the birthplace of Roy Orbison. Dixon overcame that problem by investing depositors' money in vacation houses, a mini-fleet of jets, and a yacht, which he kept on the Potomac due to lack of available docking space in landlocked Vernon. ("It served as a floating lobbying platform. Yes, the prostitutes showed up here as well," wrote Black in his account of the S & L meltdown, *The Best Way to Rob a Bank Is to Own One*.) It was also Dixon who invested bank money in a fact-finding tour of top-notch French restaurants. (Dixon's wife kept a diary of the tour, entitled "Gastronomique Fantastique!") There was not, however, any long-term solvency in the game plan, and Dixon was eventually convicted of twenty-three counts of bank fraud.

"Very Texas instincts"

Athough Texas had swung hard for Reagan in the presidential elections, at the time the S & Ls were imploding, the state's biggest power in Washington was a Democrat, House Speaker Jim Wright of Fort Worth, and Wright became a go-to guy for Texas thrift officials seeking protection from regulators who wanted to pull the plug on their doomed institutions. "The Speaker had very Texas instincts—these folks call themselves entrepreneurs who are beset by government, so they must be right," said Black.

When the Bank Board needed money to cover all the failing S & Ls, regulators believed Wright was holding up authorization while he demanded more leeway for home state businesses. (At one point, he requested more time for "Vermin.") Wright wound up being brought before the House Ethics Committee on a range of allegations, ranging from misusing his power in relation to the S & Ls, to using a congressional aide to help him write his memoirs. Wright claimed he was simply doing his duty to aid his constituents in the first case. When it came to the book, he told the committee that the aide in question was so eager to have a part in the creation of *Reflections of a Public Man* that he volunteered to do it on his own time, in the evenings and on weekends.

The Ethics Committee decided that Wright's efforts on behalf of the Texas S & Ls, while "intemperate," fell within the normal course of legislative business. Whether this makes you feel better about Wright or worse about Congress is another one of those natural-optimism tests. However, the committee did agree to pursue some of the other charges, which appeared to cluster around the sins other members were less likely to dabble in. In response, the Speaker resigned from office in 1989. It was the last time Texas would get its power on the national level through a Democrat.

For the rest of us, the repercussions of the Texas part of the S & L debacle were multitudinous. Wright's main accuser, a hitherto little-known Georgia Republican named Newt Gingrich, was catapulted into political stardom, and began his quest to turn the Republican minority into an ideologically unified attack force. At his side were allies like Tom DeLay, who turned out to be as bloodthirsty in partisan House politics as he was in Sugar Land extermination projects. Gingrich would eventually wind up before the Ethics Committee himself, topping Wright by becoming the first Speaker to be officially sanctioned by the House. But not before he, DeLay, and Armey had turned the clubby House of Representatives of yore into the partisan battlefield we all know and loathe today.

And then there was the price of Texas bidness itself. By the time the thrifts stopped imploding in the 1990s, 237 Texas S & Ls had failed, more than twice as many as in next-place California. In the end, more than half of all the money lost in the nationwide debacle was lost in Texas. As Robert Bryce notes in his Texas book, *Cronies*, Texas got $4,775 per capita in federal bailout funds, while New Jersey lost $1,074 per capita. It was one of those times when Texas politicians did not complain about massive government spending.

"I want our America back"

But back to Phil Gramm.

The other memorable point in Gramm's presidential candidacy speech was biographical—the story of how he had failed the third, seventh, and ninth grade, and how his algebra teacher told his mother that little Phil would never graduate high school. How, in a last-ditch effort to save her son's future, his mom sent him to military school under a federal program that provided scholarships for even the least promising offspring of dead servicemen. There, Gramm was turned around; his mother's fondest hopes were realized and he went to college and then graduate school, all on government money. "Too many mothers' dreams are dying too easily in America today," he would conclude. "I want our America back."

He told this story often, and once the speech was over, everyone would proceed to a press conference where reporters would get to point out that as a US senator, Gramm had supported legislative proposals that would lead to draconian cuts in federal spending on education.

"The debate is not about how much money should be spent on education and housing and nutrition," Gramm would say. "The debate is about who should do the spending. Bill Clinton wants the government to do the spending, and I want the families to do the spending."

And off he went to the next stop.

"He's been asked that one for years and he still hasn't come up with a good answer," one of the Texas reporters on the presidential tour plane said.

Gramm threw all his hopes on the Iowa Republican caucus,

where he came in fifth. Even the conservative caucus-goers, it turned out, didn't want a guy who opposed food stamp spending because "all our poor people are fat" and joked that he did indeed have a heart—which he kept in a jar in his office. Ronald Reagan occasionally made weird or offputting remarks, but he had a lovely smile. Gramm just had that turtle thing.

"I look at subprime lending and I see the American dream"

So much for the presidency. But Gramm did not go away. No, he had promises to keep, and miles to go before he retired from public service to become a lobbyist for an international megabank. He went back to the Senate, where he later became chairman of the Banking, Housing, and Urban Affairs Committee, and where his continuing quest for wide open markets played a central role in creating several major economic earthquakes for the entire nation.

When predatory lending—the practice, basically, of making home loans to people who could not afford to keep up on the payments—began to create an uptick in foreclosures in 2001, Gramm led the fight to beat back any attempts to crack down. Once again, he brought back his poor widowed mother, who he claimed was able to put a roof over her children's heads thanks to a 1950s' version of subprime lending. "Some people look at subprime lending and see evil. I look at subprime lending and I see the American dream in action," he said. It was not perhaps the most devastating blow to the nation's economic balance that he helped deliver, but it did kind of set a pattern.

Meanwhile, Gramm was a major player in writing the Commodity Futures Modernization Act of 2000, which would modernize commodities trading so thoroughly that by 2008 the nation's major banks were able to trade fiercely and unregulatedly in credit default swaps and other financial instruments so exotic that even their CEOs did not understand them. These major banks were much larger, much more too-big-to-fail than they had been in the 1980s, when the government had encouraged them to acquire failed savings and loans, some of which were, of course, in Texas.

And Gramm was also the Gramm of the Gramm–Leach–Bliley Act, which dismantled the Depression-era regulations that kept a wall between commercial and investment banks. This law was blamed by many for ushering in the crazed trading by commercial banks that led to the economic collapse of 2008. To be fair, Gramm–Leach–Etc. was the work of half of Washington. Gramm at one point even threatened to destroy the whole project because he was angry over the section of the act that required banks to make loans in poor communities, some perhaps clotted with struggling widows trying to cope with a semi-delinquent son who failed ninth grade.

In the end, Gramm did help write the bill, which was a regulatory nightmare that split up the job of watching what the newly liberated banks were doing among different agencies, creating so many loopholes and untended corners that the traders themselves could not have done it much better. That could not have been a mistake, since Gramm had made it a practice to reject requests by the Securities and Exchange Commission for more money to make sure Wall Street was obeying the law. "We have learned government is not the answer," Gramm intoned as he shepherded the massive bill through the Senate and out into the world, where it would prove that unfettered markets were definitely not the answer either.

"Oh, yuck"

And then . . . (drum roll) . . . there was the Enron meltdown. Gramm had a soft spot in his heart for the Houston-based firm, possibly because he admired CEO Ken Lay, a soul mate who, the senator enthused, was "as comfortable talking about the ancient Greeks as he is the competitive selling of electric power." Those chats about the ancient Greeks were undoubtedly a bonding factor, although there was also the thing about Enron being a very big donor to Phil Gramm campaigns.

When the helping of Enron began, the company was already well on its way to being a business of the twenty-first century—that is, a place that creates nothing whatsoever, but devotes all its time to taking stuff that other people make and putting it in various financial packages, which are then traded back and forth until their value loses all relationship to reality. "Enron's business model was built entirely on the premise that it could make more money speculating on electricity contracts than it could by actually producing electricity at a power plant," said the watchdog organization Public Citizen in a devastating report on the Gramm connection.

But to really get the trading going full speed, Enron needed to be out from under the thumb of federal oversight, unbridled and free to trot about the plateaus of online energy auctioneering, creating markets and perhaps, every now and then, withholding energy from the market entirely in order to make its price rise at a convenient moment. Happily for Enron, Gramm's wife, Wendy, was serving during the George H. W. Bush administration as the chair of the federal Commodity Futures Trading Commission.

Wendy Gramm, like her husband, has a doctorate in economics. (What is it about the mixture of economics degrees and Texas? Dick Armey has one, too.) Wendy often told the story of how, when she was being recruited for a job in Phil's college economics department, he told her, "As a single member of the faculty I'd be very interested in having you come to Texas A & M," and she in return said, "Oh, yuck." However, the Gramms apparently found accord in their mutual passion for capitalism unbound. (In a confidential e-mail while she was chair of the CFTC, Wendy Gramm told a correspondent at Enron that she was unpopular, nay *hated*, in some quarters in Washington because "I'm too free-market.")

When Bill Clinton was elected president, Wendy Gramm understood that her days were numbered. In January of 1993, six days before Clinton took the oath of office, she produced the rule

change desired by Enron, eliminating her own commission's ability to oversee energy derivatives contracts and interest rate swaps.
(The investors in these trades did not need protection, she rea-
soned, because they were "large sophisticated commercial entities,"
not "real people.") At the time, two of the five commission seats
were vacant. The three sitting members approved the plan 2–1.
Mission accomplished, Wendy resigned. A few weeks later, she was
appointed to the Enron board of directors, where she served on
the audit committee, which did such a swell job of making sure
the bankruptcy-bound corporation's accounting was accurate and
that its financial reports were on the up-and-up. For those services, Public Citizen reported, she was paid "between $915,000
and $1.85 million in salary, attendance fees, stock option sales, and
dividends from 1993 to 2001."

Who would have imagined that joining the Texas A & M faculty could have turned out to be so lucrative?

"I happen to think Gramm did not know what he was doing"

At the tail end of 2000, when Bill Clinton was preparing to leave
office, the Supreme Court was preparing to hand the presidency
to George W. Bush, and Congress was preparing to have one
of its frequent meltdowns, Phil Gramm struck again. This time,
he inserted an amendment into a federal budget resolution that
the House and Senate were struggling mightily to get passed. It
mirrored a bill he had championed earlier in the year, deregulating
certain kinds of futures trading—like the swaps that we came to
hear so much more about in 2008. The bill appeared to be dead
until Gramm successfully attached it as a 262-page amendment to
the budget resolution.

Michael Greenberger, a former director of the CFTC division
of trading and markets, told *Mother Jones* writer David Corn in
2008 that the deregulation of the swaps market under the Gramm

amendment was at "the heart of the subprime meltdown." But, Greenberger added, "I happen to think Gramm did not know what he was doing. I don't think a single member in Congress had read the 262-page bill or had thought of the cataclysm it would cause." Gramm, who never admits not knowing anything, seems to feel that his amendment made things better.

The last-minute stuck-in-the-budget amendment also included deregulation of energy futures, the very thing that Enron was hoping to make its twenty-first-century career manipulating. Energy futures were an issue of concern at the time—in fact, a special White House advisory group had just spent a great deal of time looking into it, concluding that it was very important that the future price of energy should not be deregulated in any way, never, nohow. If you did, who knew what might happen? Unprincipled people in the power market might even start manufacturing artificial shortages just to increase the cost of power.

Gramm later claimed the language, which came to be known as the "Enron loophole," did not come from him, although it was, you know, his amendment.

Soon thereafter, California, which had been having energy troubles of a serious but not desperate nature, began imploding. Rolling blackout followed rolling blackout as utilities found it impossible to get their hands on enough energy to power the state. Enron, however, was having a terrific time. "Wholesale services" revenue—which would include the profits from its energy auctions—went from $12 billion in the first quarter of 2000 to $48.4 billion for the same period in 2001.

All the fun ended in the summer of 2001, when the pressure on Washington to do something became too great to resist. The Federal Energy Regulatory Commission imposed price controls in eleven western states, ruining the Enron auction system. And shortly thereafter, the company was bankrupt. Thousands of Texans lost their jobs, their health care plan, and frequently their retirement accounts. Other firms around the country that had tried to duplicate Enron's energy trading strategy saw their stocks crater. Congress passed the Sarbanes-Oxley Act, a tough new set of accounting standards, by a near-unanimous vote. (By the 2012 presidential race, conservatives would be denouncing it as a massive bureaucratic burden on the cost of doing business.) And of course, California was still nursing its wounds.

I'm sure you'll be happy to know that Phil Gramm bounced right back. He announced that he would not seek reelection and took a job as a highly paid investment banker and lobbyist for the Swiss bank UBS, continuing to urge his friends in Congress to avoid the temptation to regulate predatory lenders. (Gramm became vice president of the UBS investment banking arm—a limb that would not have existed had the Gramm–Leach–Bliley Act not made it possible for the bank to buy Paine Webber two years earlier.) When the crash came, he was unmoved by critics of his performance as the free-market guru of Capitol Hill. The fault, he said, lay with others, including "predatory borrowers" who took out loans they couldn't afford to pay. In 2008, he became the economic adviser to John McCain's presidential campaign and blamed the meltdown panic on the fact that the country had become "a nation of whiners."

5

No Child Left Behind

*"The worst educational system
you could possibly have"*

The story of how Texas came to set the education agenda of the nation is more emotionally complicated than the one about financial regulation. Not many of us have conflicted feelings about Phil Gramm's efforts to deregulate swaps or give Enron the green light on its electricity futures trading schemes. Bad news for the bottom 99 percent. However, reforming education is another deal altogether. Let me warn you in advance that it's going to be filled with people who were trying to do the right thing—along, of course, with a passel of special interests.

This is also going to be a story about how Texas gave us a new vision of public education that involved unprecedented levels of federal oversight of local schools. *Texas!* Amazing, right? Even today there are Texas politicians who shake their head in stunned befuddlement at what they've wrought.

The very idea of Texas being at the center of a national education reform movement is counterintuitive. Nothing in its history suggests this is the place where the Lone Star State should wind up. Look at the Alamo, and you can instantly imagine a series of Texas politicians going to Washington and starting wars. On energy, you can intuit the connection. Even taxes. But Texas had not traditionally been the first, second, or twentieth name that came to mind when the subject was quality education. Back in 1920, in a cry that would be repeated throughout most of the state's modern history, the Campaign for Better Schools pushed for more funding with a flyer that read:

TEXAS
First in Size
First in Agricultural Products
First in Production of Oil
Seventh in Wealth
Thirty-Ninth in Education

When World War Two began, 23 percent of the young men being drafted or recruited from Texas were too badly educated to qualify for the military—twice the national average. After the war ended, Texas still only required that teachers have a high school education, and rural districts routinely shut down when it was time to plant or harvest the crops. "We had the worst educational system . . . that you could possibly have," recalled former House Speaker Reuben Senterfitt, who helped get the schools their first infusion of state funding. Decades later, many Texas policy-makers still believed that all you needed to make it in their state was sweat and savvy, not book learning. "When I first came to the legislature you had to have arguments with a lot of people about whether it was necessary to graduate high school," said Representative Scott Hochberg, who was first elected in 1992.

Nevertheless, Texas had joined the rest of the nation in wondering if its schools were up to snuff. The Reagan administration—not normally known to be a den of worrywarts when it came to the quality of domestic government programs—had issued a widely influential report, "A Nation at Risk," in 1983, which said that the world was becoming one large economic village, in which products of the American educational system were at a disadvantage. The hawkish White House warned ominously that the country had been "committing an act of unthinking, unilateral educational disarmament," and the more Americans looked around, the more it did seem as if other countries—particularly rather obscure Nordic countries—were doing way better at teaching reading and math, not to mention science and geography. What did Finland know that we didn't? The debate raged endlessly, as did the promises for change. The first President Bush vowed to be the "education president," to little discernible effect. And Bill Clinton ran, in part, on his pro-education record as governor of Arkansas.

Then came the 2000 election. During the campaign, George W. Bush couldn't stop talking about education. "It's important to have standards," he'd say, holding up his hand to indicate the setting of a bar—a gesture that seemed to indicate the standards he had in mind were about five feet high. During one of the primary debates, he got a little sulky when John McCain was asked about schools while he got a question on gun control. "Not about education, but go ahead," he said unhappily. As a presidential candidate, George W. Bush wasn't just issuing general promises to improve the schools. He claimed to have the secret recipe. "We think we know how to do it. Governor Bush has done it in Texas," Dick Cheney told America in the vice presidential debate.

This came up all the time. Bush, it was said, had presided over "the Texas Miracle" that turned public schools around, sent test scores soaring, and dramatically narrowed the gap between middle-class white kids and poor, black, and Hispanic students. On the presidential press buses, reporters kept asking the Texas journalists whether the state's schools had improved as dramatically as the campaign claimed. Frequently, the response was something along the line of "I guess so." Political reporters tend to shy away from in-depth analysis of education, which invariably requires a discussion of the relative value of the Texas Assessment of Academic Skills versus the National Assessment of Educational Progress.

But it really did appear that something good had happened.

"One of our better right-wing billionaires"

We need to examine the Texas Miracle, because the way you interpret the saga of how Texas pulled its schools up—and how far the pulling went—will have a lot to do with how favorably you look upon the legacy it gave the nation. When the Reagan White House started ringing the warning bell about international competition in the 1980s, Texas was still close to the bottom of the barrel when it came to the quality of education. Beginning public school teachers were paid $4,100 a year. Administrative costs were high, in part because Texas had 1,031 independent school districts, nearly 400 of which had fewer than 500 students. (In a huge lift, reformers in the late 1940s got the number down from over 2,000. Further merging was regarded as politically impossible; cynics blamed the existing districts' determination to protect the identity of their high school football teams.) Funding was wildly inequitable. The wealthiest district in the state had more than $14 million in assessed property value to tax for each child in the local public schools, while the poorest district had $20,000.

The first serious effort to change things came in the mid-1980s from Governor Mark White, a Democrat who was once described by an opponent as "one of the first nerds in Texas." White wanted to improve education as a tribute to his mother, an overworked teacher. "I've got pictures of her classroom in the first grade with thirty-four kids in it," he told reporters. To figure out what to do, he appointed the inevitable blue-ribbon commission, with Ross Perot as chairman.

Perot, a short, big-eared man with a squeaky voice, was a billionaire businessman who would later run for president as a third-party candidate, destroying the reelection hopes of George H. W.

Bush in 1992. (As a candidate, Perot's big issue was the federal debt. As a businessman, he got his big break when he snared huge government contracts to handle Medicare data processing. This would make him one of the many, many rich Texans who were deeply opposed to Washington spending money on things that did not involve them.) Before his presidential adventures, he was best known for having financed a commando raid on Iran to rescue some employees who had been jailed during the fall of the shah's government. He also once dispatched an attorney to go to England and buy an original copy of the Magna Carta. After the lawyer shelled out $1.5 million for the historic document and requested instructions on how to safely transport it home, Perot said: "Just stick it in your briefcase." Deferring to the man with the check-book, the lawyer did just that.

Perot was, in short, a man who knew what he wanted. And the education task force was one of his finest hours. "They traveled around the state and he was smart enough and wealthy enough and peculiar enough that he would say absolutely what was on his mind," said David Anderson, a former state education official who now lobbies the legislature on education and other issues. Besides spending an enormous amount of time on the project, Perot also spent $500,000 of his own money on consultants. "H. Ross took off like an unguided missile," the iconic Texas columnist Molly Ivins wrote. "I keep having to explain to foreigners that some loopy right-wing Dallas billionaires are a lot better than others, and H. Ross happens to be one of our better right-wing billion-aires. This is assuming you don't make him so mad that he goes out and buys an army and invades your country with it."

The commission report will be remembered forever in Texas for its wildly controversial "no pass, no play" recommendation, which held that students who were failing in their classes should not be allowed to take part in sports or other extracurricular activities. ("It wasn't just football," said Anderson. "Perot told a great story of a west Texas boy missing forty-four days of school showing his chicken at the various agricultural competitions.") A new bumper sticker appeared on Texas cars: "I Don't Brake for H. Ross Perot."

Less colorfully but more centrally, the commission recommended smaller classes, better teacher pay and pre-kindergarten for poor youngsters—all of which Perot personally paid lobbyists to push through the state legislature, along with a companion $4.8 billion tax bill. "In some respects we didn't move the ball very far," admitted then-Lieutenant Governor Bill Hobby, who got the legislation through the senate in an acrimonious session in 1984. "In the end, Texas still had the shortest school year of all the states, and our students spent fewer hours in class than students in other states." But it was definitely a start. And the football players did have to get passing grades.

The really big lift came in 1993, after the exasperated Texas Supreme Court threatened to close down every public school in the state if the legislature didn't find a constitutional way to equalize education funding, pronto. The resolution, a formula so stupendously complicated that only about five people actually understood it, arrived at the last possible moment, twenty-four hours short of an educational Alamo. "We have had three school finance plans that have been struck down since 1989," said Governor Ann Richards. "We pray that this fourth time will produce the charm."

The bill that averted disaster also created the Texas Miracle we would hear so much about in the 2000 presidential campaign. It did two major things. First of all, it gave the schools a lot of money. "Everybody got more," said Bill Ratliff, the Republican who was head of the state senate's Education Committee at the time. Ratliff was one of the five people who understood how the new formula for school funding worked. Most of his colleagues didn't care— they just wanted to look at the printouts that showed how much money each district would receive. "That was the famous line: 'Where's my printout?'" Ratliff reminisced. "You have to raise all boats. You just raise some more." And while everybody got something, the boats being raised the most were exactly the ones whose passengers were several years behind their grade level in reading and math.

Second, to convince people—particularly the business community—that the additional investment would be worthwhile, the school finance bill created an "accountability" system based on a series of statewide tests. This is the part that would, in the future, become the basis of President George W. Bush's No Child Left Behind law. Some of its authors are downright horrified at what they've unleashed. But we'll get to that in a minute.

During the last half of the 1990s, Texas schools did get better. It was very, very hard to figure out exactly how much better, given the amount of conflicting data floating around, but some observers were wowed by how well the students were testing. ("I couldn't believe it," said David Grissmer, who wrote or co-wrote several important education studies on the state.) Some were just prepared to thank God for small favors. (Molly Ivins called it the "story on how our schools rocketed from abysmal to only slightly below average in a mere thirty years.") The doubters would be empowered later, when reporters discovered that in some places, the results had been, shall we say, rigged.

Whether the lift was huge or modest, it had very little to do with George W. Bush, whose role as governor was to arrive at the party after the refreshments had been served and the orchestra had finished its first set. Bush was supportive, but as happened so frequently in the W. saga, his main role was that of cheerleader. "His contribution to education was to argue that it was necessary," said Scott Hochberg, the legislator who had the debates with his fellow lawmakers about whether a high school diploma was important. "And the people who needed to hear that message trusted him."

You will remember that there were two pieces to the big Texas school reform—getting more resources, especially for the poor districts, and testing/accountability. As a presidential candidate, Bush fixated on one of them. We will pause here while everyone guesses which.

"But it's not a business!"

"Testing is the cornerstone of reform. You know how I know? Because it's the cornerstone of reform in Texas," W. said in one of his debates with Al Gore. His opponent, he said, only had a wishy-washy commitment. ("You may claim you've got mandatory testing but you don't, Mr. Vice President.")

While there's absolutely no reason to doubt that Bush's interest in education was genuine, you sometimes wondered how deep his focus went. (During the presidential campaign, a high school student in Beaufort, SC, asked what could be done to push up her state's terrible college board scores, and Bush answered, "Write your governor.") He did promise to increase federal aid to education, although by less than half of what Gore was targeting. But money, he argued, paled next to the importance of his *plan*—based on tests, accountability, and giving parents the right to move their children out of failing schools. "What's more important is reform," Bush told Diane Sawyer. "You know, why pour money into a system that's not reformed?"

In the summer of 2000 the RAND Corporation came out with the study that seemed to verify the existence of a wondrous change in Texas schools, particularly when it came to closing the gap between white and minority students. "Regardless of where a child starts out in Texas, the research shows there is going to be improvement," Grissmer, the lead writer, told the Associated Press. The Bush team did a happy dance. "I am proud of the results we have achieved in education in Texas. As president, I will achieve the same results, ensuring that no child is left behind," the candidate said in a statement.

Then in October, just weeks before the election, *another* RAND study came out, this one finding that Texas had mainly taught its young people to be unusually good at taking the Texas assessment test. "It's not a miracle," said Stephen P. Klein, the lead writer. "We think these scores are misleading and biased because they're

inflated. They're improvements in scores, but not in proficiency."
RAND is less a single entity than a collection of study projects, and
it wasn't absolutely unprecedented for two of its reports to apparently contradict one another. But it certainly was confusing. The
second study was more recent, but smaller. The Bush campaign
called it "the opinion of a few researchers." The Gore campaign
passed it out to every reporter in the country.

Meanwhile, journalists started coming back from Texas with
notebooks full of complaints about the way the school curriculum
was focused on the state standardized test. ("All the emphasis has
been on scores, scores, scores," a school board member in El Paso
griped to the *New York Times*.)

Although Texas wound up having the most influence over
national education policy, it was hardly the only state that developed a testing mania in the 1990s. All around the country, cutting-
edge school districts were administering annual tests to certain
grades, and using them to determine how well individual schools
were performing. A school was only as good as its test scores. During the 2000 Senate campaign in New York, Rick Lazio, who was
running against Hillary Clinton, visited a high school that had
tested well and congratulated the kids for helping to maintain local
property values.

In the states where the test obsession was strongest, teachers
went into mourning for the days when they had been allowed to
try to make learning fun. A fourth-grade teacher in Quincy, Massachusetts, talked about the unit on Antarctica that her students
had always loved but which she had to drop from the curriculum
in favor of test drills. A middle school PTA president in Scarsdale,
NY, was upset that the kids no longer had time to learn science by
tracking hurricanes on the computer because that wasn't included
on the tests. "It's much less pleasant since the tests," said Barbara
Wilson, a high school math teacher in Boston. "Much, much less
pleasant. Extremely less pleasant. Couldn't be more less pleasant."

The tales of woe were the same in Texas. "Growing up in El

Paso, which is mostly a low-income, Latino community, I felt and still feel that most teachers were content letting most of my peers learn *just* enough to pass the TAAS test," said Brenda Arredondo, who went on to Rice University and is now press secretary for a congressional committee. (TAAS is our old friend, the Texas Assessment for Academic Skills, which the state used to judge how well a school was performing.) Arredondo, who was in the Advanced Placement program, said that when it came to the kids who weren't in AP, "it was like [the teachers] felt that it was not their responsibility to prepare students for anything beyond the TAAS test." Another Texas native, now a Washington journalist, bemoans years spent writing "hundreds of practice descriptive paragraphs." In high school, she recalled, her sophomore English teacher "leaned over the transparency machine and said: 'Everything I've been teaching you kids for the last two years on persuasive essays: Toss. It. Out. Of. Your. Brains. Now I'm going to teach you how to really write.'"

The dismay was shared by some of the people who had worked on the Texas school reforms and who had very different memories of what those tests were supposed to do. Paul Sadler, the Democrat who was head of the house Public Education Committee while Bush was governor, insists that the original intent was simply to find out whether a given child was performing at grade level, so the ones who weren't could be given help to improve. "It wasn't a throw-up exam, a your-school's-going-to-be-trashed exam," he said. Bill Ratliff, who led the education reform drive in the state senate, felt that the tests were a way to let parents, and the community, know how well a school was doing, so they could decide for themselves what measures to take if the report card was bad.

"The unfortunate thing," Ratliff added, "was we took those scores and started using them as a punitive measure. Terribly punitive in many cases."

"Everybody said we need to run our schools like a business," Sadler recalled. "I kept saying: *But it's not a business!*"

The Texas business community tended to disagree. It pushed to make the tests high-stakes, so teachers and administrators would know that a poor performance could lead to unpleasant results, up to and including closing down the school entirely. They had accountability in their companies, and they knew what it looked like. "Market discipline is the key, the ultimate form of accountability," wrote Louis V. Gerstner, the head of IBM, in a book detailing his ideas on how to run schools like a business. And while, at the beginning, testing was seen as a tradeoff for more resources, when budgets got tight, people began suggesting that accountability alone would do the trick. In 2011, the Texas Association of Business argued that a no-new-taxes state budget, which drastically cut the state's commitment to school funding, would be fine as long as Texas implemented additional accountability—say, by testing pre-kindergarten classes. "We're talking about productivity," said Bill Hammond, the association's CEO.

Whatever its flaws back home, the Texas Miracle worked great for a presidential campaign. George W. Bush's identification with good schools was particularly important to women, for whom Republican candidates were sometimes a tough sell. At a low point in the race, Bush's team reached out to Paul Sadler, who had worked successfully with the governor on education issues even though he was a Democrat. "They called and asked if I'd go to South Carolina and campaign with him," Sadler recalled. But Sadler thought the testing-and-accountability version of education reform had gone way beyond what he had envisioned. "I think you're going to create the biggest education bureaucracy in the history of the world," he said he told the soon-to-be-president's men.

"Well, maybe we'll call somebody else," they responded.

"He's a pretty relaxed guy"

If the education issue was Bush's trump card, it's possible that the last-minute questions about the validity of the Texas Miracle—the second RAND report, the complaints about all the testing—cost him enough votes at the end of the campaign to send the election into the infamous Florida recount crisis. (Karl Rove disagreed, blaming a late-breaking release of records from a long-ago DUI arrest in Maine.) At any rate, with the help of the Supreme Court, the electoral college and a screwed-up ballot that left some Florida Democrats inadvertently voting for the right-wing Pat Buchanan, Bush wound up in the White House, eager to turn his schools agenda into law.

To tell how the legislation we now know as No Child Left Behind came into being, we have to begin with some serious praise for George W. Bush.

While some other states had gotten into testing in a big way, too, there was one part of the Texas school reforms that was unusual. It's known as disaggregation. Basically, it means that a school's score on the test is based not only on how the students do overall, but also on how much the poor, black, and Hispanic kids improve. "The argument was—and I think it was a compelling argument—that in the past the schools had let some sub-populations drop through the cracks and that wasn't acceptable," said Bill Ratliff.

Disaggregation put tremendous pressure on schools to focus on bringing up their poor and minority students. Districts with large middle-class white populations hated it because their schools could wind up with a low rating even if the majority of their kids were doing well. It was a powerful club against all the subtle and not-so-subtle forces that have created unequal educational opportunity in the twenty-first century. And George Bush adored disaggregation. He loved saying the *word*. Disaggregation was what he meant when he talked about "the soft bigotry of low expectations" for poor and minority students.

There are many veterans of the Texas statehouse in the 1990s who have claimed to be the core creator of the disaggregation system, and trying to sort it out would be as futile as trying to figure out what really happened to Davy Crockett. Bush certainly didn't think it up, but as governor, he proved his commitment. When the Clinton administration ran a pilot program offering more flexibility to states that promised to improve school accountability and raise standards for all students, twelve states got the waivers to participate, but the results were underwhelming. "The only one that did anything concrete in trying to serve poor minority kids was George Bush's Texas," said Charles Barone, who was the top Democratic staff member on the House Education Committee at the time.

So Bush had every right to feel he had some serious credibility when the negotiations on a new federal education law began. Even before the inauguration, he invited a handful of lawmakers to Austin, to have lunch and talk about schools. The Republicans had control of the House and the Senate, and the guests included the education committee chairmen, Representative John Boehner, and Senator Jim Jeffords, and the ranking House Democrat, Representative George Miller.

"He asked people to say something," recalled Miller. The president-elect was in high spirits, jovially calling the senators by their last names. ("Jeffords, what do you think?")

Miller particularly remembered the way Senator Jeffords, a Vermont Republican, began his remarks by delving into his experiences with education back home in Vermont.

"Mr. President," Jeffords said rather formally, "our two states have a lot in common."

"I can't think of *anything*," Bush stage-whispered. (W., Miller noted, is "a pretty relaxed guy.")

The meeting went well, but Jeffords would soon switch parties, becoming an independent and thereby handing control of the Senate over to the Democrats and the education chairmanship to Ted Kennedy. Maybe he was wounded by the crack about Vermont.

"Either you have consequences or you don't"

The Democrats had no particular affection for Bush, and they disliked many of the Republican education priorities, particularly the idea that students should be allowed to use public money to attend private schools through the use of vouchers. But Miller and Kennedy were won over by the president's enthusiasm for disaggregation—a concept even Bill Clinton had found too hot to handle. "That was a game-changer," Barone said.

The focus on poor and minority children made it much easier for liberals to swallow the test-centric nature of the president's vision, about which Democratic allies like the teachers unions were deeply unenthusiastic. The White House wanted to see all children, particularly those in grades three though eight, take achievement tests every year. The public should be told the results. Children in low-performing schools who got bad results should be able to demand outside tutoring help—paid for out of the school budget. So far, this was basically the Texas version of how to reform education— heavy on accountability, friendly to private enterprise—and it had some inherent problems. One involved that accountability. Virtually everybody agreed that the grass roots should run the schools, and that the state's job was to set standards while the districts figured out how to meet them. But what happened if they didn't? Back in Austin, people like Ratliff and Sadler had believed pressure from the community would make things better. If the pressure didn't work, they didn't really have a next step.

The business community had always felt there had to be a stage two. "Calling things what they are is great but either you have consequences or you don't," said Sandy Kress, who was a consultant to the Governor's Business Council, which had pushed for education reform during W.'s gubernatorial years, and then one of the top White House aides handling the issue. After that, Kress became a lobbyist for Pearson PLC, one of the world's largest test publishers.

The program Congress was cobbling together was going to

involve stiff penalties for poor results. If a school consistently failed to improve, parents would have an option of demanding that their children be moved to a better-performing public school. (The White House wanted to give them vouchers to use at any school they wanted, private or public. That never made it into the Texas law, and it was never going to make it into a national one, either. Yet for voucher partisans, hope sprang eternal. Truly, if they could have figured out a way to hand kids vouchers with their flu shots, they'd have gone for it.)

The big question was how to figure out who was performing badly. That seemed simple in Texas, since all the schools took the same test. But the idea of imposing a national test on all states was anathema to many conservatives. (States' rights! States' rights!) So the bill-drafters in Washington decided that every state could write its own. No wonder the law was complicated—fifty different tests, fifty different standards for separating the winners from the losers.

When the Texas law was being written, by people who had no idea they were creating a national model, the legislators had debated whether the state should write its own test or adopt one that seemed to be working well for other states. If the second option had won out, perhaps that would have provided the juice to put a single test standard in the federal legislation. But looking back, Ratliff concluded it never would have worked. When the testing began, he recalled, Christian conservatives began spreading rumors that the new accountability had "an anti-religious agenda." There were hysterical reports that the kids were being asked questions about witchcraft, and to calm things down, the state finally decided to make its old tests public every year so the critics could see there were no references to, say, the positive aspects of devil worship. If Texas had been using a national test, Ratliff pointed out, "we never could have been able to release it and to this day we'd be having these horror stories about pointy-headed liberals that were writing these tests in New York or Iowa or wherever."

Don't blame the Texas drafters for this one—they had no idea

that the law they were passing would wind up being the inspiration for a new national schools agenda. Who knew that when you
mixed school-funding lawsuits, witch-hunting Christian conservatives, and business interests in love with the magic of the marketplace, you'd wind up with a new federal education initiative that
was based on fifty different tests?

"I think he looked on the sunny side of the street"

The Democrats won several big points during the No Child Left
Behind negotiations. Bush dropped the voucher demand as hopeless,
and he agreed to a schedule of large increases in federal education aid
that was painstakingly worked out down to the smallest detail. But
the White House won a central accountability point—if a school
consistently got bad results on the tests, children should be able to
transfer to a better school in the system. Then, the theory went,
the threat of the loss of students would force the poor schools to
pull themselves together. It was the first rule of the marketplace—
consumer demand drives everything. That law does generally
work when the product customers are judging is a television set
or an iPod. Education turned out to be more complicated. Parents
often preferred to keep their children in a familiar, easy-to-reach
school that got poor results rather than transferring them to a more
successful model in a strange neighborhood. (In New York City
in 2011, parents held demonstrations to protest city plans to close
schools that had repeatedly failed to meet the standards.)

Diane Ravitch, an education expert who had been a cheerleader
for No Child Left Behind, recalled the day her enthusiasm for the
law evaporated—at a 2006 conference at the conservative think
tank the American Enterprise Institute, in which "the scholars presented persuasive evidence that only a tiny percentage of eligible
students asked to transfer to better schools." In California, only
1 percent of kids in failing schools requested a change. In Colorado, it was 2 percent. While the advocates of choice were certain

that most families wanted the chance to escape their neighborhood schools, Ravitch recalled, real-life experience "demonstrated the opposite." And if there was no real threat of lost students, then a central accountability principle was toast.

That left only the threat that a bad test performance posed to the principals and teachers, many of whom quickly demonstrated that if the high stakes involved their own careers, they were prepared to spend large chunks of class time drilling students on how to pass. "The problem we had then was, we didn't know much about tests," said Miller. "What we've learned over time is the tests were all of different validities and values." But Miller doubted that Bush had any idea he was pushing a plan with dubious underpinnings: "I think he looked on the sunny side of the street."

The debate over the No Child Left Behind bill went on for months, but it finally was passed into law with an 87–10 vote in the Senate. It happened shortly after the 9/11 terrorist attacks, when lawmakers were yearning for a chance to show some unity. It was signed into law in January of 2002. The nation had a big new federal education program that looked very familiar to Texans.

"He simply walked away from it"

In 2003, more than a year after the plan that produced the Texas Miracle had been translated into No Child Left Behind, a Houston TV station discovered that a local school had fudged its reporting to make it look as though dropouts had just moved to another district. ("We go from 1,000 freshmen to less than 300 seniors with no dropouts. Amazing!" an assistant principal wrote to the principal, cynically.) The state responded by conducting an audit which found that in 2000–01, just as George W. Bush was getting elected president, being sworn in, and naming Houston schools chancellor Rod Paige as head of the Department of Education, more than half of the 5,500 Houston students who left the school were described as having moved to another district rather than being declared dropouts as they should have been. So much for accountability.

The Bush administration still saw the sunny side of the street. "Some people think they can damage the process of national reform and defeat the No Child Left Behind law by striking out at Texas and the Houston Independent School District," Paige told a gathering of business leaders in his home city. "They believe they can win by fighting a proxy war here. So they try to devalue the good work of the people of Houston."

By then, the president's mind was on other matters. The White House had a war or two to run, and Bush failed to deliver on his commitment to dramatically raise funding for education. "Those promises were explicit," said Miller. "You get me the reform and we'll get you the resources. He simply walked away from it."

"A federal takeover of public schools"

No Child Left Behind immediately made an impact on the nation. One of the first big changes was that nearly a third of the states lowered their standards for academic success. As an official in North Carolina explained to the *New York Times,* the states were stuck with a choice—lower standards so their students would hit the markers under the new federal law, "or do you do the right thing for kids, by setting them higher so they're comparable with our global competitors?" North Carolina went for the global competitors and actually raised its standards. Maine, Oklahoma, and Wyoming lowered the bar for all the critical tests. Many other states lowered only some or, in a real stab at creativity, raised some and lowered others.

It was impossibly complicated. As time went on, the entire nation seemed wound up in some variation on the fight over the Texas Assessment of Academic Skills versus the National Assessment of Educational Progress. In New York City, Mayor Michael Bloomberg ran for reelection in 2009 on the terrific progress of the public schools, where two-thirds of the students were passing the state English test and 82 percent were proficient in math. (Pour the champagne!) Then when the test was changed to one the teachers and students weren't already familiar with, the scores dropped back down. (Put the cork back in the bottle!)

"This doesn't mean the kids did any worse—quite the contrary," averred the mayor, as parents around the city beat their heads against the nearest wall. Meanwhile, in states like Georgia and Pennsylvania, cities had high hopes that their struggles with the No Child model were going to bear fruit, then found out that at least some of their progress was the result of educators who gave into the temptation to cheat—principals with an eraser, or teachers who gave students a sneak peek at the questions or impromptu hints during the test-taking.

You have to give Bush some credit. He got a big bill through Congress, which probably could never have happened if it hadn't been for that particular blend of business-oriented priorities which Republicans liked, along with the focus on progress by poor and minority children to bring along the Democrats. It sparked a lot of experimentation, which is good, and shook up institutions which can be really, really resistant to change.

But by its own standards, No Child Left Behind flunked. Under the law, local schools had to have all their students reading and doing math at their grade level by 2014. If not, they were supposed to face an educational nuclear meltdown, complete with closed schools and fired teachers. In 2011, Secretary of Education Arne Duncan announced that the deadlines were "a slow-moving train wreck" and predicted that if they weren't waived, about 80,000 of the nation's 100,000 public schools would fail to meet their markers.

This is a familiar pattern. One of the reasons that many veteran teachers responded with such skepticism to No Child Left Behind was that they'd seen that movie before: Ambitious school reformer arrives on the scene, offers a dramatic plan for change, complete with deadlines by which the vast majority of students will be reading at grade level. Or doing math as well as their proficient peers in Singapore. Or doing anything as well as the Finns. Perhaps some improvement occurs, but it's never as much as was advertised and by the time the deadlines arrive, everyone has retreated to their respective corners trying to pretend the whole thing never happened.

President Obama called on Congress to fix the law, but the Republicans—who had really come to loathe it—hardly seemed interested in working out a deal. So in the fall of 2011, the president invited states to apply for a waiver from many of the No Child Left Behind requirements, including the deadlines, in return for meeting a new set of objectives. The law, he said, had "serious flaws that are hurting our children instead of helping them."

"Testing our kids to death"

You may be wondering how things are going, education-wise, in the state that deeded its reform plan to the country. Paul Sadler, the Democrat who led the effort in the Texas house, complains that the state is "testing our kids to death." (Under the state's newest regimen, students take seventeen high-stakes tests between third and eighth grade, and up to a dozen more while they're in high school.) A survey by the Texas State Teachers Association showed that 43 percent of its members were seriously thinking of looking for another line of work.

Sadler still believes that the leaps made in the 1990s are holding up. "I think most of our schools do a pretty good job," he said. Other observers are, at minimum, disillusioned. "The eighth grade reading scores were exactly the same in 2009 as 1998," said Diane Ravitch, referring to the scores Texas received in the national NAEP test results. (I know we were trying to avoid them, but sometimes it's impossible.) "The whole country is now embarked on remedies that didn't do anything for Texas."

David Grissmer, the author of that glowing RAND study, says

that since 2000, when the study came out, Texas students' scores on national tests have begun to "flag." Perhaps coincidentally, 2000 was exactly the time when Bush stopped being governor and turned the state over to Perry, whose interest in K–12 education was minimal. When the state's budget developed a monster hole in 2011, Perry refused to raise taxes—or even dip into state savings—to avoid enormous cuts in school aid. As the impact began to hit the districts, schools began cutting back on programs that had been in place since the Perot commission, seeking waivers on class size and preschool requirements. Former First Lady Barbara Bush wrote an opinion piece in the *Houston Chronicle* protesting the lack of financial support for public schools. "We rank 36th in the nation in high school graduation rates," she wrote. "An estimated 3.8 million Texans do not have a high school diploma. We rank 49th in verbal SAT scores, 47th in literacy and 46th in average SAT scores."

It all sounded sort of familiar.

"Not a single person would show up"

When No Child Left Behind celebrated its tenth anniversary at the beginning of 2012, there weren't any parties. The Republican presidential candidates were denouncing it in one debate after another, and the Democrats in Congress weren't much more enthusiastic. Senator Michael Bennet of Colorado, who was the Denver school superintendent before he ran for office, said that if anyone had called for a rally to preserve the law as it stands "not a single person would show up."

George W. Bush gave a rare interview defending the law and blaming some of its problems on the teachers' union. "People don't like to be held to account," he said. However, the teachers' union's hostility was a mere peep compared to the negativity of, say, a Rick Perry. As governor, Perry refused to let Texas compete in Race to the Top, Obama's effort to get states to voluntarily meet No Child goals. He refused to let Texas join in an effort to come up with national standards that all the states could agree to—the only state, besides Alaska, that declined to take part. It was, Perry claimed, "a federal takeover of public schools." Then, of course, he ran for president himself, promising to do away with the law entirely and eliminate the Department of Education.

Given the total failure of that presidential thing, we will refrain from pointing out that back when the law was first passed, Perry had issued a press release bragging that "Texas was a model" for No Child Left Behind, and pointing out how much extra funding it would send to the state.

The law ran into an inherent conflict in the worldview of the Texas political establishment: how do you demand both limited government and accountability? Remember how the mayor of Midland was so sure his constituents would want the water conservation rules to be voluntary? Then he discovered that the public was more concerned about making sure their neighbors couldn't get away with watering the lawn on the wrong days. Accountability trumped limited government.

The authors of the Texas school reforms wanted communities to come up with their own solutions when their schools failed to meet the mark. But then business leaders worried that the communities might not do anything, or do the wrong things, and accountability rules entered the picture. Then, when the law went national, the accountability rules became incredibly complicated due to the demand that every state be able to have its own tests. The whole thing became a pain in the neck, and the conservative Republicans in particular began denouncing the entire effort. (States' rights! States' rights!)

Yet it was the statesrights capital of the country that sent us down this path in the first place. Sometimes, Texas's most important export is not oil but irony.

6

The Business of Schools

"Step up and give the Dwight Eisenhower speech"

When history students of the future look back on what the No Child Left Behind Act did to American education, what will they see as its biggest impact? (This is an important question, so perhaps it will be included on one of the standardized tests of 2112. The eleventh-grade history teacher's job may depend on everybody having the correct answer. She may be standing in the front of the class, spelling it out with semaphore flags.)

Okay, back to the point. The answer is: education privatization.

I know it's very difficult to move forward when the words "education privatization" get tossed out at the very beginning of a chapter. My suggestion is that you try to think of the privatizers in a fun way. I personally imagine a pirate crossed with a sanitizer—a guy with an eye patch and a carpet steamer.

Keeping that in mind, let's consider what's happened to public education over the last decade or so. More and more of your education tax dollars are going to for-profit companies. They write the tests, and grade the tests, and if your child fails the tests, they provide government-subsidized tutoring. If the poor kid gets really discouraged and drops out anyway, they're back with GED rescue programs. For-profits also run more and more of the public schools themselves. Really, pretty much everywhere you turn, there's a corporation with its hand out.

Perhaps this is a welcome development, which will bring the magic of the marketplace to our overly bureaucratized educational sector. Or perhaps this is a case of our corporate entrepreneurs intruding into an area where the for-profit motive doesn't work and shouldn't be all that welcome.

Just in case you were wondering, I'm once again going for the second option.

All over the country, there are people hopping up and down, waving warning flags. In Tennessee, school districts are losing state aid to private companies whose business plan calls for encouraging parents to believe their kids are best off if they don't leave the house at all, and go to class alone with their laptops in the living room. In Colorado, the state discovered that the for-profit companies providing most of the mandated after-school tutoring for struggling students were charging up to $89 an hour to little or no benefit. In Ohio, a for-profit charter operator that just happens to be owned by one of the state's biggest political donors keeps getting more contracts and bad performance ratings. And all around the country, parents of public school students complain that their kids are being squeezed out of classroom space by new charter schools, many of them run by for-profits.

"I'm waiting for someone in a prominent position to basically step up and give the Dwight Eisenhower beware-the-military-industrial-complex speech," said David Anderson, the former Texas education official. These days Anderson is a lobbyist, representing a number of private education companies. But he still worries. "Are we getting to the point where the business interests in education are overwhelming the education interests in education?"

The eye-patch-and-carpet-steamer guys are taking the public out of public education! Where did this come from? Forgive me if I take you back to Texas.

"We're market-driven Republicans"

Texas is crazy about privatizing things. The most famous recent example was the Trans-Texas Corridor, a huge highway that was supposed to run across the state and be built by private funds. It was going to be swell—a network of monster roads, linking all the far-flung parts of the state, with six lanes for cars, which would be able to go up to 85 mph. There would be four separate lanes for trucks, and room for both passenger and freight rail lines. The companies doing the construction would make their money back from tolls. And you could build up commercial development along the sides if you sectioned off a wide enough swath of land—say, maybe four football fields' worth of wide enough. Really, if the cars had little helicopter rotors for flying, the whole thing would have looked like a Road of the Future in a 1950s science fiction movie.

Rick Perry was really, really excited. "When our hair is gray, we will be able to tell our grandchildren that we were sitting in the Department of Transportation conference room when one of the most extraordinary plans was laid out for the people of the state of Texas," the governor intoned on the day of awarding the first Corridor contract in 2002.

When a reporter asked when there was going to be a highway for the ever hopeful, very needy Rio Grande Valley, the governor's good friend, Ric Williamson, a member of the Texas Transportation Commission, allowed as how he was getting a little tired of people asking when *their* turn was going to come. "And that question is predicated upon the central planning theory of government, which makes central plans for everybody to get a piece of the pie. But we're not central-planner people. We're market-driven Republicans."

The market-driven Republicans drove right over a cliff. Private enterprise liked the idea, and a construction company from Spain won the initial bid to partner with the state in making plans for the first section, from San Antonio to Oklahoma. But average Texans, it turned out, hated it. Hated having their towns and farmlands chopped up by an impassible 1200-foot-wide concrete serpent. Hated the idea of a foreign company owning a Texas thoroughfare. Hated pretty much everything but that 85 mph speed limit.

The Texas right wing once again demonstrated its genius for finding a sinister plot in everything, including a road proposed by Rick Perry. The far right decided the Corridor was actually going to be part of a "NAFTA superhighway" that would end the United States's life as a sovereign nation and turn the continent into a North American Union. At a protest march to the state capitol, radio host Alex Jones yelled, "Down with the North American Union!" and—yes!—"Remember the Alamo!" Once again we see that there is nothing that will not remind Texas conservatives of the Alamo. European golfers, airport security checks, supersized highways. Davy Crockett and Jim Bowie would have known what to do with them all.

The state legislature gave in, and finally an election-bound Perry was forced to sign a bill backtracking on the whole idea.

Privatizers were bloodied but unbowed, at least in the state legislature, which was working on a plan of its own that would put for-profit companies in charge of eligibility screening for state social services. "We're talking about a system for the future," a state official enthused when the bill passed in 2003. The plan was supposed to save the state $600 million by replacing a large number of public workers with a handful of call centers around the state, run under a contract with Accenture, a huge consulting company headquartered in Ireland. "It was like turning Texas's social service program over to Wal-Mart," sniped the *Texas Observer*.

The call centers were overloaded, the call center workers undertrained. People lost their benefits for no good reason and delays abounded. "Most infamously," noted the *Dallas Morning News*, "applicants for a time were given a wrong fax number for sending pay stubs and other private documents." The documents ended up in a Seattle warehouse, where employees tried but failed to get the state to do something about the piles of official paper pouring out of the warehouse fax. When no one paid any attention, they shredded the whole pile in despair.

The Republicans held firm for a while. In a conference call with legislative leaders, Susan Weddington, then chair of the state party, said that parents whose children lost health care coverage could just buy private insurance and "maybe have a little less disposable income, or a little less inheritance from Mom and Dad." Eventually the public outcry grew too great, and the embarrassment of the privatization disaster too . . . embarrassing. The legislature went into retreat and in 2007 the state threw in the towel, ending the contract with Accenture, which blamed state funding problems for the debacle.

"Kids that aren't practice learning!"

None of these disasters have stopped the Texas love affair with privatization, which it's helping to export to public education. For instance, Texas is now a leader in the new world of for-profit teacher certification companies—a business sector I bet you didn't know existed. Forty percent of the state's new teachers are being produced by for-profit certification, and IteachTexas, a totally online program, is now operating in Louisiana and Tennessee, with more territorial expansion in the works.

There was a time when teachers got certified through a procedure of classes, practice teaching, tests, etc., usually under the supervision of a college. But when No Child Left Behind pushed schools to put a certified teacher in every classroom, some states tried to expand the supply by creating alternative routes. Some pioneered ambitious programs to take people with careers outside of academia—particularly careers that involved math and science—and give them the training needed to transfer their skills into the classroom. Other states seem to have created alternative certification programs with requirements discernibly lower than what you need to qualify as a personal trainer at the gym.

Texas added another fillip. For-profit companies were not just allowed to run the classes. They could also decide whether the state's requirement for "field-based experience" meant supervised teaching in a class or something less structured, like chaperoning a field trip. Once students achieved the state standards as the companies translated them, they got certification that allowed them to take over a public school classroom with no regular supervision, as provisional teachers.

"Ever since then, the innovation and competition has been phenomenal," claimed Vernon Reaser, the president of A+ Texas Teachers, the largest of the state's alt-cert companies, whose ubiquitous billboards demand: "Want to Teach? When Can You Start?"

In 2011, state representative Michael Villarreal of San Antonio made the revolutionary proposal that would-be teachers should spend at least half of the required thirty hours of "field-based experience" actually doing supervised teaching in a classroom. At a hearing on Villarreal's bill in the capitol, Reaser vigorously denounced the whole idea as putting "practice teachers in front of kids that aren't practice learning!" The bill never made it out of committee. Eventually, Villarreal managed to stick in an amendment requiring that the field work at least include some "instructional or educational activities."

It's not exactly as bad as discovering that Texas brain surgeons could get their license online without supervised practice in a real operating room. But still.

"I feel fine about that"

The No Child Left Behind law opened the door to nearly endless for-profit opportunities. There was, of course, all that testing. Pearson, the London-based education giant, signed a five-year contract in 2010 to both create and administer the Texas tests. It was worth $470 million, and no one seemed entirely clear whether the state legislature's insistence on sticking to the high-stakes testing route was due to pressure from the Bush-era education reform community or Pearson's lobbying efforts. When a (doomed) bill to decrease the state's reliance on testing came up for a hearing in Austin a few years back, Representative Scott Hochberg, the Democrats' education expert, gently forced one of the witnesses testifying against it, Sandy Kress, to acknowledge that besides being an accountability advocate, he was also a Pearson lobbyist.

Kress, you will remember, is the former Bush aide who was a point man for the administration in the No Child Left Behind negotiations with Congress. "In my mind he was doing a lot of stage directing," said Charles Barone, who worked for the House Democrats on the Education Committee at the time. "I don't mean that pejoratively. There was a lot of presence." Kress was always a big advocate for the business community's accountability concerns in school reform. After leaving the White House, he became a lobbyist, representing private enterprise players in the education game. Let me see a show of hands of all you who think this is a coincidence.

Kress has no apologies. "When I got out of the White House I found a lot of people were doing important work and wanted my help in doing it better. I tend to pick clients who are working in my areas of fascination. I feel fine about that," he said.

The privatizers found another big treasure chest in the No Child Left Behind rule requiring that failing schools provide tutoring services for children with low test scores. "I think they were trying to figure out how to wrestle money out of the public schools and give it to the private sector," Representative George Miller acknowledged. The cost of those services hit $1 billion in 2009–10, and the door was opened to pretty much anybody—faith-based, for-profit, whatever—who could get on a state approval list.

Making that list was apparently not all that rigorous in most states, where overstretched departments of education already had enough on their plates before tutoring services entered the menu. In Columbus, Ohio, city officials found that more than half of the tutoring groups working with Columbus kids were "ineffective." In Colorado, a Department of Education study found that none of the tutors, whose fees ranged from $20 to $89 an hour, seemed to make much difference. There have been repeated complaints all around the country about students being lured to for-profit tutors with the promise of a complimentary cell phone or laptop. But given the options, a free laptop might be as useful a standard for choosing as any. The Obama administration found the whole tutoring program ineffective and put it on the list of federal rules for which states could request a waiver.

"It was a war every two years"

The ultimate goal for a really ambitious privatizer would be to take over the public schools themselves, with their steady stream of federal, state, and local funding. You will remember that during the No Child Left Behind debates, the Bush administration tried but failed to include a voucher plan. Vouchers were the holy grail for many social/fiscal conservatives. They didn't think of the public school system as a precious resource to be protected; they saw it as a gluttonous slug, gobbling down resources that could be better used by private, or for-profit, or faith-based alternatives. They dreamed of the day when American children would go off to shop for a school armed with their voucher, just the way they now go off to Target toting a debit card and looking for a new notebook.

"I can afford to send my children to a private school if I think that's what's best—any place they need to go. And I think that every child in America ought to have that same opportunity," voucher champion James Leininger told PBS in 1998. A wealthy San Antonio physician, Leininger was one of many extremely rich Texans who used the wide-open campaign finance rules to make his needs felt in the capital. Leininger had made his original fortune with a hospital bed that was supposed to prevent bedsores. By the 1990s he had moved into everything from real estate to mail-order turkeys to the San Antonio Spurs basketball team. He was also financing any number of conservative causes, from supporting Christian ministries to demolishing the Endangered Species Act. Above all else, however, he had two major political passions: restricting civil lawsuits through tort reform, and school vouchers. He was very generous to Texas politicians who shared his sentiments.

In 1998 Leininger provided Rick Perry, who was running for lieutenant governor, with a last-minute $1.1 million loan for a final media buy that may have made the difference in Perry's narrow victory over Democrat John Sharp. (Perry, who continued to be a beneficiary of Leininger's generosity, once traveled with his wife to the Bahamas on the magnate's dime. There Perry and Leininger joined with anti-tax crusader Grover Norquist for what Perry called a "real, progressive conversation" about school finance.) The ever-popular Wendy Gramm once served on the board of Leininger's corporation, Kinetic Concepts, and went on to chair the think tank he founded and endowed, the Texas Public Policy Foundation. Arlene Wohlgemuth, a former right-wing state legislator who had championed that dreadful plan to privatize social service eligibility screening, became director of the foundation's Center for Health Care Policy. George W. Bush, another recipient of Leininger's donations, once sat on the foundation's board of advisors.

As soon as Bush was inaugurated governor in 1995, Leininger got his reward. You will remember that one of his obsessions was tort reform. Bush jumped into that battle, declaring the state's judicial system to be in a crisis from which it could only recover if the legislature immediately made it difficult for consumers to sue companies that sold them defective products or services. It worked.

Vouchers turned out to be a much tougher sell. In Texas, as in most places, there are quite a lot of people who *like* their local public schools and are resistant to any plan that might take money away from them. The voucher proposals came up regularly in Austin and failed just as consistently, although usually by narrow margins. (In 1999, Perry blamed the loss to a random senator who had "flaked" at the last minute.) "It was a war every two years," said Carolyn Boyle, who assembled a cadre of anti-voucher groups called the Coalition for Public Schools. "We worked our asses off."

To inspire lawmakers to rethink their opposition, Leininger unveiled a $50 million pilot program in San Antonio that made available more than 2,000 vouchers a year for low-income students who wanted to leave their local public schools. "If you got to meet the kids and talk to them you would do anything you could for 'em, just like I would," he told the Associated Press.

But the bill never passed and in 2008, Leininger pulled the plug on his San Antonio voucher program.

"He said, 'Let's get the charters'"

George W. Bush gave up his own personal voucher crusade much sooner. In 1999, when the newly reelected, suddenly-looking-at-the-presidency governor was trying to put together a big Texas education bill, Bill Ratliff, the Republican chair of the senate Education Committee, told him that he would have to choose between vouchers and charter schools because he definitely could not get both.

"He said, 'Let's get the charters,'" Ratliff recalled.

This is an important moment. One of George W. Bush's contributions to American education was to take the struggling voucher movement and turn it into a burgeoning national charter school crusade. He wanted to bring the accountability and efficiency of the business world into the public education mix, and if vouchers didn't work, charter schools would be fine.

Charter schools are another way to get choice, or new ideas—or, if you're somewhat paranoid, the clutches of moneymakers—into public education. They're part of a public school system, but sometimes only in a very tenuous way. They generally get most of the standard per-pupil aid, but they're exempted from the regular rules and oversight in favor of a special charter written by the sponsors.

Encouraging charter schools became an important part of Bush's proposals for the No Child Left Behind law. Democrats, who desperately wanted to avoid vouchers, were receptive. "Charters were sort of a middle ground. They're part of the public school system," said George Miller. "And we were trying to make room for some entrepreneurs." They're still a bipartisan favorite in many parts of the country today. When the Obama administration tried to tweak the federal education initiative with its Race to the Top contests, room to expand charter schools was a critical way to make points and win big federal grants.

When the federal government started prodding the states to do charters, the states got considerable leeway in how closely they wanted to monitor what the charters were doing. The Bush vision was to have as little bureaucratic oversight as possible. We can see that from what W. did during his last days as governor, when the Texas charter plan was being approved. "I tried to get a lot of protections from the beginning," said Representative Hochberg, who had been an early charter school advocate. "The governor's position was basically that we should have no rules. They wanted to eliminate the requirement that kids have immunizations."

Within a few years, Texas had about 200 charters, and many disasters, some due to ineptitude and some due to corruption. A reporter visiting a school in Arlington found "no desks, no chairs"—only a single aged sofa and an expansive cement floor on which to sit. The building also lacked a lunchroom, computers, textbooks, chalkboards, and a well-functioning bathroom. A school in Dallas called P.O.W.E.R. had done its budgeting based on an enrollment of 300 but recruited only what the state counted as thirty-five students. (P.O.W.E.R. officials said there were 129 but that they couldn't back up their numbers because a burglar had stolen the attendance records.) In 2001, a Houston TV station ran film of students at Prepared Table, a large charter run out of a church, where students slept, talked, or sat on the floor while they used the pews as worktables and teachers attempted to run several different grades in the same space. The founder of Prepared Table died before he could be tried, but three of his relatives eventually pled guilty to swindling the state and federal government out of at least $5 million.

Texas was hardly the only place where minimal oversight produced maximum headaches. Over in Florida where the president's brother, Jeb Bush, was overseeing his own education initiatives well before No Child Left Behind became law, nearly a quarter of the charters that were opened wound up shutting down. That meant chaos for the schools that had to accept the suddenly homeless students, and often heartache for the students themselves, who sometimes wound up having to repeat one or more grades.

Starting a successful charter school turned out to be way more difficult than some people had imagined. The president, however, didn't look back. And he kept walking on the sunny side of the street. By 2010 there were 5,000 charter schools operating around the country, educating about 1.5 million public school students

"You can take this to the bank"

We can argue for hours—days!—months!—about whether charters are a good thing. Overall, the evidence seems to suggest that charters are, on average, having about the same success as the public schools they're supposed to be replacing. The best charters do an absolutely terrific job. But the jury is still out on whether they do so well because they're not under the thumb of the regular school bureaucracy and the teachers' unions, or because they receive extra financial support from enthusiastic donors and have charismatic principals and dedicated staff—something that also makes for stupendous traditional schools.

One thing that definitely wasn't part of the original Bush sales pitch to the public was that charters would allow public schools to become private profit centers. Even some of the people who put the law together seemed to have no idea. "There was a lot of discussion on how to make states more receptive to charters, but for-profits were not part of the conversation," said a Democratic staffer who was involved in the negotiations.

Yet there they are. It turned out that under the law, a for-profit company could get a non-profit group to serve as sponsor for a charter that was almost, or entirely, the creature of the for-profit operator. While some of the sponsors were deeply involved in their schools' operation, others were perfectly happy to sit back and collect a sliver of the taxpayer funding for lending their names.

By the No Child Left Behind law's tenth anniversary, nearly 400,000 children around the country were being educated in public elementary, middle, and high schools run by for-profit companies. Studies suggested that the results weren't all that terrific. But hedge funds and other investors were wriggling with excitement about the long-term financial prospects. "You get a steady stream of funding—you can take this to the bank," said Diane Ravitch, the No Child Left Behind critic.

One of the big names in the business is K^{12} Inc., a company co-founded by William Bennett, who was Secretary of Education in the Reagan administration, with an infusion of cash from the former disgraced junk-bond king Mike Milken. (Bennett resigned as chairman in 2005 after he remarked, on his radio show, that "you could abort every black baby in this country, and your crime rate would go down.") With or without Bennett, K^{12} found that it could use the charter school system championed by No Child Left Behind to establish statewide cyber-schools. It quickly became a leader in one of the fastest-growing segments of the charter world. By 2011, there were an estimated 116,000 students going to school full-time in online programs run by for-profits. And the number kept going up. The profit margins could be huge—just think, no physical plant, no gym teachers or cafeteria workers. Many of the online teachers had far more students and made less money than their peers who worked in actual classrooms. However, K^{12} would want you to know that they are no longer outsourcing student essays to India for correction. Really, that was just a trial run. It was discontinued. Isn't happening any more. Honest.

In Tennessee, K[12] enrolled 2,000 students from around the state in the Tennessee Virtual Academy in 2011–12. The sponsor of the virtual charter was the Unity School District, located in a sparsely populated rural area whose county seat, Maynardsville, has a population about the same size as the Virtual Academy's student body. K[12] recruited students from around the state, making particularly enthusiastic pitches in poor urban areas, where it stressed to parents how safe their children would be if they stayed home with their computers all day instead of venturing into the streets and the local public schools. For each child who was enrolled, K[12] got $5,387 in state aid, minus a modest fee to the school district for its cooperation. All in all, K[12] took in nearly $10 million in 2010–11, and Tennessee public schools, of course, lost nearly $10 million.

In Pennsylvania, K[12] earned more than $70 million running the Agora Cyber Charter School, where a *New York Times* study found nearly 60 percent of the students were behind grade level in math, and almost half in reading. The prospects for future growth looked so sweet that the second-largest cyber-school business, Connections Education, was purchased for $400 million by Pearson, the for-profit education company which hired as a lobbyist the guy who helped lead the White House negotiations on the No Child Left Behind law.

A study by the National Education Policy Center at the University of Colorado found that only about a quarter of for-profit virtual schools met federal standards for academic progress. But, you know, it's all about choice.

7

The Textbook Wars

*"What happens in Texas doesn't stay in Texas
when it comes to textbooks"*

The saga of textbooks and Texas is one of the most action-packed parts of this story. No matter where you live, if your children go to public schools, the textbooks they use were very possibly written under Texas influence. If they graduated with a reflexive suspicion of the concept of separation of church and state, and an unexpected interest in the contributions of the National Rifle Association to American history, you know who to blame.

When it comes to meddling with school textbooks, Texas is once again both similar to other states and totally different. It's hardly the only one that likes to fiddle around with the material its kids study in class. The difference is due to size—4.8 million textbook-reading schoolchildren as of 2011—and the peculiarities of its system of government, in which the state board of education is selected in elections that are practically devoid of voters, where wealthy donors can chip in unlimited amounts of money to help their favorites win. Those favorites are not shrinking violets. In 2009, the nation watched in awe as the state board worked on approving a new science curriculum under the leadership of a chair who believed "evolution is hooey." In 2010, the subject was social studies and the teachers tasked with drawing up course guidelines were supposed to work in consultation with "experts" added on by the board, one of whom believed that the income tax was contrary to the word of God in the Scriptures.

Ever since the 1960s, the selection of school books in Texas has been a target for the religious right, which worried that schoolchildren were being indoctrinated in godless secularism, and political conservatives who felt their kids were being given way too much propaganda about the positive aspects of the federal government. Mel Gabler, an oil company clerk, and his wife, Norma, who began their textbook crusade at their kitchen table, were the leaders of the first wave. They brought their supporters to public comment portions of the State Board of Education meetings, unrolling their "scroll of shame," which listed objections they had to the content of the current reading material. At times, the scroll was 54 feet long. Products of the Texas school system have the Gablers to thank for the fact that at one point the New Deal was axed from the timeline of significant events in American history.

The Texas State Board of Education, which approves textbooks, curriculum standards, and supplemental materials for the public schools, has fifteen members from fifteen districts whose boundaries don't conform to congressional districts, or really anything whatsoever. They run in staggered elections that are frequently held in off years, when always-low Texas turnout is particularly abysmal. The advantage tends to go to candidates with passionate, if narrow, bands of supporters, particularly if those bands have rich backers. All of which—plus a natural supply of political eccentrics—helps explain how Texas once had a board member who believed that public schools are the tool of the devil.

Texas originally acquired its power over the nation's textbook supply because it paid 100 percent of the cost of all public school textbooks, as long as the books in question came from a very short list of board-approved options. The selection process "was grueling and tension-filled," said Julie McGee, who worked at high levels in several publishing houses before her retirement. "If you didn't get listed by the state, you got nothing." On the other side of the coin, David Anderson, who once sold textbooks in the state, said if a book made the list, even a fairly mediocre salesperson could count on doing pretty well. The books on the Texas list were likely to be mass-produced by the publisher in anticipation of those sales, so other states liked to buy them and take advantage of the economies of scale.

"What happens in Texas doesn't stay in Texas when it comes to textbooks," said Dan Quinn, who worked as an editor of social studies textbooks before joining the Texas Freedom Network, which was founded by Governor Ann Richards's daughter, Cecile, to counter the religious right.

As a market, the state was so big and influential that national publishers tended to gear their books toward whatever it wanted. Given the high cost of developing a single book, the risk of messing with Texas was high. "One of the most expensive is science," McGee said. "You have to hire medical illustrators to do all the art." When she was in the business, the cost of producing a new biology book could run to $5 million. "The investments are really great and it's all on risk."

Imagine the feelings of the textbook companies—not to mention the science teachers—when, in response to a big push from the Gablers, the state board adopted a rule in 1974 that textbooks mentioning the theory of evolution "should identify it as only one of several explanations of the origins of humankind" and that those treating the subject extensively "shall be edited, if necessary, to clarify that the treatment is theoretical rather than factually verifiable." The state attorney general eventually issued an opinion that the board's directive wouldn't stand up in court, and the rule was repealed. But the beat went on.

"Evolution is hooey"

Texas is hardly the only state with small, fierce pressure groups trying to dictate the content of textbooks. California, which has the most public school students, tends to come at things from the opposite side, pressing for more reflection of a crunchy granola worldview. "The word in publishing was that for California you wanted no references to fast food, and in Texas you wanted no references to sex," laughed Quinn. But California's system of textbook approval focuses only on books for the lower grades. Professor Keith Erekson, director of the Center for History Teaching and Learning at the University of Texas at El Paso, says that California often demands that its texts have a California-centric central narrative that would not be suitable for anywhere else, while "the Texas narrative can be used in other states." Publishers tend to keep information on who buys how much of what secret, but Erekson said he's seen estimates that the proportion of social studies textbooks sold containing the basic Texas-approved narrative range from about half to 80 percent.

Some extremely rich Texans have gotten into the board of education election game, putting their money at the disposal of conservative populists. No one has had more impact than our friend James Leininger, the San Antonio physician who took such an intense interest in school vouchers. He backed a group called Texans for Governmental Integrity, which was particularly active in state school board elections. Its most famous campaign was in 1994, when it mailed flyers to voters' homes in one district, showing a black man kissing a white man and claiming that the Democratic incumbent had voted for textbooks that promoted homosexuality. Another organization Leininger has supported, the Heidi Group, sent out a prayer calendar in 1998, which unnervingly urged the right-to-life faithful to devote one day to praying that a San Antonio doctor who performed abortions "will come to see Jesus face to face."

The chorus of objections to textbook material mounted. Approval

of environmental science books was once held up over board concern that they were teaching children to be more loyal to their
planet than their country. As the board became a national story, and
a national embarrassment, the state legislature attempted to put a lid
on the chaos in 1995 by restricting the board's oversight to "factual
errors." This made surprisingly little impact when you had a group
of deciders who believed that the theory of evolution, global warming, and separation of church and state are all basically errors of fact.

In 2009, when the science curriculum was once again up for
review, conservatives wanted to require that it cover the "strengths
and weaknesses" of the theory of evolution. In the end, they settled
for a face-saving requirement that students consider gaps in fos-
sil records and whether natural selection is enough to explain the
complexity of human cells. Don McLeroy, the board chairman
who had opined that "evolution is hooey," told *Washington Monthly*
that he felt the changes put Texas "light years ahead of any other
state when it comes to challenging evolution."

The process by which the board came to its interesting decisions
sometimes seemed confused to the point of incoherence. Things
would begin tidily, with panels of teachers and expert consultants.
Then the expert consultants multiplied, frequently becoming less
and less expert, until the whole process ended in a rash of craziness.
The science curriculum was "this document that had been worked
on for months," Nathan Bernier, a reporter for KUT in Austin,
told National Public Radio. "Members of the [teachers' associa-
tion] had been involved. People with PhDs had been involved in
developing these standards. And then at the last second, there was
this mysterious document that was shoved underneath the hotel
doors of some of the board members and this document, at the very
last minute, wound up—large portions of it wound up making its
way into the guidelines."

In 2010, the board launched itself into the equally contentious
sea of the social studies curriculum, and the teacher-dominated
team tasked with writing the standards was advised by a panel of

"experts," one of whom was a member of the Minutemen militia. Another had argued that only white people were responsible for advancing civil rights for minorities in America, since "only majorities can expand political rights in America's constitutional society."

"The way I evaluate history textbooks is first I see how they cover Christianity and Israel," McLeroy told *Washington Monthly*. "Then I see how they treat Ronald Reagan—he needs to get credit for saving the world from Communism and for the good economy over the last twenty years because he lowered taxes."

In their first year of work on social studies, the board agreed that students should be required to study the abandonment of the gold standard as a factor in the decline in the value of the dollar. If the students were going to study the McCarthy anti-Communist witch hunt of the 1950s, they were also going to contemplate "how the later release of the Venona papers confirmed suspicions of Communist infiltration in the U.S. government." The changes often seemed to be thrown out haphazardly, and to pass or fail on the basis of frequently opaque conclusions on the part of the swing members. "As a State Board of Education, I think we need to give more solid kinds of rationales why things should be included or deleted, as opposed to the subjective, personal—'I like,' 'I don't like,' 'My favorite'— those kinds of things," said member Mavis Knight. (In 2010, the board tossed out books by the late Bill Martin, Jr., the author of *Baby Bear, Baby Bear, What Do You See?*, from a list of authors third graders might want to study because someone mixed him up with Bill Martin, the author of *Ethical Marxism*.)

The final product the board came up with called for a curriculum that would make sure that students tasked to analyze economic issues of the late nineteenth century would not forget "the cattle industry boom" and that when they turned to social issues like labor, growth of the cities, and problems of immigrants they also took time to dwell on "the philanthropy of industrialists." When it came to the Middle Ages, the board appeared to be down on any mention of the Crusades, an enterprise that tends to reflect badly on the Christian side of Christian–Islamic conflict. And when they got to the Cold War era, the board wanted to be sure students would be able to "explain how Arab rejection of the State of Israel has led to ongoing conflict." Later, they were supposed to study "Islamic fundamentalism and the subsequent use of terrorism by some of its adherents." And that appeared to be pretty much all young people in Texas were going to be required to know about Arab nations and the world's second-largest religion.

For the most part, however, the board seemed determined just to sprinkle stuff its members liked hither and yon, and eliminate words they found objectionable in favor of more appealing ones. Reading through the deletions and additions, it becomes clear that a majority of board members hated the word "democratic," for which they consistently substituted "constitutional republic." They also really disliked "capitalism" (see rather: "free enterprise system") and "natural law" ("laws of nature and nature's God").

Study of the first part of the twentieth century should include not only the Spanish–American War and Theodore Roosevelt but also Sanford B. Dole, a Hawaiian lawyer and son of missionaries. When teachers get to Clarence Darrow, Henry Ford, and Charles Lindbergh, they'd also better not forget Glenn Curtiss, who broke early motorcycle speed records. For the modern era, they needed to study "the conservative resurgence of the 1980s and 1990s," including Equal Rights Amendment opponent Phyllis Schlafly, the Contract With America, the Heritage Foundation, the Moral Majority, and the National Rifle Association. And when students learn how to describe the impact of cultural movements like "Tin Pan Alley, the Harlem Renaissance, the Beat Generation, rock and roll," the board demanded that they also look into "country and western music."

That last one actually seems totally fair.

The social studies curriculum was perhaps the last hurrah for the extreme agenda that Don McLeroy, the anti-evolution dentist, had championed. When the discussions began, he could frequently rally a majority on the fifteen-member panel, with the consistent support of people like Cynthia Dunbar, who once said that sending children to public schools was like "throwing them into the enemy's flames, even as the children of Israel threw their children to Moloch." (She also once called Barack Obama a terrorist sympathizer.) In 2011, Dunbar announced her retirement; she had been commuting between Texas and Virginia, where she taught at Jerry Falwell's Liberty University School of Law. After McLeroy himself lost a Republican primary to a candidate who believes in evolution, Barbara Cargill, his successor as board chair, expressed concern that she was left with only "six conservative Christians on the board."

"Readable? I've never heard a discussion of that"

These days the Texas board is far less powerful than in its heyday. But in a way, it's more influential than ever.

The state legislature has diluted the board's ability to control what books local districts pick. And the expanding Web-based curricula make it easier for publishers to work around the preferences of any one state, no matter how big. But students all around the country will be feeling the effect of Texas on their textbooks for years, if not generations. That's because the school board's most important contribution has not been to make textbooks inaccurate. It's been to help make them unreadable.

"Readable? I've never heard a discussion of that," said Julie McGee.

The typical school textbook is composed of a general narrative sprinkled liberally with "boxes"—sidebars presenting the biographies of prominent individuals, and highlighting particular trends, social issues, or historical events. As the textbook wars mounted, those boxes multiplied like gerbils. It's the ideal place to stash the guy who broke the motorcycle speed record, or the cattle boom or, perhaps, the gold standard. (It's also where, in bows to gender and racial equality, mini-biographies of prominent women and minorities can be floated.) In an era of computerized publishing, changing the boxes is easy. The problem comes when the publisher has to change the narrative, something endless committees of experts may have labored over at the cost of millions of dollars.

All the bickering and pressuring over the years has caused publishers to shy away from using the kind of clear, lively language that might raise hackles in one corner or another. The more writers were constrained by confusing demands and conflicting requests, the more they produced unreadable mush. Texas, you may not be surprised to hear, has been particularly good at making things mushy. In 2011, the Thomas B. Fordham Institute, a conservative education think tank, issued an evaluation of US history standards for public schools. The institute was a long-time critic of curricula that insisted that representatives of women and minorities be included in all parts of American history. But the authors, Sheldon Stern and Jeremy Stern, *really* hated what the Texas board had done. Besides incorporating "all the familiar politically correct group categories," the authors said, "the document distorts or suppresses less triumphal or more nuanced aspects of our past that the Board found politically unacceptable. (Slavery and segregation are all but ignored, while religious influences are grossly exaggerated.) The resulting fusion is a confusing, unteachable hodgepodge."

All around the country, teachers and students are left to make their way through murky generalities as they struggle through the swamps of boxes and lists. "Maybe the most striking thing about current history textbooks is that they have lost their compelling narrative," wrote historian Russell Shorto.

And that's the legacy. Texas certainly didn't single-handedly mess up American textbooks, but its size, its purchasing heft, and the pickiness of the school board's endless demands—not to mention the boards' overall craziness—certainly made it the trend leader. Texas has never managed to get evolution out of American science textbooks. It's been far more successful in helping to make evolution—and history, and everything else—seem really, really boring.

8

Speedy the Sperm and Friends

*"If you teach kids about sex,
kids will start having sex."*

And now . . . Texas and sex. Once again, we are not going to worry all that much about whether the state's agenda is making its own residents happy, or even whether its behavior is constitutional, although I am going to go way out on a limb and say that I doubt that even the current Supreme Court would approve of a public school sex education class that urges students to ask themselves, when evaluating a prospective spouse, "Is Jesus their first love?"

No, we're just going to concern ourselves with how Texas's attitudes affect the other forty-nine states—some of which, if we're going to be honest here, have state legislatures that can occasionally make the one in Austin look like a Woodstock reunion.

Texas is, nevertheless, pretty darned conservative. One of the interesting things about the empty-place ethos is that the theory about leaving people alone to do whatever they want does not apply *at all* when it comes to sex. Long after the Supreme Court struck down the state's anti-sodomy law as unconstitutional, the legislature still refused to take it off the books. Texas regulations on abortion are among the most draconian in the country, and it pushes abstinence-only sex education in its public schools. It refuses to accept federal funding for sex education programs that teach kids how to avoid pregnancy and sexually transmitted diseases with tactics other than celibacy. Carrie Williams, a spokeswoman for the Department of State Health Services, explained this last one by saying that the state's "first choice is that teens choose not to have sex."

If we lived in a world where parents and teachers always got their first choice when it came to teenagers' sexual behavior, Texas would be so in the vanguard.

The state does not actually dictate what kind of sex education public schools should offer, beyond requiring that abstinence must always be presented as the best choice, and until recently, no one had any real notion of what was going on in all these classes. Then in 2009, the Texas Freedom Network, a liberal nonprofit, funded a herculean effort to come up with some answers. David Wiley and Kelly Wilson, two professors of health education at Texas State University, contacted every district and requested information on their sex instruction programs, under the Texas Public Information Act. Wiley said he was drawn to the subject since his undergraduate students regularly told him that they got little or no sex education in school, even though the state's education code requires that it be part of the curriculum. Also, he said, "Last year a sincere male student asked aloud, 'What is my risk for cervical cancer?'"

They got documents from more than 96 percent of the districts. After plowing through the information, the professors concluded that "abstinence-only programs have a stranglehold on sexuality education in Texas public schools." More than 94 percent gave that instruction exclusively, while a small percentage completely ignored the rule that said they had to have *something*. ("We're a small rural school district and we don't follow laws we disagree with," wrote a superintendent from a small district in west central Texas. "Drug problems only arose when we started teaching about drugs, and if you teach kids about sex, kids will start having sex.")

"Speedy the Sperm"

Most districts got their materials—and sometimes their speakers—from private vendors marketing programs like "Worth the Wait," "Aim for Success," or "W.A.I.T. Training." If non-abstinence methods of preventing pregnancy came up in the class material at all, the researchers found, it was almost invariably in terms of condom failure rates. "Students, condoms aren't safe. Never have been, never will be," one abstinence speaker warned her classes. Students in another program were told to pass around a leaky balloon to illustrate the danger of using condoms. The teacher was instructed to tell the student left holding the deflated balloon at the end that "if he had been the one to get a leaky condom it could have meant he was at high risk or even death." Another curriculum, "Why kNOw?" has the poor teacher construct an 18-foot-long model known as "Speedy the Sperm" to demonstrate condoms' alleged failure to guard against STDs.

"There's this huge myth that if you promote condoms it gives kids a false sense of protection," said Dr. Susan Tortolero, an expert in pregnancy prevention issues. "Seat belts have a higher failure rate." The only foolproof way to avoid pregnancy is, of course, not to have sex. But once that horse is out of the barn, there doesn't seem to be any effective way to get kids to refrain from having it again. That's the point at which it becomes important that they understand the dangers of unprotected sex, and that sex with a condom is far, far safer than sex with nothing at all.

Almost 30 percent of Texas school districts simply relied on one of the four state-approved health textbooks, whose publishers generally opted for self-censorship and obfuscation. Three of the four never mentioned the word "condom." (The other brought it up exactly one time.) The most widely used book, the imaginatively named *Health*, warned that "barrier protection is not 100 percent effective in preventing the transmission of STDs," but never explained what "barrier protection" was. Another, *Lifetime Health*, listed "8 Steps to Protect Yourself from STDs," none of which involved using condoms. One of the steps was "get plenty of rest," which the book suggested would lead to better decision-making.

Besides incoherence, there was also the stuff that was flat-out wrong. "After analyzing sexuality materials turned over by school districts under the Texas Public Information Act, we were able to document a factual error in 41 percent of school districts in the state," the Wiley report said.

Quite a bit of the information Texas students are getting seems to have arrived from another era. An abstinence-only program used in three districts assures them that "if a woman is dry, the sperm will die"—which harks back to colonial-era theories that it was impossible for a woman to get pregnant unless she enjoyed the sex. There are repeated suggestions that premarital sex could have fatal consequences—reminiscent of the 1950s' legends about couples who had illicit sex in the back seat of a car and then were murdered by the Lovers Lane Maniac. (A video used in three Texas districts has a boy asking an evangelical educator what will happen if he has sex before marriage. "Well, I guess you'll have to be prepared to die," is the response.)

"Our schools are failing Texas families by turning out generations of sexually illiterate young people at a time of high rates of teen pregnancy and STDs," Wiley and Wilson wrote mournfully.

In an effort to improve things ever so slightly, Representative Michael Villarreal of San Antonio proposed a bill in 2011 that would have required that the information taught to public school students in sex education class be medically accurate. (Villarreal, you may remember, is the guy who wanted to require that practice teaching involve being in a classroom. The man has a genius for proposing that Texas do things the outside world presumed it was doing all along.) The bill failed to even make it out of committee. The legislator who cast the swing vote against it was a pediatrician.

"We basically lost two-thirds of the budget"

The biggest problem with trying to frighten kids, or shame them, into not having sex is that it doesn't work. The schools may assure students, as one program does, that "divorce rate for two virgins who get married is less than 3 percent." But most Texas high-schoolers are not virgins. Slightly over half of ninth- to twelfth-graders reported having had sex in 2009—higher than the national figure of 46 percent. By the time they're seniors, 69 percent of Texas students are sexually active, and they indulge in risky behavior like sex with a large number of partners at rates higher than the national average.

The state has the third-highest rate of teenage births in the country, and the second-highest rate of repeat births to teenage girls. Sixty-three out of every 1,000 girls between fifteen and nineteen years old become mothers. That compares to 5 out of 1,000 in the Netherlands, and 42 in the United States as a whole. Texas is also well ahead of Rwanda (44), Micronesia (51), and Egypt (50).

It doesn't have to be that way. Back in 1992, California's teen birth rate was about the same as that of Texas—74 births for every 1,000 women between fifteen and nineteen, while Texas had 79. Then California committed to do something about the situation. "The thing is, we know how to prevent teen pregnancy," said Tortolero, who is director of the Prevention Research Center at the University of Texas. "It's being done all over the world. It's being done in other states." California refused to take any money for abstinence-only education. It required all of its public middle and high schools to teach HIV/AIDS prevention, in a way that stresses the superiority of the abstinence option while also giving kids all the facts about the importance of using condoms if one decides to be sexually active. (The information also has to be medically accurate.) Family planning services are extremely easy to obtain. By 2008, when Texas's teenage fertility rate was 63 per thousand, California's was 39.5 and continuing to drop.

We know the consequences of a large number of teenage births. The young mother is more likely to drop out of school, live in poverty, and remain a single parent. The teen fathers have a similarly dismal prospect, which includes being unusually likely to conceive children with multiple women and engage in substance abuse. The children themselves are more likely to experience abuse or neglect, end up in foster care, and, if they're male, end up in prison.

Still, if you didn't know better, you'd think there was a concerted effort going on in Texas to increase the number of children being born to teen parents. The state is also one of the most restrictive in the country when it comes to teen access to birth control. Even if a teenage girl has already given birth, she can't get state-funded contraception services without a parent's consent. And Texas is one of only four states that don't cover contraception under the federal Children's Health Insurance Program.

In 2011, the legislature also decimated funding for family planning programs for adults. "We basically lost two-thirds of the budget," said Fran Hagerty of the Women's Health and Family Planning Association of Texas. Family planning money, which used to be a miserly $99 million for the state's two-year budget cycle, was slashed to $38 million. It was impossible to get rid of the last bit, since it comes from a federal program for family planning and family planning alone. "But there's been some discussion that they might not renew the grant," Hagerty added grimly.

The lawmakers were driven in part by an antipathy toward Planned Parenthood, which provides a large chunk of the state's family planning services and also performs abortions under a separate funding stream. "I'm in politics primarily because of the life issue. Protecting life has got to be the government's highest responsibility," said Representative Bryan Hughes, who made it clear that he opposed abortion even in cases of rape. (Governor Perry made an exception for victims of rape and incest until he began courting the evangelical vote in Iowa, at which point he announced he had undergone a "transformation.") However, the antipathy toward family planning was also driven by a less-often-vocalized dislike of contraception in general. "They talk about Planned Parenthood, but there's a faction that basically doesn't like access to birth control," said Hagerty. State Senator Bob Deuell, a Republican physician who opposes abortion but supports family planning, said he hadn't gotten direct criticism for his position from pro-life groups. But he hadn't exactly gotten any rewards from the movement for his work on making contraceptive services more available. "No, I guess you've got a point there," he said.

"A terrible recipe for the future"

The result of all this is not just teen pregnancy but a huge number of poor women of all ages giving birth. Texas has the second-highest birth rate in the country after Utah, and nearly 60 percent of the women giving birth are low-income enough to qualify for Medicaid. While the state makes every conceivable effort to keep its Medicaid spending low, the overall bill for pre-and postnatal care and delivery is about $1 billion a year.

Now we're getting into the national impact of the way Texas goes. Medicaid is a federal program, and more than half of that billion-dollar bill is paid by federal taxpayers. Happy to be of help—but don't the rest of us have a right to demand that Texas at least make sure poor women who don't want to be pregnant have easy access to federally funded contraception?

And let's take this further. We've been looking at the way the Texas version of states' rights has affected the rest of the country directly, in everything from other states' banks to other states' schools. But there's also the matter of our shared future. Texas has had an 800,000 increase in the number of schoolchildren in the last decade, and all those youngsters aren't going to be spending their lives within the state's borders. Eventually, more than a tenth of the national workforce will be Texas-born.

Which is not necessarily good news. Funding for schools hasn't kept up with the booming population, and lately the state has not just been failing to fund the increased costs, but cutting back on its financial support altogether. "The decisions we're making today really give me concern about the world we're creating," said Representative Villarreal. "Legislation gutting our family planning service program and cutting education to the bone. That's a terrible recipe for the future."

For the country's future as well. When Texas decisions stay in Texas, the rest of us might be willing to let the state do what its elected officials like, even if that means educating its children that condoms kill and frigid women can't get pregnant. But the decisions made about Texas sex education have echoes. They reverberate through the educational system, and then into the national workforce and the national economy a couple of decades down the line.

SINCE THE TEXAS Freedom Network issued its terrifying report on the state of sex education in the public schools, there's been a jump in the number of districts offering programs that go beyond Speedy the Sperm to more sophisticated "abstinence-plus" approaches. That's got to be good news, but they aren't getting any encouragement from the governor.

"Abstinence works," Perry told the *Texas Tribune*'s Evan Smith during his reelection campaign in 2010.

"But we have the third highest teen pregnancy rate in the country," Smith pointed out, suggesting that the abstinence education part didn't seem to be working at all.

"It works," Perry said doggedly. "Maybe it is the way it's being taught, or maybe it is the way it is being applied out there, but the fact of the matter is it is the best form to teach our children."

"Can you give me a statistic suggesting it works?" asked Smith.

"I'm sorry, I'm going to tell you from my own personal life. Abstinence works," said the governor.

9

Cooling to Global Warming

"The worst possible sin"

There's no better empty-versus-crowded divider than environmentalism, no federal bureaucrat more despised in the empty-place world than the one who wants to tell developers that they can't expand their suburb into the wetlands, or orders farmers not to clear woodlots where an endangered species has set up shop.

"In their eyes, we have committed the worst possible sin, of being not in compliance with federal regulations," Governor Perry once said of the Environmental Protection Agency, in tones of great aggravation. Since the EPA's preeminent responsibility is, um, making sure everyone is in compliance with federal regulations, you would be sort of worried if its officials felt that the worst possible sin was drinking on the Sabbath.

Texas has a long history of hostility to environmental regulation, as befits its status as a place where everybody feels as if they're in the wide open spaces—even if they actually happen to be in Sugar Land or Plano or some other mega-suburb in which the neighbors take strong exception to an out-of-the-norm mailbox or an untended lawn. Still, there's *space*. You would not be driving sixty miles to work in the morning if there weren't

126

plenty of space. And the great tradition of Texas has been not to protect, but to extract. Oil, gas, minerals, timber—whatever you can wrestle from the land, you take it away and sell it. Screw the blue-pelted ferret. As Marshall Kuykendall, a famous white-haired Texas property rights activist, warned his fellow Texans, the federal government "can send guys down here with pistols who can fine you hundreds of thousands of dollars for stepping on a snail." (Kuykendall is best remembered for having once compared the freeing of slaves to the unconstitutional taking of property.)

"The environmental consciousness is less in Texas than the rest of the country," acknowledged Tom Smith, the executive director of Texas Public Citizen. Not to say there aren't green patches in the state. Folks in urban areas recycle; everybody's sensitive to wasting water in a drought, and while Texas probably doesn't have the highest proportion of scenic beauty per acre in the country, people treasure what they've got. But still. "Texans had spent most of five generations trying to wring a living out of the land, and they associated environmentalism with flower children and other nonsense," wrote historian James Haley.

Amazing, then, that Lyndon Johnson rolled up such a strong environmental record when he was president: the Water Quality Act of 1965, the Air Quality Act of 1967, the Solid Waste Disposal Act of 1965, the Highway Beautification Act of 1965, the Land and Water Conservation Fund Act, the Endangered Species Preservation Act, and the Wild and Scenic Rivers Act. He signed or otherwise endorsed 1,112 international treaties, agreements, conventions, and protocols dealing with the environment. "There was more environmental legislation passed than in all previous administrations combined," said Martin Melosi, a professor of history at the University of Houston.

But Lyndon Johnson was one of a kind. It was also another era. It took a while for the people in the empty places to realize that all the feel-good talk about highway beautification might have an impact on their property and their businesses. Back in the day, Richard Nixon had a great environmental record, too.

"A cocked gun aimed at Texas"

There is, naturally, no part of environmental policy that touches as deep in the heart of Texas as energy policy. The last Democratic presidential candidate to win the state's affection did it, in part, by sweet-talking the gas barons. "First," Jimmy Carter wrote to Governor Dolph Briscoe when he was campaigning for president, "I will work with the Congress, as the Ford administration has been unable to do, to deregulate new natural gas." The price of natural gas was controlled under a complicated system that allowed Texas producers to charge what they wanted in-state while most of the rest of the country paid artificially lower prices. Carter seemed to be leaning toward what Washington called "the Texas position," which was that there would be no restrictions anywhere. The state's power structure was in love with the idea. They responded to Carter's overtures by handing over a ton of campaign donations, and Texas voters followed their lead, giving Carter the state's twenty-six electoral votes in his 1976 victory over Gerald Ford.

The romance was brief. Within months after the inauguration, Texas had metaphorically returned the fraternity pin.

You may remember, if you're old enough, that 1976 was the middle of an energy crisis of epic proportions. The United States spent much of the decade wrestling with the Middle East oil embargo, gas shortages, soaring energy prices. The government, shocked into action, had done everything from setting a 55 mph speed limit on highways to year-round daylight savings time. Richard Nixon imposed price controls. But we still had inflation, as well as a recession. So just a few months after his inauguration, Carter went on television to announce that the energy crisis was the "moral equivalent of war." He urged Americans to "reduce demand through conservation" by giving up their big gas-guzzling cars, to car-pool and take mass transit, to turn their thermostats down to 65 during the day and 55 at night. He was even wearing a sweater.

If Carter had announced a *real* war he might have roused some Texan enthusiasm. But a state that sold energy for a living had no particular desire to see people buy less of it. Plus, where was that clarion call for deregulating natural gas? Briscoe called the speech "a cocked gun aimed at Texas."

Carter acknowledged that he'd promised to try to deregulate natural gas prices, but noted that he didn't say when. He also held a press conference where he warned about "potential war profiteering" by the energy industry which, he predicted, could develop into "the biggest ripoff in history." By that point Texas Democrats and the White House were having one of the worst breakups in the history of politics—they might as well have been sitting in front of the TV sobbing and eating butter brickle ice cream. Remember that story about Bill Clements, the first Republican governor since Reconstruction, who started his campaign in 1978 by promising to wrap Jimmy Carter around his Democratic opponent's neck? (It will be forever emblazoned in our minds as the "throwing a rubber chicken across the dinner table" incident.) It worked.

Texas voters paid Carter back in 1980, deserting him for Ronald Reagan in huge numbers. Carter took others down with him, hastening the Democrats' decline. Among the victims was Representative Bob Eckhardt, a veteran Houston congressman who had calculated that legislation he passed to control oil prices, particularly the Energy Policy and Conservation Act of 1975, had saved consumers nearly $64 billion over the years. Eckhardt had been a favorite of consumer protection groups, whose support had previously protected him from being unseated, though not for the energy industry's lack of trying. "If you can't get Bob to vote with us, we're just going to have to beat him," Houston oilman Jack Warren had warned Eckhardt's wife.

You might say the oilmen had tied the proverbial chicken around Eckhardt's neck. His opponent was twenty-eight-year-old

Jack Fields, a lawyer who had avoided any candidate debates but spent twice Eckhardt's money. "I think the worst part about it is the oil industry can basically say they beat a congressman," said Representative Jim Mattox of Dallas. Fields was appointed to the House Committee on Energy and Commerce.

So out went Jimmy Carter and in came Ronald Reagan, whose energy policy transition team was made up of oil company executives and geologists, led by Michel Halbouty, a Texas wildcatter, who helped produce an analysis of the Carter energy policy that concluded, "Instead of unleashing the resources of a wealthy nation, we have, in the name of saving energy for some unspecified future time, tucked energy away like a rare bottle of wine." The new president would eventually sign legislation restoring many of the tax breaks that oil producers had lost in the 1970s. He also took down the solar panels Carter had installed on the White House roof.

"We say to the lobbyists, 'Help us'"

Ronald Reagan was hardly what you'd call an environmentalist— he once told reporters that trees cause more pollution than automobiles. After eight years with him, almost anybody might have looked good to the environmental lobby. But George H. W. Bush actually seemed better than not-as-bad. "I call him Bush the Good," said James Marston of the Environmental Defense Fund.

"I never thought of him as a Texan—I just thought of him as a great guy," said Sherwood Boehlert, a former Republican member of Congress from upstate New York who did endless battles against his party's leadership on behalf of clean air and water.

When H. W. ran for president in 1988, the Republican platform—a document useful only for taking the party's emotional temperature—supported the need to protect the air and water, and even mentioned climate change. The first President Bush said he wanted to be known as an environmentalist and the White House extolled his efforts to promote issues like reforestation, noting the president's "personal commitment to planting trees." More significantly, he approved the 1990 Clean Air Act, which significantly expanded on the versions passed during previous administrations, particularly in matters like acid rain. Its goal, the *New York Times* reported on the day Bush signed the bill into law, was "to cut acid rain pollutants by half, sharply reduce urban smog and eliminate most of the toxic chemical emissions from industrial plants by the turn of the century." Never quite got that far, but a lot of progress was made thanks to that legislation.

Bush was certainly not an enemy of the oil industry. He was *of* the oil industry, and many of his biggest campaign donors were Texas energy barons. If you were feeling benevolent, however, you could argue that the first Bush mimicked the LBJ strategy in making sure that Texas's many variations on the theme of Halliburton were taken care of when it came to federal contracts, while looking out for the country when it came to broader environmental policy. But H. W. had his limits, particularly when it came to global warming. He was reluctant to even attend the Earth Summit in Rio in 1992, and when he got there, he refused to sign a treaty on biodiversity. He approved the global warming treaty only after it had been seriously watered down. "The American way of life is not negotiable," he said. During his campaign against Bill Clinton in 1992, he would memorably lash out at Clinton's running mate, Al Gore, as "ozone man." ("This guy is so far out in the environmental extreme we'll be up to our necks in owls and outta work for every American.")

As a campaign strategy, the ozone offense apparently had its limits. Bush lost. Bill Clinton became president, bearing with him a strong environmental agenda that ran aground after the Republican landslide in 1994. The new leadership was topped by Newt Gingrich and the two Texans we've met before—Dick Armey as majority leader and Tom DeLay as whip. It was a perfect Texas moment, heavy with triumphalism. No more the disempowered minority, embracing bipartisanship for the sake of a few scraps from the table of the perpetually-in-charge Democrats. It was time to kick ass.

As if this wasn't enough of a nightmare for the environmental community, the new chairman of the House Energy and Commerce Committee was another Texan, "Smokey Joe" Barton. He was just back from an unsuccessful attempt to move into the Senate, in a campaign that lives on in memory for his argument against gay rights: "If homosexuality was normal, we wouldn't any of us be here." These days, Barton tends to be known best for his famous public apology to BP for the Obama administration's attempt to get it to pay for the damage caused by its Gulf oil spill. ("I do not want to live in a country where any time a citizen or corporation does something that is legitimately wrong, is subject to some sort of political pressure that is, again, in my words—amounts to a shakedown, so I apologize.") He later apologized for the apology. Barton represents the town of Midlothian, which is known as the Cement Capital of Texas, and he was particularly fierce about protecting the cement industry's right to pollute. A cement company paid for his college education, for heaven's sake.

The new Republican leadership attached seventeen addenda, known as riders, to the annual appropriation for the EPA. Known as the "Riders from Hell," they were aimed at gutting the Clean Air Act and other legislation the new right loathed by cutting the agency's money and prohibiting it from using what funds it had left to enforce certain regulations—like the ones relating to, um, pesticides and cement kilns. Although DeLay was of course getting tons of money from polluting industries for himself and his various political action committees, he wanted to make it clear he was doing this out of love: "You've got to understand, we are ideologues. We have an agenda. We have a philosophy. I want to repeal the Clean Air Act. No one came to me and said, 'Please repeal the Clean Air Act.' We say to the lobbyists, 'Help us.'"

The period after the game-changing 1994 election was the first bellow of the louder, more aggressive, and far more conservative new Republicanism. The great realignment of the American political parties that began after Lyndon Johnson pushed the Civil Rights Act into law was handing over the South to the GOP while the Democrats took control of the old centrist strongholds in the Northeast and West Coast. The two parties would fight on, over a handful of toss-up states, in campaigns that sometimes seemed to be conducted entirely in Ohio and Florida. Meanwhile, the conservative Southern Democrats and the moderate Republicans would fade away, to whatever lobbying firms constitute the political equivalent of an elephant burial ground.

It was all coming on fast, but in the mid-1990s, the changes hadn't quite solidified, and there was still a substantial contingent of moderates in the GOP House ranks. Frequently the thing that defined them as moderate was a positive attitude toward environmental legislation. Many of them represented suburban districts, and the whole point of the suburbs, when you got right down to it, was grass and birds and a breathable atmosphere. "I could sometimes count on as many as fifty [Republican] votes to go along with something my staff and I agreed was important to the environmental community," said Sherwood Boehlert, the New York Republican who mobilized the opposition. DeLay—usually such a canny vote-counter—overestimated the support for the Riders from Hell and watched in shock as his fellow Republicans voted them down.

Boehlert, who was chair of the Science Committee, said he generally got along with DeLay, who tended to respect a worthy opponent and who appreciated the fact that Boehlert, if asked, would give him an accurate count of the votes that were against him. Dick Armey was a different matter. "Armey had these cowboy boots with the member of Congress seal on them," Boehlert grumbled. "Glad I never took an economics course from him. DeLay was much more engaging."

Engaging, in an enraging sort of way. "They came up with this cockamamie idea—let's abolish the EPA," Boehlert recalled. "I fought them all the way, and they were surprised to get opposition from the business community, but many in the business community felt they'd rather have one national standard to deal with than fifty states." In the end, the main result of all of the Texans' efforts was to move the center of debate further and further to the right, while stopping any future environmental legislation in its tracks. Presidents would come and go, but Congress would never pass a law to control the carbon output of American industry. Tom DeLay didn't get his Riders from Hell, but he helped create a new discourse, in which the political debate about global warming, when it comes up at all, is usually about whether or not it exists.

"Let Texans run Texas"

By 2000, when George W. Bush was running for president, the days when Republicans could burble about protecting the forests and stopping climate change were pretty much over. The environmental discussion shifted to the need for "market-based incentives" and the rights of local communities. The 2000 Republican platform promised that the party nominee would approach environmental issues "just as he did it in Texas." That sounded rather ominous, since at the time Texas ranked first in airborne carcinogens, first in ozone components, first in toxic air releases. Houston had the nation's dirtiest air and Texas was number one when it came to unhealthy ozone levels.

Early in his days as governor, George W. had set the tone with his appointments to the Texas Natural Resource Conservation Commission, the state environmental agency. The TNRCC is run by three commissioners, and Bush chose:

1) A cattleman
2) A former employee of the state agriculture department, who

    was known for his attempts to loosen the rules governing the
use of pesticides

3) A career lobbyist for the Texas Chemical Council who had
once testified in Congress that ozone was "a relatively benign
pollutant"

To be fair, Governor Bush had an environmental plus side—sort
of. When the pollution in Dallas became so bad that the federal
government threatened to cut off road construction funds, Bush
backed efforts by the state legislature to require power plants to cut
their emissions dramatically by 2003—a year that he didn't plan to
be around to check on compliance. The state also tried to impose
a new motor vehicle inspection program, but it ran into opposition
from right-wing talk radio and the governor canceled it. When the
firm that had won the contract to implement the program sued, the
state settled for $130 million, which it paid for with funds from a
state environmental protection program.

    Bush's one genuine environmental enthusiasm was alternative
energy, or at least one form of alternative energy. "Pat, we like
wind," Bush told Pat Wood, the chairman of Texas's Public Utility
Commission, who he urged to "go get smart on wind." It made
total sense—if God had wanted to create a wind-power-generating
heaven, it would have looked a lot like Texas. And it was apparently Bush's enthusiasm for wind that caused him to order the creation of the Texas Renewable Portfolio Standard, which has one
of those names that make you understand why some people hate
government bureaucrats. It was basically a set of goals for production of renewable energy, which Texas more than met.

    "That led to a great investment in wind power," said Daniel
Weiss, a senior fellow at the Center for American Progress. "But
at the same time, when it came to a conflict between oil company
profits and Texans' health, the government has always chosen oil
company profits."

    In general, the Bush refrain when it came to the environment was "Let Texans run Texas." There it was again, that self-conscious appeal to the state's identity, which happened to work in concert with industry's desire to be let alone. The state's air pollution problems were made considerably worse by the more than 800 plants that had been built before Texas passed its Clean Air Act of 1971, which only applied to businesses to be constructed in the future. When Bush was governor most of the older plants were still in service, happily polluting away. Bush decided to resolve the problem with what his campaign would come to describe as "a healthy mix of voluntary and compulsory regulations." Under a law that was written with the help of executives from oil and chemical businesses, he exempted the plants from state regulation in return for their promise to clean up voluntarily. The problem with voluntary was that you didn't have to do it, and very few plants did.

"Basically, what you had is a guy from Marathon and a guy from Exxon sending out a proposal to this secret group of companies affected saying, here's the way we should approach this," said Smith.

Under Bush, the state stopped making surprise inspections of the plants it *did* regulate. And there weren't enough state employees to oversee the program anyway. "We have our limits," then Texas Natural Resource Conservation commissioner Ralph Marquez told the *Washington Post* in 2000. Marquez was a former lobbyist for the Texas Chemical Council, a trade organization whose members were, at the time, responsible for 74 percent of all EPA-tracked toxic chemical emissions in the state, 98 percent of the toxic water pollution, and 67 percent of the toxic air pollution.

"It is a darn good bill"

When Bush was elected president, for once a plank in a political platform got carried out. He did indeed continue the Texas strategy. He championed a Clear Skies initiative which, Al Gore grumbled, "actually allows more toxic mercury, nitrogen oxide and sulfur pollution than if we enforced the laws on the books today." There was a Healthy Forests initiative to allow more logging. The environment in general accounted for only 5 percent of Bush's presidential radio addresses. Given the fact that he gave one a week for eight years, it was a wonder his speechwriters didn't just turn to it more in desperation.

Meanwhile, the energy industry lobbyists were being assured that they would have the president's ear. During the transition, Bush's primary policy advisor on energy issues was Hunter Hunt, son of oil baron Ray Hunt. At the Department of the Interior, environmentalists learned to their horror that the number two man was going to be J. Steven Griles, an energy industry lobbyist.

"Not since the rise of the railroads more than a century ago has a single industry placed so many foot soldiers at the top of a new administration," said *Newsweek*.

And then—oh joy and bliss beyond compare for Texas—Bush made Vice President Dick Cheney his energy czar. "Conservation may be a sign of personal virtue but it is not a sufficient basis for a sound, comprehensive energy policy," the vice president said, in a hint that what was coming would not involve turning down the thermostat or turning in the Hummer.

Cheney is from Wyoming, one of the emptiest places in the country, a state with a population of 544,000 that sends as many senators to Washington as California, with a population of roughly 37 million. And unlike Texas, Wyoming is not showing any signs of ever getting crowded. Cheney represented Wyoming in Congress, was secretary of defense under George H. W. Bush, and then left politics to become CEO of the Houston-based energy giant Halliburton. So let's consider him an honorary Texan.

The vice president's task force, the National Energy Policy Development Group, ran for about three months. Enron officials met with the task force at least six times in person as well as a number of times on the phone. Ken Lay, who Bush called "Kenny-boy," got a meeting to discuss energy policy in California, where

Enron would eventually use the magic of the marketplace to create a catastrophic spike in electricity prices. In 2003, the General Accounting Office looked back on how the energy group had operated, and reported that one of Cheney's advisors "solicited detailed energy policy recommendations from a variety of nonfederal energy stakeholders, including the American Petroleum Institute [and] the National Petrochemical and Refiners Association." It hardly seems necessary to point out that while Bush was pushing out his energy policy, the oil industry was spending seven times as much as environmental groups on lobbying.

"We'll have a strong conservation statement," the president promised as the world awaited the Cheney energy policy's arrival. Later that day, White House spokesman Ari Fleischer was also asked whether Bush would be calling on Americans to use less energy, and took the opportunity to clarify his boss's statement a tad. "That's a big no," Fleischer said. "The president believes that it's an American way of life, that it should be the goal of policymakers to protect the American way of life. The American way of life is a blessed one." God, it seemed, smiled upon the Hummers in his flock. He looked upon the empty room with a burning lightbulb and found it good.

The plan that arrived from the Cheney task force, to the surprise of no one, was all about more drilling and pipelines and power plants. Also, about the importance of removing burdensome clean air regulations. In 2005, Congress followed up by passing an energy plan that was basically a Texas model with a nod to the plains states' desire to have something that involved using a whole lot of corn. There were huge breaks for energy producers, plus provisions to help create markets for ethanol and wind power. "It is a darn good bill," said Smokey Joe Barton, the lead sponsor. Texas was getting what it came for. A report by the Congressional Budget Office found that while American business in general is taxed at an overall 25 percent rate, oil field leases and drilling equipment were taxed at an effective rate of 9 percent. For small and midsize companies, whatever taxes existed were eliminated by various credits, giving them a return on investment that can actually be greater after taxes than it would have been before.

"Only nature can change the climate— a volcano for instance"

If the Texas Republicans hated all things EPA, there was no subject on which they were more rabid than global warming. "It's the arrogance of man to think that man can change the climate of the world. Only nature can change the climate—a volcano for instance," said DeLay. Armey, who disagreed with his fellow Texan on quite a lot, was in exactly the same camp. At a hearing on climate change legislation in 2009, Armey equated a belief in man-made global warming with a lack of faith in God. "It is quite pretentious of we little weaklings here on earth to think that, that we are going to destroy God's creation," he testified.

Christie Todd Whitman, the former governor of New Jersey, was Bush's original head of the Environmental Protection Agency. She was a moderate East Coast Republican, and it didn't require a crystal ball to figure out she was not going to fit in. Not long after the inauguration, Whitman made a trip to Italy, where she emphasized to Europeans that the administration was committed to controlling greenhouse gases—something the president had said himself before the election. Environmentalists had hung on desperately to that campaign comment, but the W. portfolio of compassionate-conservative commitments was a mixture of things the new president seemed to really believe in, like education reform, and the stuff that was just thrown out there for the moment. Everything relating to global warming, it turned out, was in Category Two.

The White House announced that a cabinet-level review of its energy policy had convinced the president that there should be no federal attempt to cut carbon dioxide emissions. It could not have been more humiliating for Whitman, particularly given the fact that this particular cabinet-level review had not included the head of the Environmental Protection Agency. "When I made the statement in Italy that something might happen on CO_2, the utility industry got really engaged, and all of that caused a rethink," Whitman told *Rolling Stone* much later. The magazine acquired a memo from a team of Cheney loyalists in the White House, which posited that whatever Bush had said about greenhouse gasses during the campaign "did not fully reflect the president's position" and that "it would be premature at this time to propose any specific policy or approach aimed at addressing global warming."

Many people, from Whitman to the administration's first secretary of the treasury, Paul O'Neill, have argued that George W. went into the presidency planning to do something about climate change, but that Cheney stole the issue away from him. Doesn't matter. In policy, good intentions—especially good intentions that aren't followed up by any attempt at action whatsoever—don't count. The bottom line was that the idea of doing anything serious about global warming got trashed, pounded into the ground, pulverized, vaporized, and expelled into the already rather heavily polluted Washington air. And in 2002, when the EPA issued a report that said climate change was probably due to human activity, Bush said dismissively, "I read the report put out by the bureaucracy."

The White House did eventually set a goal of reducing the growth of greenhouse gas emissions by 18 percent by 2012. It's always hard to get a fix on goals that involve reducing the rate at which something is growing. So when Bush held a press conference in 2008 to announce that his initiatives were going great, I did some calculations. If Bush, that well-known fitness buff, had discovered two years into his job that he had gained 40 pounds and resolved to deal with the problem by reducing the rate at which he was gaining weight by 18 percent, he would have weighed 400 pounds in 2012.

When delivering his good news about global warming, Bush also vowed to stop the growth of US emissions entirely by 2025. Setting aside the fact that Bush was only going to be president for nine months of that next seventeen years, and that the president warned that the "wrong way" to accomplish this goal was "to raise taxes, duplicate mandates or demand sudden and drastic emissions cuts," you were still talking, in my original model, about a 486-pound ex-president.

"The science is actually going the other way"

In the real world, W. was the same size as always when the White House changed hands in 2008. The Bushes returned to a quiet life in Texas and Barack Obama came roaring into Washington promising aggressive action on environmental issues, almost nothing of which made it into law. The White House claimed it had accomplished quite a bit through executive orders, but there is a limit to how much you can do without any congressional help whatsoever.

The surging Tea Party movement helped pressure Senate Republicans into delaying or derailing everything possible, and when the Republicans recaptured the House in 2010, they marched through the agenda that DeLay had once pursued. The Democratic minority on the House Energy and Commerce Committee tallied "191 votes against environmental protection" in the first year of Republican control, which would have averaged out to more than one anti-environmental vote per day. The House majority knew that virtually none of their environmental rollbacks had a chance of going anywhere in the still-Democratic Senate. But if you envisioned the environmental legislation that had been set into place since the days of Lyndon Johnson as bowling pins, the House Republicans were very happily knocking them down, just to show they could: weaken the Clean Air Act, weaken the Endangered Species Act, defund and declaw the EPA, and, of course, liberate the cement industry. Also, refuse to acknowledge that the globe is warming. "The science is not settled and the science is actually going the other way," said Joe Barton, who had, in the wake of the

BP apology dustup, been kicked upstairs to Energy Committee Chairman Emeritus. Texan Ralph Hall, who had taken over Sherwood Boehlert's old post as chair of the Science Committee, told the *National Journal* that he was "pretty close" to the Rick Perry theory of climate change as baloney that research scientists were tossing out to qualify for federal funding. "I don't think we can control what God controls," Hall added, scientifically.

The environmentalists were stuck in a world where a victorious day was one in which something had been stopped from happening.

"One contrived phony mess"

To judge how badly things were going for the clean-air-clean-water crowd, you just had to look at Texas, where the torch had been passed on to Rick Perry.

One big difference between George W. Bush and his successor as governor was their perceptions of how the nation in general felt about the environment. When Bush began positioning himself to run for national office, he got greener. The man who, as governor of Texas, had once expressed serious doubts about the whole climate change issue announced as a presidential hopeful that after consulting some experts he had decided that yep, global warming was out there. Environmental groups were thrilled when his staff started asking the experts sophisticated questions about methane emissions and black carbon particles and the candidate himself announced he wanted to do something about controlling carbon emissions. It never came to anything, but still it did indicate that Bush felt you needed to at least go through the motions. Perry, who had won his first statewide office by opposing a rule requiring that farm workers be kept out of the fields when they're being sprayed with pesticides, started out further to the right on environmental issues, and when he began thinking about a national run, he only got more so.

Perry had an ongoing fight with Lisa Jackson, the Obama

administration's Environmental Protection Agency head, over air quality rules. (The EPA, Perry wrote in his campaign book, *Fed Up*, is "destroying federalism and individuals' ability to make their own economic decisions.") But it was once again on the issue of climate change that Texas really went to war with Washington.

Texas produces the most greenhouse gases in the nation, what with one thing (energy production) and another (energy use). All those cars aren't just there for decoration. But Perry didn't put any stock in climate change—an aide told the Austin *American-Statesman* that the governor was "not convinced that it's an issue." In *Fed Up*, Perry was a little more forthcoming, describing global warming science as "one contrived phony mess that is falling apart under its own weight."

During the George W. Bush presidency, the post-Whitman EPA had announced that it had no authority to regulate carbon dioxide and other greenhouse gas emissions in order to halt climate change. Massachusetts and eleven other states filed suit, and in 2007 the Supreme Court ruled that greenhouse gases counted as pollutants. The states won; the EPA, after a fair bit of foot-dragging, including a totally futile attempt to find some scientific proof that greenhouse gas emissions were harmless, announced its regulatory plans. Texas was the only state that refused to join in the program. Instead, it led its own consortium of states in suing the EPA.

Announcing the action, Texas attorney general Greg Abbott said the EPA was relying on global warming information that was tainted by "cover-ups and the suppression and destruction of scientific evidence." In response, climate scientists from the state's major universities published an op-ed in the *Houston Chronicle* pointing out that no climate scientist in the state agreed with the suit's premise.

"To me, it's a sign of an extremely weak position, to start attacking the process. And if you read the petition—I was just amazed," said Larry Soward, a former member of the Texas Commission on Environmental Quality who had been appointed by Perry, and who called the governor "a dear friend."

At this particular point, Soward said, his dear friend was being "short-sighted."

"Texas is the largest emitter of carbon dioxide in the nation," he continued. "We're the—I can't remember if it's the eleventh or twelfth or whatever in the world—and nobody can reasonably tell me that if we didn't reduce our carbon dioxide emissions in the atmosphere that it wouldn't have a positive effect locally."

By the end of 2011, Perry took his anti-environmental regulation crusade national, through his much-ballyhooed, though ultimately deeply humiliating, presidential race. Meanwhile, Perry's national ambitions were having an impact back in Texas, where the state's Commission on Environmental Quality took a blue pencil to a 200-page scientific study it had commissioned on the deteriorating condition of Galveston Bay, editing out every mention of climate change and sea-level rise. Every scientist involved in the project demanded his or her name be removed.

"I like to tell people we live in a state of denial in the state of Texas," said John Anderson, an oceanographer at Rice University.

PART THREE
THE TEXAS MODEL

10

The Texas Miracle, Part II

"America's new land of opportunity"

In the depths of America's post-recession recession, Texas looked like a proverbial jobs oasis. What were they doing right? Non-Texans were unnerved—maybe humbled—by the idea that the state had discovered the secret sauce for fixing the American economy. First they want to secede; now they want to grow all the jobs. What gives?

"For the last few weeks, I've been unable to get a startling statistic out of my head: Since the recession officially ended [in 2009], Texas has created more than four out of every ten new jobs in America," wrote Rick Wartzman of Claremont Graduate University's Drucker Institute in the summer of 2011.

Four out of ten! Or maybe more. "Since June 2009, about 48 percent of all the jobs created in America were in Texas. Come add to it," Perry told Glenn Beck in June of 2011.

"Thank you. I'd love to," Beck responded. And indeed, after his unceremonious departure from Fox, the loud, emotional, right-wing populist announced he was moving to Dallas. Gone To Texas.

Or even more! "Approximately 70 percent of the jobs created in the US from November 2007–8 were in Texas," announced the governor's office in 2009, as it reported on a Perry speech crediting

"Texas's low taxes, reasonable regulatory structure and economic development incentives" for this wonderful achievement—which, it turned out, was actually based on statistics from only fourteen other states. "In fact, if you throw out just thirteen more inconvenient states, Texas accounted for 100 percent of all new US jobs," snarked Texans for Public Justice.

Obviously, we are paddling in statistically challenging waters. But whatever the jobs number was, the Texas Miracle seemed impressive. (When good news comes to other states, it's an uptick. In Texas it's always a miracle.)

"There is still a land of opportunity, friends. It's called Texas. We're creating more jobs than any other state in the nation," said Rick Perry during his last gubernatorial campaign. "Would you rather live in a state like this, or in a state where guys can marry guys?"

Okay, not normally what you would think of as alternate career paths.

OVER THE PAST decade Texas has replaced New York as the nation's second largest economy. California, which is still first, has been struggling and Texas, which has spent most of its modern history resentfully sitting in California's shadow, has been known to gloat. "As the state of California continues to support legislation that causes undue burden and taxation on companies doing business in the Los Angeles area, I invite you to consider your future in America's new land of opportunity, the state of Texas," Perry recently wrote to companies in the California town of Vernon. (He was attempting to profit from the bad feelings that arose over a bipartisan attempt in Sacramento to deprive Vernon of its status as an independent municipality, for no good reason except Vernon's enormous political corruption and lack of actual residents.) And in 2006, when a trade association paid for a private jet to fly Perry and his family to the Rose Bowl (U. T. was playing!), a gubernatorial spokesman suggested the real reason for the trip was to hold a barbecue during which the governor would persuade California companies to relocate.

Texas has been named the best place to do business by so many publications, it has come to resemble an irritating kid who wins all the awards at graduation and then devotes the valedictorian speech to his secrets for success.

- In *Forbes*, columnist Joel Kotkin put Austin first on his "next big boom town" list, giving the number four slot to San Antonio and number five to Houston.
- CNBC chose Texas as the top state for business in 2010, citing the state's first-place ranking in the categories of overall economy and transportation. Texas came in thirtieth in education and twenty-ninth in quality of life, but you can't have everything.
- A magazine called *Site Selection* awarded Texas its Governor's Cup for the most new and expanded corporate facilities in 2010. Sending a shout-out to his fellow governors, Perry said: "It's a clear challenge to improve the business climate in their states to put pressure on Texas to be more competitive."
- *Chief Executive* magazine, in a 2011 article naming Texas the best state for business for the seventh consecutive year, deemed it a "Periclean Athens" compared to archrival California.

Perry did love to boast about the companies he'd snatched away from California, although critics claimed he frequently confused "moving to Texas" with "opening a modest-sized branch in Texas." But sometimes it did seem as if California couldn't do anything right. In 2011, the *Houston Business Journal* reported that Andrew Puzder, the CEO of Carl's Jr., a fast-food chain that boasts a six-dollar bacon-burger, was in town scouting sites. Carl's Jr. was headquartered in Carpinteria, California, but the lure of the Lone Star State, Puzder said, was compelling: "People in Houston love their meat."

Take that, you West Coast vegans.

California's deepest humiliation came in April of 2011, when a delegation of its state legislators, led by Lieutenant Governor Gavin Newsom, came to Texas claiming they wanted to learn what their state was doing wrong. (Their motivation wasn't entirely clear, although the desire to drive Governor Jerry Brown crazy must have figured in there somewhere.) The group was organized by Dan Logue, an assemblyman who had put together a similar pilgrimage to booming Nevada two years earlier. Since then, the Nevada economy had tanked so deeply that it had the highest unemployment rate in the country and was in worse shape than California. However, Logue told the *Los Angeles Times* that Nevada would come back faster "because it has a business-friendly climate."

We will stop for a moment to mull how a state with such an estimable attitude toward the free market managed to get in such a hole in the first place.

But about the legislators' visit to Texas: The gang was trotted from one meeting to the next, where the message, as Nolan Hicks of the *Houston Chronicle* described it, was always pretty much the same: "Lowering taxes, handcuffing trial lawyers and a 'business friendly' (or lax) regulatory climate were the keys to Texas's success and could be the keys to boosting the California economy." At one stop, Governor Perry joined the fun, listening to the speakers sing his state's praises while he sat, cowboy-style, legs crossed, the boots Liberty and Freedom on display, with his arm around the back of Newsom's chair.

Perry's worldview was simple. Texas had lower taxes, less regulation, and more business-friendly incentives like its Enterprise Fund, which offered money to sweeten the deal for firms looking to move in. So it was growing business. And if the rest of the country would follow its lead, they, too, would create lots and lots of jobs all over. And the whole country would be booming. "As well as Texas has done in the past and in 2010, we're not going to be what we can be, or as strong as we can be, unless we have competition from other states," Perry told *Site Selection* in his victory interview. In other words, Texas was doing the rest of the states a favor. And the governor was dying for the other forty-nine to get in the game and try to snitch Texas jobs, too. Really, nothing would make him happier.

"It started up as a good plan and it wound up a mess"

It was an early clarion call for what would become a national debate during the presidential election year. Perry might have been gone from the scene, but the Republican argument over how jobs could be created was still built around the Texas model—low taxes, low regulation, special incentives to lure businesses to move in.

There are a couple of ways to look at Perry's idea for a national competition among the states to see who could develop the most business-appealing environment. Perhaps Texas has the recipe for growing the national economy. Great! On the other hand, maybe job growth in Texas is mainly due to accidents of the state's location, and the competition is just a way to blackmail other states into bankrupting themselves for no good reason whatsoever except corporate greed.

Of course, the truth could lie somewhere in the middle. That's always a good bet, but for the moment, I'm going with the blackmail-and-bankrupt scenario.

Tax-wise, the thing businesses love most about Texas is that it has no income tax, and is highly unlikely to have one in the future. As former Lieutenant Governor Bob Bullock once said, you're more likely to see a Russian submarine invade Houston. Supporting a state income tax is considered such political suicide that when Bullock called for one during the Ann Richards administration, word spread that he had thrown political caution to the winds due to a terminal illness. The entire experience was so traumatic that the lieutenant governor, in one of those deeply Texas impulses,

expressed his frustration over the lack of an income tax by engi-
neering the passage of a constitutional amendment requiring a
voter referendum before an income tax could ever be put into law.

Unless such a referendum passes, an event slightly less likely than
that submarine attack, an income tax is officially unconstitutional,
right up there with same-sex unions and state officials who don't
believe in God.

For revenue, Texas relies heavily on the sales tax, as regressive
a levy as you can invent short of a tax on children. It averages out
at more than 8 percent once the local governments get their extra
taste. "When we were faced with the necessity of passing a tax bill
in the legislature, we would talk about this idea and that recommendation and in the end it all came down to the same thing—add
a quarter penny to the sales tax," former Lieutenant Governor Bill
Hobby recalled.

So as it turns out, Texas is a low-tax state only for people with
lots of income. A study by the Institute on Taxation and Economic
Policy found that the bottom 20 percent of residents pay more
than 12 percent of their income in state and local taxes, while the
top 20 percent pay about 3.3 percent. After the report came out,
the *Dallas Morning News* interviewed a former state House Appropriations Committee chair, Talmadge Heflin, who denounced the
study for praising states like New York and Vermont for their
more even-handed taxation systems. What Texan would want to
be like New York or Vermont? "The data show emphatically that
people want to live and do business in states with low overall taxes
and no income tax," Heflin concluded.

Rule One: To join the Texas job-growth derby, begin by making sure poor people pay a disproportionate share of the freight.

On the business side, Texas had long made its money off a complicated levy known as the franchise tax, which fell heavily on some
firms while leaving many others untouched. Meanwhile, the locali-
ties and school districts got their funds mainly from the property
tax, which was also relatively high on average in Texas, and hard on

large-space enterprises like manufacturing. The Council on State Taxation, an organization representing business taxpayers, estimated that in 2010, Texas ranked nineteenth highest in what it called its "total effective business tax rate," slightly above the national average.

So, rule two in the economic development sweepstakes is to lowball the taxes you're actually imposing. Those pilgrims from the California state legislature eventually made a stop at the Texas Taxpayers and Research Association, which broke the news that the business tax numbers of the two states were actually pretty similar. They left "kind of in shock," said Dale Craymer, the association's president.

In 2006, under the gun to do something about the level of property taxes Texans were paying to fund their schools, the legislature undertook a big, ambitious reform. "They needed to create a business tax that was fair. The franchise tax only taxes one in four," said Bill Ratliff, the former Republican state senator who was once acting lieutenant governor. The endeavor, he said unhappily, "started up as a good plan and it wound up a mess."

The franchise tax was out, and something called the margin tax on business profits was in. The Tax Foundation, a conservative Washington think tank that's generally been a big fan of Texas fiscal policy, denounced the new tax as "a failed experiment desperately needing reform" that had already "become notorious for its complexity." Politicians' passion for passing exemptions for favored businesses, the Foundation noted, was so fierce that "in 2009 alone, an additional 100 proposals to modify the tax made their way through the Texas state legislature." But the biggest defect was in the math. The lawmakers refused to believe the comptroller when she said the new tax structure would raise around $12.5 billion a year less than they were counting on. Which was exactly what happened.

But nobody's perfect. And remember, no income tax.

"A smoking gun of bad economic development"

When it comes to job growth policies that businesses really love, there are few more attractive than the idea that states should simply give them a bunch of money to move in. No part of Rick Perry's vision of a national job-attraction competition sounded more delicious than the idea of a perpetual bidding war.

In Texas, the cash used to bribe—um, *incentivize*—businesses to relocate is called the Enterprise Fund. In recent years it's been the largest program of its kind in the country, handing out more than $400 million in taxpayer dollars to encourage corporations to create jobs in the state. The Fund is Governor Perry's particular brainchild, one he protected even in 2011, when the legislature was forced to slash other programs, including public schools, in order to create at least a pretense of having balanced the budget without tax hikes. There is also an Emerging Technology Fund and a special fund for moviemaking which critics say is actually more like a special fund for subsidizing the filming of corporate TV commercials.

The Fund was supposed to be a "deal-closer" that would win over firms that couldn't quite decide whether Texas's award-winning business friendliness was really enough to make a move there worthwhile. It has zero oversight beyond needing the approval of the three top elected state officials, all currently Republican. Negative minds have been known to refer to it as "the governor's slush fund."

"If you're looking for a smoking gun of bad economic development, that's it," said Don Baylor of the Center for Public Policy Priorities, an Austin-based think tank. "It's state money—and it's money, not tax credits. On top of local tax incentives. It's a one-, five-, twenty-million-dollar cherry on top of the sundae."

Now, people, how many of you would like to think that the company you work for might pull up stakes and move someplace else because another state offered them a bunch of money to do it? How many of you would like to spend your own tax dollars one-upping the bids so hometown firms will stay put?

Let me see a show of hands. Just as I thought.

If we're going to give public funds to businesses, shouldn't it be going to the ones that can actually create new jobs rather than the ones that are just prepared to ship their existing ones across state lines? "Nationally, all we are doing is moving companies around and giving them huge incentives to do what they were probably going to do anyway," Robert Orr of the North Carolina Institute for Constitutional Law told the *Dallas Morning News*.

And if we're thinking about the welfare of the country as a whole, shouldn't we be discouraging states from this kind of wasteful competition? Instead of demanding that every state have an Enterprise Fund like Texas, shouldn't we be considering whether to make things like the Enterprise Fund illegal? Instead of trying to amend the Constitution to make it impossible for states to permit gay marriage, shouldn't we be looking at an amendment that would make it illegal for one state to use public money to pay another state's businesses to move away?

The Enterprise Fund strategy doesn't even seem to be working out all that well for Texas. Reporters discovered that the Texas Institute for Genomic Medicine—a biotech effort at Texas A & M that received $50 million from the state and allegedly created 12,000 jobs—only actually employed ten people. The *Wall Street Journal* determined that the state had been counting every biotechnology-related job created anywhere in Texas since 2005, including employment in areas like dental equipment and fertilizer manufacturing. In the case of another $25 million for a medical-imaging research facility at a Houston cancer center, Perry took credit for 2,000 jobs created which, the *Journal* noted, included virtually any position added anywhere in the giant cancer center for anything, including "a plumber and a chaplain, along with nurses, social workers and other staffers." Alec MacGillis of the *New Republic* went to the Houston suburb of Sugar Land to check out the Texas Energy Center, an awardee that was supposed to have created 1,500 jobs, and discovered it existed only on paper, through the efforts of the president of the local economic development council, who appeared to be getting a slice of the $3.5 million Enterprise Fund grant mainly for figuring out how to credit the Center with job creation.

We will pause here to contemplate whether Texas's love affair with the imaginary extends to economic statistics.

One of the most infamous Enterprise Fund deals involved Cabela's ("Quality Hunting, Fishing, Camping and Outdoor Gear at Competitive Prices"), which got $600,000 to build stores in Fort Worth and Buda, a city just south of Austin. The retailer also received whopping local incentives, including $40 million from Fort Worth to help pay for property acquisition and construction.

"I know I speak for thousands of fellow hunters when I say we have waited anxiously for this to arrive, like a kid on Christmas Eve," said Perry, announcing the Buda deal.

The stores arrived but the jobs never really did. Cabela's eventually lost the last of its $200,000 in state grants and had to pay back $70,000 of what it originally took home because it fell far short of creating the 400 jobs it originally promised. "But the property is already bought, the store built and the company saved a couple of million dollars it would have had to pay in salaries and benefits to those 126 mythical workers. Not a bad bottom line," said the *Fort Worth Weekly*. Also, the other stores, hotels, entertainment parks, and restaurants that the state expansively predicted would follow the Cabela's openings never materialized.

But there's still all that outdoor gear. At competitive prices.

"The most important thing that's happened to us"

Next stop, regulation.

Among the many, many benefits which Rick Perry sees from a cutthroat economic development competition among the states is the way it would force the competitors to reduce unnecessary regulation. And that could indeed be a good thing. Nobody likes unnecessary regulation. Although of course the last thing in the world we would want is to see rogue companies try to avoid righteous penalties for their bad behavior by decamping to a place that seems intent on allowing them to do whatever the hell they want if only they'll move in. Obviously.

Let's take a look at what Texas has been up to.

Given its let's-whack-California inclinations, the Perry administration was particularly thrilled to announce in 2005 that Hilmar Cheese Company of central California was going to build its new plant in Dalhart, on the Texas panhandle. The lure, said Hilmar officials, was Texas's "common-sense approach to regulation." They were presumably thinking of the record $4 million fine Hilmar had gotten in California for befouling the local drinking water with the waste from its cheese-making. The wells of Hilmar's neighbors were contaminated with arsenic, barium, and salts, and the water had become undrinkable. When people in the Hilmar zone washed themselves or their laundry, the salt content in the water was so high that "it leaves a residue of white, chunky crystals," reported *Environmental Health News*.

It wasn't as if California regulators had been going out of their way to crack down on Hilmar, whose co-founder was Governor Arnold Schwarzenegger's undersecretary of agriculture. Water quality enforcers had pretty clearly been looking the other way until the *Sacramento Bee* published a story with the uncheery title "The World's Biggest Cheese Factory Fouled Air and Water for Years." Then came the fine—which Hilmar settled for $3 million—and next thing you knew, the firm's chairman, Richard Clauss, was in Texas, saying he had "never got a welcome like that in California."

Which was probably true, since Perry's Enterprise Fund gave Hilmar $7.5 million to build its new factory in the panhandle, a move the cheese-makers said would create 376 new jobs and another 1,586 "associated" jobs at dairies that would naturally spring up to supply Hilmar. Three years later, the new factory had actually produced 169 direct jobs and 326 associated jobs.

WHEN TEXAS OFFICIALS brag about their hatred of business-unfriendly restrictions, they don't generally point to, say, lax enforcement of laws against water pollution—although the state didn't claw its way up to the number one spot in toxic discharges into the waterways without a good deal of effort. And God knows what they say in private to chemical firm executives looking to move. But in public, the emphasis is often on the way the state has clamped down on frivolous lawsuits.

"The most important thing that's happened to us is tort reform," Richard Fisher, the head of the Federal Reserve's Dallas branch, told Rick Wartzman in that *Los Angeles Times* piece. Fisher added that he believed companies like John Deere have expanded in Texas because they were "largely driven by steps the state has taken to cap non-economic damages in medical malpractice suits and to make it harder to bring product liability and class-action cases."

Tort reform was one of George W. Bush's big issues in his 1994 campaign against Governor Ann Richards, the famous race in which Bush astonished the political world with his ability to make the same four points over and over without collapsing from boredom. (The other three, in case anyone ever asks, involved juvenile justice, schools, and welfare.) And he had a point. Even people who believed strongly in the importance of civil suits in protecting the public against defective products and services sometimes admitted that the Texas system could indeed use a little reining in. After Bush was elected reforms ensued, limiting the amount juries could award in punitive damages and making it harder for lawyers to go venue-shopping for the most sympathetic locations for their trials.

Then in 2003, the legislature went tort reforming again, and threw out the proverbial baby with the judicial bathwater.

"Here is what can happen to you in Texas today," Mimi Swartz of *Texas Monthly* wrote in 2005. "If you go to an emergency room with a heart attack and the ER doctor misreads your EKG, you must prove, in order to prevail in a lawsuit, that he was both 'wantonly and willfully negligent.'" Swartz went on to a long list of depressing and distressing outcomes. ("If your child is blinded at birth because of medical malpractice, there is a good chance that her only remedy is to receive a few hundred dollars a month for the rest of her life.") Then she pointed out that even getting a tiny settlement was dependent on being able to find a lawyer—a difficult project, since under the new regime, few lawyers were willing to take on clients who could only pay a percentage of their final court settlement. Finally, Swartz added that if you did manage to find a lawyer and miraculously win the case, the other side could always appeal. In which case, the odds of your winning were about 12 percent.

And there you are. "Our tort policy has improved the business climate," said state representative Mark Strama of Austin. "But it's also the reason one of the mothers in my district whose four-year-old daughter checked into the hospital with a cold and never checked out can't even get a lawyer to find out why."

The caps on malpractice awards were supposed to draw more doctors to Texas, and it is true that they're flocking in. But the rural areas that were underserved by physicians when George W. Bush was governor are still pretty much in the same boat. "The doctors are by and large coming to the places that already had them," said Alex Winslow of Texas Watch, a consumer advocacy group. The undersupply of doctors, Winslow argues, was never really due to malpractice issues as much as to the state's low Medicaid reimbursement rates, which discourage doctors from going to any part of the state where there are a lot of poor people—especially a lot of poor people spread far apart. "And overall health care spending has risen more in Texas than the national average," he added.

(The idea that Texas is innately efficient when it comes to health care delivery lies in the same category as the idea that it has a right to secede. In a much-noted article in *The New Yorker* in 2009, Atul

Gawande pointed out that the border town of McAllen was the second most expensive health care market in the country after Miami, despite what would seem to be a relatively low cost of living. "In 2006, Medicare spent fifteen thousand dollars per enrollee here, almost twice the national average," Gawande wrote. "The income per capita is twelve thousand dollars. In other words, Medicare spends three thousand dollars more per person here than the average person earns." The reason, Gawande found, was simply that medical practitioners and their suppliers organized everything to maximize financial returns—"a medical community came to treat patients the way subprime-mortgage lenders treated home buyers: as profit centers.")

Once again, we should recall that these are our federal dollars. Which we are happy to see spent on seniors' health, although not so much to maintain the high incomes of the medical community of McAllen. Particularly not if their state is going to constantly brag about how thrifty it is.

The Bush administration claimed tort reform would save consumers $3 billion a year in insurance premiums, but in 2010, Texas had some of the highest premiums in the country for family health insurance plans and also among the highest deductibles. "High premiums and skimpy coverage," summarized Sara Collins, vice president for the Affordable Health Insurance program at the Commonwealth Fund. In 2010, Texas families spent a higher percentage of their household income on health insurance premiums than any other state but Mississippi and Arizona. Meanwhile, the pressure on other states to follow Texas's example on tort reform—and then perhaps a second level of mega-tort reform—continued unabated.

"Don't get hurt in Texas"

Next business-friendly example: Only one state in the union doesn't require large employers to take part in a state-regulated workers' compensation system, which provides people with medical benefits and support if they're injured on the job. We will take a moment's rest here while everybody guesses which state that is.

Not Vermont. Be serious.

Yes, in Texas—which has the lowest workers' compensation coverage in the country—about a third of the businesses have left the state workers' compensation system and gone off on their own. "There are two categories of employers who don't carry workers' comp," says Rick Levy, the legal director for the Texas AFL–CIO. "One is small employers who operate on the margins. Unfortunately, that's a lot of the most dangerous occupations, like construction. And increasingly, there are Fortune 500 companies."

Since the late 1980s, the state legislature has reorganized, fiddled, and otherwise changed the workers' comp system, always with an eye to reducing insurers' costs and keeping the injured employees from getting legal representation. In Texas, as in many parts of the country, there is an ongoing war between the Republican Party and the trial lawyers, in part because Republicans connect the lawyers with business costs, and in part because the trial lawyers tend to be big Democratic donors. Texas law now limits lawyers' compensation in these cases so drastically that few will take them. "Where previously hundreds of Texas lawyers had significant workers' comp practices, there now are about 30," wrote Terry Carter in the *American Bar Association Journal*. If an insurer wants to fight an injured worker's claim—and the insurer has every reason in the world to give it a shot, or delay resolution for as long as possible—the worker is unlikely to have anyone on his side of the battle. Most Texas workers aren't unionized, and now the chances of getting a lawyer are small, particularly for a low-paid worker with an unsensational injury.

"The moral of the story is, don't get hurt in Texas," said Richard Pena, a former president of the state bar of Texas, who still takes some workers' compensation cases. Pena said that in the cases for which he gets paid at all, he typically receives about $630 per case—for nine weeks' work and hearings.

Big employers in Texas often set up their own privatized workers' compensation system, Levy said. Those plans aren't under state regulation. They often provide limited benefits and have narrow windows of opportunity to qualify. In some, workers have to file a written complaint before the end of the shift in which they're hurt.

As an example, Levy cited a woman who worked for a hospital, and hurt her back doing lifting. The woman told her supervisor, who suggested she go see a doctor. Leaving work for the day, she saw the doctor, went home to rest, and woke up the next morning unable to move. "She needs surgery," said Levy. "She filed and the company denied her any benefits because she didn't report it in writing on the day she was injured.

"It's an unregulated Wild West," he continued. "The employer gets to make up all the rules. And what's interesting now is, we're seeing these companies attempting to export this model to other states. It's like rolling back the clock ninety years."

And yes, the corporate community sees this as a model for improving the business climate in the rest of the nation.

"It's all about air conditioning"

If deregulation and low taxes were the real keys to job growth, wouldn't Mississippi be setting records? Before anybody joins in the race to out-Texas Texas, we'd better consider the possibility that there are other reasons for job growth there. And there are plenty. If your state really wants to follow Texas's lead, it probably ought to:

Have oil. When energy prices go up, the economy suffers. Unless you happen to be in a state that's pocked with oil wells and shale drilling sites. In the long run, the Texas economy tends to follow the price of oil.

Avoid being in the Snowbelt. The most spectacularly boring explanation for the Texas job surge is that it's just a part of the long-running migration to the Sunbelt. "Because we have population growth down here, there's a growth in leisure, health care—those are trends following the people," said Christopher King, an economics professor at the University of Texas at Austin. "So really, it's all about air conditioning."

Abolish sex education. Texas's population is also young—the state median age is 33.2, compared to 36.8 for the country as a whole—and everybody knows that young people like to spend money more than seniors. Besides immigration, Texas's secret is a booming birth rate, which was propelled along in part by that abstinence-only sex education in the schools and the antipathy toward family planning funding in the state legislature.

Share a border with Mexico. "Texas does a huge amount of trade with Mexico, and Mexico is the gateway to the rest of Central and South America," said Michael Brandl, an economics professor at Ohio State University who spent much of his career in Austin. A lot of that is the result of the North American Free Trade Agreement. NAFTA's impact on, say, Michigan may have been problematic, but in Texas everything's good. "NAFTA, that's the export story," said Mine Yücel of the Dallas Fed. "We send about a third of our exports to Mexico. That's taken off since NAFTA."

The total impact of Mexico on the Texas economy is impossible to account, given that billions of it involves the illegal drug trade. But on the legal side, just the trade between violence-torn Juarez, Mexico, and El Paso (fourteen murders in 2011, lowest crime rate for any American big city) is more than $70 billion. And, if you want to be really, really depressed, there's the revenue from the sale of guns to Mexican drug lords.

Hitch a free ride. Finally, the whole idea that other states could do what Texas is doing is flawed by the fact that Texas is doing it on their backs. Take higher education. Texas doesn't spend much on it, relatively speaking. The state has only two tier-one public universities, while California has ten and New York eight. All the four-year institutions in Texas only graduate about 140,000 people annually, but the state has been able to lure in another 170,000 graduates a year from elsewhere. "People in Ohio and Wisconsin and Pennsylvania provide the great education, and then the graduates leave, and Texas gets this educated population for which they don't have to pay anything," said Brandl.

In other words, if all the states started bribing businesses to move from other states, saving tax money by skimping on higher education, and filling high-end jobs with college graduates from other states, the whole shebang would implode. It's what economists call the fallacy of composition. "A classic example is when you're driving down the road and the sign says, 'Left Lane Closed,'" Brandl continued. "If everybody sticks to the right lane, things are fine. If you as an individual go in the left lane, all the way to the orange barrel, and then cut back over, you'll be in front. But if everybody tries to do it, it's gridlock."

"Government doesn't create any jobs"

Just as an aside, let's remember that a big source of new employment in Texas is the dreaded government.

"In Texas, public employment makes up about 17.8 percent of the workforce, compared to 16.9 percent in the country as a whole," said Leslie Helmcamp of the Center for Public Policy Priorities. Moreover, she added, "The Texas public sector created over 47 percent of the net new jobs since the beginning of 2007."

Counting in a different way, as these issues seem to demand, the *Wall Street Journal* estimated that Texas gained more than a million jobs since the end of 2000, about 300,000 of which were in government, mainly in public schools.

In some parts of the state, these jobs are on the federal government's tab, in the form of military bases. In 2008, the Texas comptroller estimated that Fort Hood alone added $10.9 billion to the state's economy. And in 2011, the federal government announced plans to move 6,000 more soldiers to Fort Bliss, outside El Paso, beyond the 14,000 it had added over the previous three years.

Meanwhile, in yet another interview on *Glenn Beck*, Governor Perry told his host, the soon-to-be-Dallas resident, "Government doesn't create any jobs. They can actually run jobs away."

Our men in uniform aside, you can see why Perry liked that government-has-no-relation-to-job-creation thought stream, since school districts were about to start laying people off in Texas to compensate for state budget cuts. (A gubernatorial spokesman told the *Wall Street Journal* that the cuts wouldn't hurt the state economy because "the key to prosperity is the growth of the private sector, not the government sector.")

But let's at least remember that Texas was built by government assistance of one kind or another. A massive federally funded infrastructure, including the great New Deal rural electrification and the Eisenhower-era roads, brought the state out of the semifeudal condition it had existed in from the time of Sam Houston. For most of American history, Texas was a place that sent raw material off for some more advanced place to turn into valuable products. The federal government lifted it out of that trap, all the while subsidizing the crops it produced, and doling out massive tax credits to the oil it pumped from the ground.

Not looking for thanks, really. Or maybe just a little.

"Everybody else is baking these muffins"

Let's go back to the Texas recipe for national prosperity: Spurred on by the wholesome national competition to steal each other's employers, every state in the union should repeal all income taxes, make it extremely difficult for people to sue the company that sold them the canned hash flavored with ground glass, relocate to somewhere in the Sunbelt, preferably with a border on Mexico, and sneak into the left lane until they get as close to the orange barrel as possible.

Then we will be going like Texas! Jobs jobs jobs. Our governors, too, will be saying the word in every sentence.

But about those jobs . . .

One of the economic Oscars that Texas hasn't been bragging about is its long-standing first-place ranking for jobs at or below minimum wage—although in 2011, it finally managed a tie with Mississippi for the honor.

Nearly 10 percent of the workers who are paid by the hour in Texas (and Mississippi!) get $7.25 an hour or less, which translates into less than $300 for a forty-hour week. Of all the jobs Texas added in 2010, 37 percent were in this category—which is also, of course, the group that winds up paying 12 percent of their income in state and local taxes.

California, Florida, and Illinois combined did not have as many people as Texas did earning the minimum wage or less in 2010. In part, that's because the state makes it very hard for workers to unionize—a factoid that always gives it a bump on those best-state-to-do-business polls.

Maybe what Texas has been working on is really the recipe for still more, still worse, national economic inequality. The state has a massive number of badly educated adults prepared to work for very low wages, plus laws that make it next to impossible for labor to organize and press for better salaries, plus a tax system that favors the wealthy. What's not to like?

"We've got a split economy," says Christopher King, the economics professor. He's sitting on the porch of a nice café that overlooks Lake Austin and features gourmet coffee and upscale muffins. King is drawing a picture from Kurt Vonnegut's *Player Piano*, of a world divided between the elite scientists and the miserable masses. "It's a vision I can see without squinting too hard," he says, waving a fork. "Dell [Computers] isn't growing here. They've shifted their assembly overseas. Some of the design stuff is here. Everybody else is baking these muffins."

11

The Other Side of the Coin

"From the perspective of a disembodied soul"

P olicy wonks have always described Texas as "low tax, low service." While the state's leaders like to brag about the first part, they don't generally broadcast the rest. There are no signs announcing, "Welcome to Texas. You Won't Pay Much and You'll Get What You Pay For." But it's hardly a secret.

If we're looking at Texas as a model of the empty-place vision of how to succeed, it seems only fair to look at both sides of the coin. Some Texans, particularly the wealthy, pay low taxes. But virtually no one gets much support from the state. Even if they're poor. Or need services.

When that famous California what-are-we-doing-wrong delegation made its trek through Texas, one of the many, many people the lawmakers talked to was Representative Mark Strama, a Democrat from Austin. "I told them, maybe a better way to look at this is through the prism of what John Rawls called the veil of ignorance," Strama recalled. "You should look at public policy questions from the perspective of a disembodied soul that doesn't know the body with which it's going to incorporate."

John Rawls was an American moral philosopher, and I think we can all assume this is the only time he ever came up during any event related to the Texas legislature.

This was the test Strama was posing: if you got to pick the place where you were born, would you be less enthusiastic about Texas if you had no idea if you were going to be a future software entrepreneur or a future teenage unwed mother? "Your chances of being employed in Texas are three to four percentage points better than if you're in California," Strama continued. "Your chances of not having a doctor when you need one are substantially higher, too. If your soul happens to be born in a body that doesn't work below the waist, or that doesn't have vision, the chances that you'll have a meaningful life are probably better in California."

Despite this unique opportunity to combine a visit with Rick Perry and a discussion of the veil of ignorance on the same trip, the delegation was not all that thrilled with Strama's presentation. "What I remember is one of the guys interrupting me and rejecting the premise because he didn't like the outcome. He said: 'That's an argument for the welfare state!' "

"Everything's bigger in Texas, including our poverty and hunger"

One of the high points of every session of the Texas legislature is the release of "Texas on the Brink," a production of the liberal-leaning Legislative Study Group in the house of representatives, which compares their state to the other 49 in categories ranging from average hourly earnings of production workers on manufacturing payrolls (38th) to percentage of the population who visit a dentist (46th). Unless you're the sort of person who roots for your state to make it to the top in number of executions, the report is never happy tidings. "Texas has the highest percentage of uninsured children in the nation," the 2011 report read. "Texas is dead last in the percentage of residents with their high school diploma and near last in SAT scores. Texas has America's dirtiest air." Also the dirtiest water, if you're talking amount of toxic chemicals released into it. Texas has the lowest percentage of pregnant women who get prenatal care in the first trimester. It ranks fourth worst when it comes to the percentage of children living in poverty, and second worst in the percentage of the population with "food insecurity," which basically means not having enough to eat. "Everything's bigger in Texas, including our poverty and hunger problems," said Paige Phelps of the West Texas Food Bank, who pointed out that in one west Texas county, Presidio, more than 44 percent of children don't always have enough food to meet their basic needs.

This is very bad news for more of the country than just Texas. The dirty air does tend to flow elsewhere. The people entering the workforce without a high school diploma are going to be a drag on the entire national economy. And if we're citizens of this country, it's hard to be comfortable about pregnant American women who aren't being cared for by a doctor, or children who don't know where their next meal is coming from.

"This report makes for some interesting trivia, but if Texas is such a horrible place, why have 4.5 million people moved here in the last decade?" retorted Arlene Wohlgemuth, who was the executive director of the conservative think tank the Texas Public Policy Foundation, when "Texas on the Brink" was released. You may remember her as a leading architect of that social services privatization hell.

"We're not going to find out about it, either"

When we think about what a low-service state fails to do, we tend to focus on social services. But there are a lot of other things that we instinctively expect to be taken care of, and Texas doesn't. Necessarily. In all cases.

For instance, there's the matter of weather-tracking. Weather is no small matter in Texas, which actually has some of the worst in the country, what with hurricanes, floods, droughts, and wildfires.

In 2011, it was hit by a killer dry spell that decimated much of the farmland in the state, and half the population was awake nights worrying about how long this would last.

Yet Texas spends virtually nothing trying to keep track of weather and climate data. The *Houston Chronicle* noted that "the Texas state climatologist has a staff of three part-time students. The Oklahoma Climatological Survey has a staff of forty-eight scientists and technicians and sophisticated data collection in every county in the state." You do not think of Oklahoma as a big spender when it comes to state services. Yet Oklahoma manages to cough up enough cash to try to figure out where the next disasters are going to strike, and warn its citizens about what might happen and how to prepare for it.

Or on doctor-tracking. In 2011, reporters from the *Duluth News Tribune* decided to write a "Where is he now?" about a former Minnesota surgeon who had left the state after being disciplined by the Minnesota Board of Medical Practice for "unprofessional and unethical conduct." During their investigation, they determined that although the Texas Medical Board was supposed to review a doctor's disciplinary history every two years during license renewal, it did not make use of the National Practitioner Data Bank, which keeps track of such things. A spokesperson for the Texas Medical Board said that would be too expensive for the state, because the Data Bank charges a fee.

"If the doctor doesn't want to tell us and is not truthful when he renews his license, then we're not going to find out about it either," she said.

"Things start to look like rationing"

Still, the low-service-state story is mainly about things that happen to the poor and helpless. Let's start with mental illness. If you're poor and mentally ill in Texas, you had better be suffering from schizophrenia, bipolar disorder, or severe depression, because those are the only conditions the state is really prepared to treat. Most mental health care for low-income Texans comes through thirty-nine community mental health centers and in 2003, when the state was having one of its regular budget crises, the legislature decided to reduce the number of eligible patients—an initiative that seems to have permanently nailed down the fiftieth place spot for per capita mental health spending. "When you have more need than resources, things start to look like rationing," said David Evans, the CEO of Austin Travis County Integral Care, which runs the community mental health center and related services. The state gives the organization funding to care for about 3,000 adults, but in 2011, it was serving 6,800.

It's kind of ironic that Texas Republicans were bounding up and down, denouncing the Obama health care plan as "rationing," when so much of it was already going on back in their home state. (Senator John Cornyn, the up-and-coming power in the Texas congressional delegation, urged the country to "resist the movement toward a single-payer socialized system that will inevitably lead to rationing and a lower standard of care for most people.") But, as we've noted before, irony is a commodity not in short supply in the Lone Star State.

Under the new state order, unless a victim of mental illness was threatening to harm himself or others, the centers weren't supposed to treat people who weren't schizophrenic, bipolar, or suffering from severe depression. In theory, that would leave lots more resources available to victims of the three covered conditions. In 2009, the Department of State Health Services did a study to see how the changes were going. They found that even people suffering from schizophrenia, bipolar disorder, or severe depression were sometimes waiting more than a year to get treatment.

Texans with mental illness were estimated to be eight times more likely to end up in jail than in a mental hospital. That ranked as the forty-eighth worst odds among the states. (Thank you, Nevada and Arizona.) "The largest psychiatric facility in the state of Texas is not a hospital or a clinic or an outpatient center. It's the Harris County jail, which treats and houses, on a daily basis, about 2,500 mentally ill people," reported Patricia Kilday Hart in *Texas Monthly*.

Poor people with severe mental illness are supposed to be sent to one of the state's mental hospitals, but there are only forty-three of them, and 5,450 psychiatric care beds, for a state of over 25 million people. A patient in distress may wind up being transported hundreds of miles to get care—if there's care available anywhere. "We have days when there are no beds available anywhere in the state," Evans said. "Then the only choice becomes, stay too long in the emergency room, or be taken to jail, or in an untenable family situation, or become homeless."

Of all the many, many horror stories that haunt Evans, one of the worst is that matter of the mentally ill person who winds up being picked up by the cops: "The individual goes to jail, but might not be competent to stand trial. Folks have averaged something like thirty-seven days in jail, in psychiatric distress." Texas has a history of class action suits filed by advocacy groups on behalf of mentally disturbed prisoners, and Evans is torn between rooting for their successes and worrying that if the jailed mentally ill are put at the front of the line for treatment, other people with an equally desperate need will have to wait still longer.

"Treatment works; recovery is possible," he said. "But the real hope lies in access on demand."

"I was there two and a half days waiting for treatment"

There's a support group meeting in a church on the west side of San Antonio. The sponsor is C.O.P.S./Metro Alliance, a local community organization. The subject is jobs. Nobody in attendance seems to have heard of the Texas Miracle.

A young father has lost his construction job ("hard labor but good money") and worries about the stress on his wife and family. A middle-aged woman with a background in data processing just visited the unemployment office and was depressed when she saw that the notices for available jobs appeared to be the same ones that had been hanging there when she last visited two years before. A balding man who had worked in civil service for eighteen years was let go four months ago and had gone back to living with his mother. A woman who had worked cleaning motel rooms ("they pay you for twenty minutes a room") quit when she realized her child care bills were higher than her salary.

The one theme that runs through all their stories is lack of health insurance. "She worries because I'm not insured," says the man who works construction, gesturing to his wife, who seems to be near tears. "But my health is okay for now."

"I'm diabetic," says the woman who worked in data processing. "Can I afford to buy my medicine? Definitely not." The former civil service employee needs medication for depression that costs $500 a month.

Lack of health insurance is a common problem in the families of unemployed people around the country. It's just that in Texas it's bigger. Way, way bigger, since 26 percent of the people there are uninsured—including a third of all working-age adults. It's the highest proportion in the country and Texas, as we've been reminded quite a bit, is a really large state. We're talking more than 6.2 million uninsured Americans. Americans who will grow up—and grow old—with untreated and chronic conditions like diabetes and asthma. Some of them will then move to other states where their built-up medical issues will become the problem of emergency rooms in Chicago or Atlanta or Denver.

One of the reasons so few Texans have health insurance is the much-touted business-friendly culture that shies away from the idea that employers have any responsibility to their workers beyond the occasional paycheck. Another is that the state is second from the bottom in its spending on Medicaid. (Pressed on this matter during the presidential campaign, Perry alternately blamed federal bureaucracy and Washington's unwillingness to hand over all the Medicaid funds in a block grant for Texas to use as it saw fit.) If a working mother with two children makes $5,000 a year, she can't qualify for Medicaid coverage.

Texas isn't the only state attempting to keep everybody but indigent adults off Medicaid. Four states make the cutoff even lower—Arkansas, Alabama, Louisiana, and Missouri. That's very tough on the residents of those states, but even if you add all four together you are talking about less than half the uninsured people wandering around Texas, perhaps trying to control their tubercular symptoms with cough syrup. (Also, we have not been having a national debate about whether the country could create more jobs if everybody else behaved more like Louisiana or Arkansas.) On the other hand, there are also states working under the assumption that everybody is better off when as many people as possible are insured. In Minnesota, the most liberal place in the nation when it comes to Medicaid eligibility, that working parent's income just has to be below $41,043.

What do all those uninsured Texans do when they get sick? If they live in an urban area, the most likely recourse is the county hospital, which is obliged to treat everyone who comes in the door, although it reserves the right to charge the people who don't qualify for free treatment.

"When the bill comes, I don't open it," admitted Amira, one of the participants at the C.O.P.S./Metro Alliance community meeting. A widow with four kids, she's studying to become a nurse.

The quality and efficiency of health care provided to uninsured patients varies from city to city. In rural areas, the nearest hospital that will provide treatment can be hours away. In San Antonio, if the stories at the community meeting are any indication, anyone who tries to use the emergency room as their physician will pay in waiting time. "I went to the emergency room when I was very sick," Amira tells the group. "I was there two and a half days waiting for treatment. It's terrible not to have insurance and be in Texas."

No matter how great the hospital's effort, it falls short of the vast, uninsured demand. Harris County, which encompasses the city of Houston, has a county hospital system that runs three public hospitals and thirteen clinics. The county also has a $1.2 billion budget, much of which comes from local property taxes. Nevertheless, uninsured patients complain about waiting weeks or months to get a clinic appointment.

The biggest worry for the health care professionals, however, is the people who never show up at all.

"Honestly what keeps us up at night," said David Lopez, the CEO of the Harris County Hospital District, "is that you have 1.2 million people who are uninsured. As busy as we are, if we were to count noses it's about 325,000 uninsured people a year. That means the balance aren't being seen." And the ones who do come in often delay the visit so long that their problems have become acute. "Cornell has asked to send residents down here because the pathology we see is great for teaching purposes," Lopez reported.

If you're a young doctor in search of unusual cases, however, the place to go in Texas is the *colonias*—about 2,300 extremely poor communities along the border, some of which lack running water, solid waste disposal, and paved roads. Some have rates of tuberculosis four times the national rate, and there are seldom-seen-in-this-country diseases like dengue fever and leprosy. Most of the residents are citizens—uninsured citizens. Once a year Operation Lone Star, a training exercise run by the state and the military, provides free basic medical and dental treatment in the *colonias*, and people sometimes wait overnight to get a place in line.

Here's what all this means to the rest of us: We've got untreated carriers of communicable diseases, along with many, many people with untreated chronic conditions. All of them have every right, as Americans, to move to other states and present themselves to the local emergency room or state-funded clinic. Maybe they've moved to Minnesota, which makes so much effort to provide health care for every family that needs it. Minnesota didn't create their untreated–diabetes problems, but Minnesotans might have to pay to treat them.

You'd think the fairest thing would be for the country to come up with a plan that makes sure everyone has health insurance. Then people who have the capacity to pay for their coverage will have to do so. Those who don't will get help. No matter where Americans are living, they'll get an equal chance at proper medical treatment. And then when our citizens move from state to state, they won't be bringing their untreated health problems along with them.

But wait. That's what Barack Obama's health care reform was all about. And in Congress, Texas was overwhelmingly unenthu-siastic. *Rationing!*

PART FOUR
WHERE
WE'RE GOING

12

We've Seen the Future, and It's Texas

*"A bunch of drunks and crooks
and slaveholding imperialists"*

Lionel Sosa, the man who's credited with showing Ronald Reagan and George W. Bush how to woo the Hispanic vote, is sitting in a very nice café in San Antonio, mulling over the Alamo.

"History is always told by the winner," he says. "Mexicans were the bad guys and Texans were the heroes. That's the way everyone learned it."

Sosa was born in San Antonio on the Hispanic west side of town, and for years he has been trying to get hold of a copy of the book on Texas history he read in the eighth grade in 1952. "*Texas History in Pictures*—it was done comic-book style," he says, nibbling at his mussels in white wine sauce. "I know I didn't imagine it because it made such an impression on me. The Mexicans all looked like bad banditos."

A soft-spoken marketer who spent the early 2012 presidential primary season trying to sell Hispanic voters on Newt Gingrich, Sosa lives in a world that is mainly made up of Democrats, and he is good at making his point without raising hackles. When it comes to the Alamo, others are less diplomatic. "They used to take us there when we were schoolchildren," the activist Rosie Castro told the *New York Times*. "They told us how glorious that battle was. When I grew up I learned that the 'heroes' of the Alamo were a bunch of drunks and crooks and slaveholding imperialists who conquered land that didn't belong to them. But as a little girl I got the message—we were losers. I can truly say that I hate that place and everything it stands for."

I haven't mentioned that Rosie Castro is the mayor's mother. San Antonio is a really interesting city.

"TO THIS DAY I don't know if my grandmother came here legally or illegally," says Joaquín Castro, a state representative from San Antonio. His twin brother, Julián, is the mayor. They are in their mid-thirties, graduates of Stanford and Harvard Law School, sons of a single mother whose own mother came from Mexico as an orphan and only made it to the fourth grade. "She was a babysitter, cook," Castro says of his grandmother. "She never owned a car, never owned a house." But she raised a daughter who made it through college, became a leader of La Raza Unida, the Mexican American civil rights party, had an affair with another community organizer, and gave birth to two wildly overachieving sons.

The brothers—who look so much alike there is at least one verifiable instance in which they switched places to accommodate a tight schedule of appearances—went to public schools. Joaquín says he started his educational career at Edgewood, which was so poor it became the test case over which several generations of litigation on the funding of Texas education has been fought. "When I went to Stanford I had only been out of San Antonio half a dozen times," he recalled.

State Representative Castro was sitting in a bare-bones office in his district on this particular day, amid the computers and coffee cups, while his youthful aides plotted a possible congressional race. His brother the mayor, who everybody is talking about as perhaps the first Hispanic governor of Texas, was out of town on business. "The year before we went," he said, recalling his college career, "my mom made less than $20,000, and she's sending two sons to university. My dad bought us the cheapest plane tickets he could find. We stopped twice." When he went to register for classes, Joaquín didn't know how to work the computers because the ones at his high school had been too basic to include a mouse: "I couldn't move the cursor with the keyboard, so I picked up the mouse and started moving the balls with my hand." Nearly two decades later, he's still obsessing about a friend he made at Stanford who turned out to have taken twelve Advanced Placement classes. ("I think I took two out of the three AP classes at my high school. He'd taken *twelve*. The guy had *twelve*.")

But things worked out. Really, really well, in fact.

San Antonio, the seventh largest city in the United States, is already majority Hispanic, moving toward two-thirds. It's a good example of how varied the portrait of Mexican American Texas can be. While a great many of the Latino residents are poor and undereducated, there are also rich refugees from the violence in Mexico, tootling happily around their gated communities under the watchful eye of security patrols, and plenty of middle-class professionals. Many of them, like the Castros, had grandparents who fled Mexico during the long-running revolution of 1910. Sosa's parents were also among those émigrés. "As a consequence, they didn't have a good image of Mexico," said Sosa. "But they said, never forget your history. Never, never lose your language."

The language thing is a little delicate. "The city I've lived in that has the highest proportion of Hispanic residents who don't speak Spanish is San Antonio," says Steve Murdock, the demographer and Rice professor. That should be a comfort to people who are afraid that Mexican Americans won't assimilate as easily as immigrants whose homeland was an ocean away. But it's problematic for young people who have to celebrate their ethnic pride in English, particularly for those who work in fields where they need to interact with an older generation that expects to be communicated with in Spanish. Like . . . politicians. "I understand it better than I speak it," said Joaquín Castro. His brother the mayor is preparing for whatever campaigns his future holds by improving his conversational skills. As the *New York Times* reported, "Rosie Castro's son is now being taught Spanish by a woman named Marta Bronstein."

"These folks don't want a wall"

The Castro story is not all that different, in many ways, from that of Barack Obama. (If the president's mother had wound up in San Antonio instead of Hawaii, her story would undoubtedly have involved a few picket lines at the Alamo.) And it's hard to find any part of America that doesn't boast of a humble-roots-to-Harvard political success story. But trust Texas to have *twins*. Anything worth doing is worth doing large.

It's going to take a whole lot more than the Castro brothers, however, to get Texas into the future. Before long, this is going to be a majority Hispanic state, and there's no way the political or business leadership reflects that fact. "There's a lot of nodding heads, 'Yeah, it's happening.' But people don't understand the impact," said Robert Sanborn, the children's advocate from Houston. "Maybe it's just human nature that we think things are always going to be the same as they are now."

Texas is already a majority minority state—whites compose less than 50 percent of the population. But there's a second shift coming, in which Hispanics will be the majority all by themselves. Steve Murdock, the Rice University professor, says it will happen by 2030; some Latinos think it will be much sooner. So there are two Texases—the cowboy/oil baron/Rick Perry version that the rest of the country instinctively envisions, even when we know better, and the demographic one, which is mainly young and Latino.

"We live in a bipolar state," says Castro.

Racial tolerance has not historically been one of Texas's strong suits, but the surging number of Hispanics does not seem to have made the average Anglo Texan particularly crazy. (Mexican Americans have often been discriminated against, but they have also generally been regarded as white by the establishment. The Texas legislature actually passed a resolution saying so in the 1940s.) While Tea Party wall-builders are amply represented in the Texas Republican Party, the general tenor in the state is nothing like the anti-immigrant paranoia elsewhere along the border. "I've spoken several times in Arizona and each time I feel like I'm going back about twenty years in Texas," says Murdock. "I don't think Texas is anything like Arizona."

During one of the first Republican presidential debates, when Rick Perry was trying to make his name as a wild man of the Republican right, the Texas governor ran into fire for his support of a Texas law granting in-state college tuition to high school graduates who were undocumented immigrants. Perry blinked, looking a little surprised as the rest of the pack laced into him for condoning illegal behavior and possibly "amnesty." He had, after all, just been doing what he usually does, which is to follow the money. The Texas business community, worried about the shortage of college graduates in the workforce, was behind the in-state tuition plan, which passed the legislature by near-unanimous votes in both chambers. Dick Armey ran into the same problem with some of his Tea Party rivals, who pointed out that he had called the whole wall-building strategy "just stupid."

"Unlike Arizona, we've had this big border area that's been pretty well populated since the nineteenth century," said former lieutenant governor Bill Hobby. "Those folks don't want a wall. The farther you are from the border, the more you want a wall."

During the 2011 state legislative session, a ton of Tea Party-inspired bills on the subject of immigration were introduced, including a much-publicized proposal by the famous Representative Debbie Riddle which would have made hiring an "unauthorized alien" punishable by up to two years in prison and a fine of up to $10,000—with an exception for cleaning women and gardeners. There was a bill to deny undocumented residents access to state colleges and universities, a bill making English the

official state language, and another by Riddle to require state
agencies to report how much it costs them to provide services for
the undocumented. But only one got very far—a proposal to out-
law "sanctuary cities" in which police are prohibited into inquir-
ing into the immigration status of arrestees. Perry—generally so
weirdly moderate on immigration issues that actually mattered—
declared resurrecting it to be a matter so critical that he put it on
the agenda as an emergency matter for the legislature's special
budget session. It died in a house-senate squabble, leading Tea
Party groups to call for a second special session just for the sanctuary city bill.

Even Rick Perry wasn't that crazy.

"Illegal immigration is a big problem," wrote Rick Casey in the
Houston Chronicle as the governor and the Republican legislators
were blaming each other for the bill's demise. "Sanctuary cities
are not, as is indicated by the fact that Perry couldn't name one in
Texas."

What Perry did get, which was far more important to his fellow
Republicans, was the toughest law on voter identification in the
nation, prohibiting anyone from getting access to a ballot unless
he or she had either a driver's license or a very limited number of
other types of government-issued photo IDs. (A license to carry a
concealed gun was good enough for the law's backers. A university
student ID wasn't.)

"Voter fraud is a problem," wrote Casey, "but mostly through
mail ballots that don't require IDs to be shown."

Voter identification laws are almost always Republican initiatives, since the people most likely to be confused or frightened
away from the polls tend to be poorer, and Democratic. "It's a calculated effort to diminish Hispanic turnout," said Joaquín Castro.
"They say 90 percent of people have ID cards. But you're trying to
shave off the 8 to 10 percent who don't."

Texas's low cost of living and doing business is directly related to
its huge supply of cheap labor, much of it Hispanic. Cynical minds

might suggest that the state's political and business establishment celebrates its growing population of Hispanic workers; but as to the growing population of Hispanic voters . . . not so much.

"They know the demographics"

Lionel Sosa got his real start from the first-Republican-senator-since-Reconstruction, John Tower. "John Tower called me out of the blue," Sosa recounts. "He said, 'Lionel, I'm going to be in town for a couple of days. Take me to the beer joints on the west side of town. I want to talk to some guys.'" Sosa made sure he had a really good list of the Hispanic working-class drinking places, but in touring the neighborhoods with Tower, "I discovered all kinds of Mexican bars I never knew." Tower was a familiar face in many of them. He must have enjoyed the evening, because he hired Sosa to work on getting him the Mexican American vote. Tower won a sliver of a majority over Democratic congressman Robert Krueger in 1978, and Sosa was more than rewarded for his efforts: "In three months I had Coors Beer, Bacardi, Coca-Cola. My little ad agency quadrupled and it totally changed my life." Then Tower called again and said, "Lionel, there's a fundraiser in Dallas. I want you to come and meet somebody."

That was how Sosa met Ronald Reagan, who told him that "Latinos are Republicans. They just don't know it yet." As Sosa remembers it, Reagan asked him what values his parents taught him, and when Sosa replied, "Hard work, faith in God, and love of family," Reagan said that was the GOP all the way. "Figure out how to tie me to those values," he directed.

Now, Democrats might point out that they tend to believe in hard work, faith in God, and love of family, too. Plus health care, generous aid to education, and affirmative action to make sure minorities can get into good colleges. But you work with what you've got.

The relationship between the Republican Party and Texas Hispanics peaked in 1994, when George W. Bush won the gover-
norship with 49 percent of the Hispanic vote. "He went out and
asked for the vote. Nobody else has come close," said Sosa. The
relationship foundered on the shoals of Tea Party cries for border walls or, in the case of former presidential candidate Herman
Cain, a border moat full of alligators. The Republican majority
in Congress helped seal the deal with its opposition to the Dream
Act, which would allow young people who were brought here as
undocumented children to qualify for citizenship by serving in the
military or attending college. It's a variation on the bill that Rick
Perry thought was so natural to sign for Texas—until he tried running for national office.

These days in Texas, the growing Hispanic population tends
Democratic, and it's pretty much the only hope the Democrats
can look to. The party is now on its back, as flat as a flounder, and
yearning for the time when the majority Latino population will
send it back into power. How could their star not be rising? The
state is already majority minority. Its population is much younger
than the national average, and young people tend to vote Democrat. The cities are growing and the conservative rural towns are
shrinking. The suburbs are strongly Republican, but the newest
suburban arrivals are likely to be Hispanic, too. "You got a lot of
hysteria among my colleagues," State Senator Ellis said cheerfully
of the Republicans. "They know the demographics."

But for the Democrats, the big problem is that Hispanic Texans
who are registered voters are even less likely to go to the polls than
registered Anglos—who are not exactly beating a path to the ballot
box. And no matter how the sponsors parse it, those voter ID bills
are intended to make sure that continues to be the case.

So far, despite its huge Hispanic population, Texas has only
elected one Latino to statewide office—Dan Morales of San Antonio, who was the attorney general back in the 1990s. This is a story
Democrats don't talk about all that often. In 2002 Morales ran for

governor, losing the primary to Tony Sanchez, a Laredo business-man. Then he was indicted on twelve counts of tax and mail fraud, conspiracy, and lying on the loan application for his house. He eventually pled guilty to mail fraud and filing a false tax return.

Tony Sanchez doesn't come up in Democratic conversations all that often either. He turned out to combine the Democrats' fond-est dreams (Mexican American/really, really rich) with the party's worst nightmares (terrible, terrible candidate). But Henry Cisne-ros always does. "I believe if Henry Cisneros had run in the early nineties, the trajectory of Texas politics would have changed," said Joaquín Castro. "We haven't had a popular Hispanic run for gov-ernor or senator, ever. If Henry had run back then it really would have changed things."

Cisneros was mayor of San Antonio from 1981 to 1989, the first Hispanic to run a major American city. He was smart and issue-oriented and very rooted in his community—to this day, his principal residence is a modest house on the west side that his grandfather once owned. People believed he would be governor. Or senator. Or vice president, in which case, inevitably, the first Hispanic in the Oval Office. "Ann Richards came to me and said, 'I won't run for governor if you run,'" Cisneros says now. "But I said no, I have personal things to deal with . . . It's yours."

He quit politics and went into the asset-management business, and although he put in a tour as Bill Clinton's secretary of housing and urban development, Cisneros never ran for office again. Part of the personal things he had to deal with was the illness of his son, who was born with a serious heart defect. But the big, whopping personal thing was Cisneros's stupendously messy affair with his chief fundraiser, which became public and the source of a fam-ily crisis and several long-running though ultimately meaningless federal investigations.

"It should have been Henry," said Lionel Sosa, talking about when Texas would get its first Hispanic governor. "Henry cares for the community more than anybody I know. But he screwed up."

Julián Castro is sometimes referred to as the great Hispanic hope who "won't screw up." But the question of when Mexican Americans will get their natural share of top offices is not just a matter of finding the right candidates. It also involves the Anglos who still make up a majority of the state's voting population and the politicians who currently run the state in Austin. How much do they want to let Latinos have the biggest prizes? After the 2010 census, Texas was awarded four new congressional districts thanks to its enormous—and largely Hispanic—population growth. The Republican-dominated legislature promptly drew the new districts in a way that made only one ripe for minority takeover. The whole issue sparked a raft of court cases, but the message was pretty clear. The Hispanic community "went forward in good faith," said Steve Murdock. "And I think they feel like they got nothing."

"We've run out of white folks to flee"

Murdock, the former state demographer turned sociology professor, was sitting up in his aerie at Rice University in Houston, at the top of a remarkable old building that boasts only a small, balky elevator. (For a while, Rice liked to put its sociologists up where only the eagles could get at them. Sadly, Murdock and his colleagues have now been moved to a more normal perch.) His desk and bookcase were filled with printouts. Murdock, who was also once head of the US Bureau of the Census, thinks a lot about numbers— births, deaths, migration patterns. "Texas's future is clearly tied to its minority populations. In particular, how well Hispanic and African American populations do is going to be how well Texas does in the long run," he said.

There's nowhere that points to the future more than Houston, where the exurbs keep growing but the new arrivals from the city are different from the generations that preceded them in one way: they're Asian, Hispanic, and black. "We've run out of white folks to flee," said Richard Murray, director of the Survey Research Institute at the University of Houston.

Harris County, where Houston is located, is now less than one-third Anglo. And all the trend lines point in the same direction: nearly three-quarters of the county's residents sixty years of age and over are white non-Hispanics, while more than two-thirds of adults under thirty are Hispanic, Asian, or African American. "I think older people tend to think they're not going to be around to see the most dramatic transitions," says Murdock. "The younger population not only knows from the numbers, they know from looking around in their classes, in the places they go. The younger population is much more open to diversity. But whether they'll be more accepting of power sharing when they move along—we'll see."

Murdock has made it his great mission to educate the state about what's coming. The degree to which Texas is prepared to become a majority Hispanic state, he feels, will decree the success to which the state will march into the future.

And where Texas goes, so goes the nation.

"This is the US," says Murdock, pointing to one of his many piles of printouts. "Look at the under-eighteen. Had there not been Hispanic growth in the number of children, we'd have had the largest decline in the number of children since the 1930s."

"Hablamos rocketry"

If there's a single thing that will decide which way Texas goes, it's the schools. But the dropout rate, particularly among minority kids, is huge. "We're very proud in Texas," said Sanborn. "We really want to believe Texas is the best. If we're bad in something, there must be something wrong—the statistics are lying. And part of the reason is we don't want to spend the money to fix it."

What happened to the Texas Miracle? Well, there are some terrific public schools in Texas. Houston has some great magnet schools. Austin has places like the Ann Richards School for Young Women Leaders, where the students, who are almost all economically disadvantaged, are as curious and outgoing as the best-socialized prep school students in the state. Down by the Rio

Grande in west Texas, the students and teachers of Presidio School District gear up for a new academic year with the overheated obsession of a Texas football team preparing for state finals. "I don't buy into the testing system—I'm more concerned with how many kids are ready to go to college," says Dennis McEntire, the superintendent. He's a large guy with a bristly head of grey hair who wears a jacket and tie in the stupendous late summer heat.

In the summer of 2011, the Presidio schools made something of a splash when McEntire was quoted as saying that he might ask the state for a waiver to drop down to a four-day week in order to deal with state budget cuts. He was not, he admits now, seriously considering it. But there was reason to pay attention, since seven years before Presidio had shocked the Texas world when it balanced the school budget by doing away with football.

Presidio is not at the top of the heap when it comes to the all-powerful state test scores, but it does pretty well for one of the poorest districts in the state. McEntire says the graduation rate is high, and that 77 percent of graduates go on to further education. After classes end there is tutoring until five o'clock, and the cafeteria ceiling has vanished behind all the college banners draped there. Presidio, which has a history of getting, and leveraging, government grants, also has an award-winning rocketry program. "Hablamos rocketry," says Shella Condino, the science teacher who mentors it. "The kids I work with—they're in English as a second language. They're not the brightest in the class. But they can write technical reports for NASA."

The city of Presidio has one of the highest hunger rates, and poverty rates, and everything-else-depressing rates in the state, but the school district had socked away a rainy day fund to get it through the first shock of the state education cuts in 2011. Other districts that were less blessed with government largesse or less willing to give up football were reeling from the $4 billion the state legislature cut from education funding. This was after the legislature made its disastrous attempt to reform the business and property taxes and wound up with a huge void in the place where revenues and expenditures were supposed to meet.

Rather than raise taxes, Rick Perry and Co. cut what amounted to $537 per student in state education aid. Soon, the Ross Perot reforms of 1984 began to teeter. One was the legal limit of twenty-two elementary school students to each teacher, as the state began handing out waivers like popcorn, having added "financial hardship" to the special reasons why classes could be made larger. The uncapped higher grades exploded. Meanwhile, the inequality between rich and poor districts was sparking another wave of legal action.

While Presidio's football-cutting option did not seem popular, school districts were laying off faculty and support staff, and imposing new charges on students' families. A district north of Fort Worth announced it would bill students $185 a semester if they wanted to ride the school bus. Other districts dropped their pre-K programs back to the minimum the state required—part-time, for only the poorest of students.

A little north of Presidio, there's Marfa, an absolutely fascinating little place that you might call the Texas version of Taos, except for the definite lack of ski slopes. Marfa has attracted an influx of artists, but its school population is mainly children of local agricultural workers and the Perry cuts left its budget in crisis. It, too, was looking at bus service. "We will no longer bring in the children from town," said Teloa Swinnea, the school superintendent. "It's not the law. The parents think it is, but it's not." Next stop, Swinnea said grimly, was football. But nobody else in the home of the beloved Marfa Shorthorns seemed able to imagine that could happen.

Things seemed likely to get much worse as the schools' rainy day funds dried up. Texas was already forty-seventh in the nation when it comes to state aid per pupil, forty-third in high school graduation rate, and forty-fifth in SAT scores. It's hard to call that leading the way.

"Failure to provide equal and quality education—it's really tragic," said Cisneros. He recalled a conversation with a businessman who runs a major consumer goods firm with outlets all around the state. "He told me they were consciously moving downscale in their marketing, in their product mix, because every analysis they have tells them incomes are going to be declining because of the gap in education."

BUT TO GET back to where we started, I asked Cisneros about the Alamo. "I came to terms with it a long time ago," he shrugged. "It's not about wars or Mexicans versus Americans or victory or death. It's just something that happened."

In a way, it's what's still happening now. The modern battle for the soul of Texas began with Ross Perot and his commission, and it was fought over the question of whether all the state's children would be seriously, rigorously, and perhaps even expensively, educated, or whether those privileges would be reserved for a wealthier, mostly Anglo minority while the masses of Texas young people just learned to be literate enough for manual labor and the low-end side of the service economy. Right now, Texas seems to need a leader who's ready to draw the line and dare the people to step over. Victory or death.

Epilogue

It seems only fair to leave Texas with the Alamo. But where does Texas leave the rest of us?

If you're a diehard states'-righter, as most of Texas's leading politicians are, the answer would probably be that this is the wrong question. What Texas does is its own business, they say, since the states are individual boats, each bobbing along on its own—although certainly prepared to join together in times of national crisis when the country needs the whole fleet. But not some made-up crisis, like the collapse of the auto industry. Serious, manly crises, like wars, hurricanes, and forest fires.

Personally, I prefer to think that all Americans are in the same boat. And Texas has a lot to do with where we're heading. We've seen how Texas politicians played central roles in the deregulation of financial markets and the near elimination of energy conservation as a national policy, and how the state served as the model for federal savings and loan deregulation and federal education reform. (Neither one quite worked out the way their architects imagined, but as we have noted a number of times in this journey, nobody's perfect.) Texans also led the way in the destruction of all major legislation aimed at dealing with global warming, even as their home state was alternately being drowned by hurricanes and dried to a crisp with droughts. But of course that has nothing to do with the ozone layer. Only God can change the planet's temperature. Like with a volcano or something. Just ask Tom DeLay.

It's lucky that Texas has such a hard time growing presidential candidates, that Phil Gramm lacked charm and Rick Perry was so short on coherence. Otherwise, we might have had nothing but Texans in the White House for the last thirty years or so. As it was, the two we did have got us into three wars in the Middle East, while extricating us from a grand total of one.

Now, as the country lurches through the second decade of the twenty-first century, Texas politicians and business leaders have tried to define the debate on growing the economy, arguing that the right formula is as close to zero taxes and zero regulation as possible. Governor Perry has declared his right—he seems to regard it as a kind of moral duty—to poach jobs away from states that follow a different model. But while Texas may look like a corporate dream, it's a high-tax state for low-income workers. The lack of regulations puts it near the top of the pile when it comes to unenviable achievements like air and water pollution or on-the-job worker fatalities. Jobs—particularly low-wage jobs—may be easier to find than in some other states, but health care benefits, unemployment compensation, and disability coverage are considerably tougher to locate. When the number of white-collar jobs for college-trained workers grew, they were filled in large part by young people who had been educated in other states, on other taxpayers' dimes.

The country as a whole has been watching the gap between the privileged minority and the struggling majority grow, and Texas has been doing way more than its share to keep pushing us in that direction.

Texas frames its political worldview on the ideology of empty places, which holds that virtually any amount of government is too much government. *Plus nobody needs it anyway because there's plenty of room. You leave me alone and I'll leave you alone.* It's an inarguable worldview unless a) There really isn't plenty of room, or b) You are not actually leaving me alone.

We feel Texas's influence in our lives every day, but we'll be feeling it much more in the future, due to its enormous population growth, helped along by those interesting sex education classes and the almost complete lack of state family planning funds. To be fair, it's hardly the only state where public schools teach their students that sexual relations should be regarded in about the same way as transmission of the Ebola virus. And Texas does have a harder educational challenge than many, due to the enormous number of poor minority students. But that's really sort of the point. It's that huge Latino-fueled population growth that gives the state's businesses an edge and creates the pool of low-wage workers that helps fuel that famous economic miracle. In return, the great challenge for Texas is to educate its children to do better, to replace the 170,000 college graduates the state imports every year from other states with a Texas-grown generation of professional workers of tomorrow.

Very few people seem to feel particularly confident that's going to happen.

So there we are. Texas can use its great advantages—the space, the cheap housing, the exploding population—to create a model of possibilities for the twenty-first century. It can prepare its young people so well that in a generation they'll be taking off to fill jobs all around the country, the way places like New York and Illinois are sending their college graduates to Texas now. Or it can just demonstrate how easy it is to create a two-tiered economy in which the failing underclass looks resentfully at the happy sliver on the top.

The rest of the country can't do all that much to dictate where Texas goes, what with states' rights, states' rights, states' rights. But if Texas goes south, it's taking us along.

Acknowledgments

Normally, this is my favorite part of writing a book—when you get to thank all the people who helped you along the way. In the case of this particular book, however, I got assistance, advice, support, and good information from so many incredibly smart and helpful people it's a little embarrassing.

The idea for *As Texas Goes . . .* came from Bob Weil at Liveright Publishing/W. W. Norton, who was also, to my incredible good fortune, my editor at every step along the road. Although it's certainly true that without him the book would never have been written, I'd rather point out that without him the book would have been unreadable.

At the beginning of this project, Abby Livingston of *Roll Call* did me the enormous favor of recommending a fellow Texan, Annie Boehnke, as a researcher. Before she went off to pursue an advanced degree in architecture at Harvard, Annie got me through all the initial chapters, as well as the education section. I would not have survived her departure if it hadn't been for another Texas native, the incomparable Amanda Sterling. Besides Annie and Amanda, I got invaluable research help from Sean Beherec, Alexa Garcia-Ditta, Rachael Greenberg, Isabella Moschen, and Katherine Stevens.

Thanks to James Haley for his suggestions and help with Texas history, to Bob Semple for doing the same when I got to the environment, and to Joe Nocera when it came to financial deregulation. Trish Hall got me through the first chapters, and special thanks to Evan Smith for reading the whole thing and for introducing me to Mimi Swartz and John Wilburn, who took me on an enlightening tour of Houston. It convinced me great cities can thrive without zoning, although I still don't think I'd want a tire recapping business to set up shop on my block.

I cannot possibly thank all the Texans who were generous with their time and expertise. The whole project was inspired by a column that was inspired by a suggestion from Sylvia Acevedo, who has now been a source of information and ideas for two of my books. The very fact that I got to spend time with Paula and Nizar Djabbarah was an incentive to do the project. Many thanks to the hospitable people of Marfa, Texas, especially Tom Michael and Katherine Shaughnessy Michael. Also on the gracious-host-and-guide front, I am grateful to Jan Demetri, Mary Margaret and Ray Farabee, Bill Hobby, Steve Klineberg, Kathy and Don Mauro, John Mixon, and Jan Jarboe Russell. Thanks to all the amazing journalists I met in Texas, and the hundreds of others whose work I read and used shamelessly.

The people I interviewed who were quoted directly in the book are listed in the notes for each chapter, but please do not hold any of them responsible for my conclusions. Dozens of others also generously gave me their time, and the information they shared informs every page. I can't name them all, but they know who they are, and I hope at least some of them will be pleased with the way this all came out.

Finally, thanks to Alice Martell, who has been way more than an agent for my entire book-writing career. And above all, to my beloved husband Dan, who really does put up with a lot.

NOTES

Except when otherwise noted, direct quotes are taken from interviews by the author. The names of interviewees are at the beginning of each chapter.

Prologue

3 "We didn't": Rick Perry, speech at Tea Party rally, Austin, April 15, 2009, available at: http://www.youtube.com/watch?v=dbWz1RYGE3Q.

4 "We've got a great": Associated Press, "Colorful Quotes from Rick Perry Throughout the Years," *Texas on the Potomac* (blog), chron.com (*Houston Chronicle* online edition), August 2011.

4 "Man allegedly beat": Gail Collins, "Day of the Armadillo," *New York Times*, November 2, 2011.

7 "Dead armadillos": Ibid.

1: Remember the Alamo

Interviews: Frank Cahoon, James Haley, Stephen Harrigan, Jan Jarboe Russell, Karen Thompson.

12 "We are very": "Governor says Texas is one state that could leave the union, though he's not pushing it," W. Gardner Selby and Jason Embry, *Austin American-Statesman*, April 17, 2009.

12 Rasmussen poll: "Texas Secession Poll," *Huffington Post*, May 18, 2009.

13 to nominate Donald Trump: "WSJ/NBC Poll: Donald Trump No. 2," *Los Angeles Times*, April 7, 2011.

13 "Texans, more so": Brian McCall, *The Power of the Texas Governor: Connally to Bush* (Austin: University of Texas Press, 2009), 58.

15 clause prohibiting atheists: Texas state constitution, Article 1, Section 4.

20 Bush . . . sent a copy of Travis's letter: Don Van Natta, *First Off the Tee*, (New York: PublicAffairs, 2003), 280.

21 "donning the patriotic trappings": Joe Holley, "Sen. Dan Patrick Goes Beyond Talk in the Legislature, *Houston Chronicle*, July 4, 2001.

21 "House Republicans felt": Justin Sink, "House GOP Tax Cut Negotiator Says Debate Was Like 'Reenacting the Alamo,'" *The Hill*, December 22, 2011.

22 "Where did this idea": Lou Dubose and Jan Reid, *The Hammer* (New York: PublicAffairs, 2004), p. 207; Gary Scharrer, "Legislator Questions Border Health," *El Paso Times*, March 6, 2003.

22 Pamela Mann: James Haley, *Passionate Nation* (New York: Free Press, 2006), 187, 193.

24 Molly Ivins watched: *Molly Ivins Can't Say That, Can She?* (New York: Vintage, 1991) 18.

2: Empty Places

Interviews: David Crossley, Tom Dunlap, Bill Hobby, Ray Kelly, Christopher King, Stephen Klineberg, Lois Kolkhorst, Bob Lanier,

Martin Melosi, Tom Michael, John Mixon, Richard Murray, Wes
Perry, Chris Steinbach, Tom Smith, Ronald Welch.

27 "the big empty": Jake Silverstein, "Boy's Life," *Texas Monthly*,
    June 2010.

28 "reckless and irresponsible": Gary Scharrer, "Perry Vetos
    Texting While Driving Legislation," *Houston Chronicle*, June
    17, 2011; "Gov. Perry Vetoes HB242," Office of the Gover-
    nor, June 17, 2011.

28 Freedom and Liberty: Kevin D. Williamson, "Rick Perry's
    Tenth Commandment," *National Review*, April 4, 2011.

28 "If you've got a car": Glenna Whitley, "Texas Concealed
    Gun Laws Loosen," *Dallas Observer*, October 25, 2011.

29 Bob Bullock: Dave McNeely and Jim Henderson, *Bob Bull-
    ock: God Bless Texas* (Austin: University of Texas Press), 121.

29 California has the most stringent gun laws: Statistics from
    Bureau of Alcohol, Tobacco, Firearms and Explosives,
    quoted by Mayors Against Illegal Guns, available at: http://
    www.tracetheguns.org/#/states/TX/exports/.

29 nearly 15,000 guns: Statistic from Bureau of Alcohol,
    Tobacco, Firearms and Explosives, quoted by Mayors Against
    Illegal Guns, available at: http://www.mayorsagainstillegal-
    guns.org/downloads/pdf/issue_brief_mexico_2010.pdf.

30 "Studies show": "Smith Supports Right-to-Carry Bill,"
    press release from Congressman Lamar Smith, November 16,
    2011.

31 The Texas constitution: There have been 643 proposed
    amendments, 467 approved and 176 rejected.

31 in the constitution: William Earl Maxwell et al., *Texas Politics
    Today* (Boston: Wadsworth, 2010), 52.

31 lobbyists far outnumber the legislators: "Austin's Oldest Pro-
    fession," Texans for Public Justice, 2010.

32 "Texans know how": Rick Perry, speech at Tea Party
    rally, Austin, April 15, 2009, http://www.youtube.com/
    watch?v=dbWz1RYGE3Q.

32 farmers in the Texas hill country: Robert Caro, *The Path to Power* (New York: Knopf, 1982), 528.

32 transfer of payments: Environmental Working Group, farm subsidy database.

32 One of the beneficiaries: R. G. Ratcliffe, "Will Subsidies to Farmer Perry Come Back to Haunt Presidential Hopeful Perry?" *Austin American-Statesman*, August 7, 2011.

33 Thousands of doctors: Ralph Blumenthal, "In Houston Astrodome, Safe but Restless Refuge," *New York Times*, September 4, 2005.

33 A year after Katrina: Amy Strahan, "Houston Tires of Katrina Evacuees as Crime Rises, Few Find Jobs," *Bloomberg News*, August 24, 2006.

33 stupendous lack of enthusiasm: "Texas on the Brink," Texas Legislative Study Group, February 2011, available at http://texaslsg.org/texasonthebrink/?p=1. See Appendix.

35 "raping and pillaging those hills": Matt Dellinger, *Interstate 69: The Unfinished History of the Last Great American Highway* (New York: Scribner, 2010), p. 186.

38 "We don't respond": Kate Galbraith, "Drought-Plagued Midland, Texas, is Running Out of Water." *Texas Tribune*, April 22, 2011.

39 "I am rejoiced": Davy Crockett, letter to his children, January 9, 1836, available at: www.thealamo.org/battle/letter-Crockett.php.

3: It's My Party

Interviews: Frank Cahoon, Robert Caro, Joaquín Castro, Rodney Ellis, Jim Marston, Norman Ornstein, Bill Ratliff, Jan Jarboe Russell.

42 101 members: Dave Mann and Abby Rapoport, "Let's Get This Party Started," *Texas Observer*, August 8, 2011.

43 As a drama: Dubose and Reid, *The Hammer*, 212.

45 "destroyed": Peggy Fikac: "Nail Lid Shut: Senate's Two-thirds Rule Dead," *Houston Chronicle*, June 20, 2011.

45 "a big hurricane": McCall, *The Power of the Texas Governor*, 64.

45 "Well, I don't have": Ibid., 68.

46 "Everyone wanted to let": Mimi Swartz, "Ann Richards: How Perfection Led to Failure," *Texas Monthly*, October 1990.

46 "If it's inevitable": McCall, *The Power of the Texas Governor*, 98.

46 When Perry announced: Justin Elliott, "Have You Ever Had Sex With Rick Perry?" *Salon*, August 18, 2011.

46 "hairy-legged lesbians": McNeely and Henderson, *Bob Bullock*, 216.

47 "ain't never done nothin'": Charles Ashman, *Connally: The Adventures of Big Bad John* (New York: Morrow, 1974), 284.

47 Bullock endorsed George W. Bush: McNeely, and Henderson, *Bob Bullock*, 274.

47 "It's the last copter": Paul Burka, "Right Place, Right Time," *Texas Monthly*, February 2010.

47 Or a pitcher: Patrick Cox, "Not Worth a Bucket of Warm Spit," George Mason University History News Network, August 20, 2008.

50 In 2010, Maine: "America Goes to the Polls," Nonprofit Voter, 2010.

51 Tom DeLay: Dubose and Reid, *The Hammer*, 43–44.

52 Armey and DeLay: Michael Sokolove, "Dick Armey Is Back on the Attack," *New York Times Magazine*, November 4, 2009.

52 "None that I can": Dubose and Reid, *The Hammer*, 102.

52 "He was innocent": Carl M. Cannon, Lou Dubose, Jan Reid, *Boy Genius* (New York: PublicAffairs, 2003), 44–5.

53 a fiend for privatization: ibid., 84–5.

54 "What's a little pain": Hilary Hylton, "Hammered: What Punishment Will Tom DeLay Get? *Time*, November 25, 2010.

54 "Armey and FreedomWorks": Sokolove, "Dick Armey Is Back."

4: Financial Deregulation—the Texas Angle

Interview: Bill Black.

60 "What we have to share": Phil Gramm, "Announcement of Candidacy," February 24, 1995, available at: http://edition .cnn.com/ALLPOLITICS/1996/candidates/republican/ withdrawn/gramm.announcement.shtml.

60 "When I am on Wall Street": Eric Lipton and Stephen Labaton, "A Deregulator Looks Back, Unswayed," *New York Times*, November 16, 2008.

61 One historic state thrift: James O'Shea, *The Daisy Chain* (New York: Simon & Schuster, 1991), 62–66.

61 set their own interest rates: Norma Riccucci, *Unsung Heroes* (Washington DC, Georgetown University Press, 1995), 25.

62 The lawyer for the thrift's: Martin Mayer, *The Greatest Ever Bank Robbery* (New York: Collier Books, 1992), 9.

62 the most profitable S & L: O'Shea, *The Daisy Chain*, 124.

63 no actual money: William K. Black, *The Best Way to Rob a Bank Is to Own One* (Austin: University of Texas Press, 2005), 107.

63 Dixon overcame that problem: Ibid., 108.

63 "It served as": Ibid.

63 Dixon's wife: Ibid., 109.

63 any long-term solvency: Riccucci, *Unsung Heroes*, 42.

63 requested more time: Black, *The Best Way*, 107.

64 told the committee: Irvin Molotosky, "House Committee Votes to Conduct Inquiry on Wright," *New York Times*, June 11, 1988.

64 The Ethics Committee: "Two Trials for Speaker Wright," *New York Times*, April 24, 1989.

64 Gingrich would eventually: John E. Young, "House Reprimands, Penalizes Speaker," *Washington Post*, January 22, 1997.

65 $4,775 per capita: Robert Bryce, *Cronies* (New York: Public-Affairs, 2004), 139.

65 The other memorable point: Gail Collins, "Dems Say: Go!" *Newsday*, February 26,1995.

66 "all our poor people": Lipton and Labaton: "A Deregulator Looks Back."

66 he did indeed have a heart: Richard L. Berke, "Tough Texan: Phil Gramm," *New York Times Magazine*, February 19, 1995.

66 "Some people look": Lipton and Labaton, "A Deregulator Looks Back."

67 threatened to destory: Stephen Labaton, "Deal on Bank Bill was Helped Along by Midnight Talks," *New York Times*, October 24, 1999.

67 reject requests: David Corn, "Foreclosure Phil," *Mother Jones*, July/August 2008.

67 "We have learned": Lipton and Labaton, "A Deregulator Looks Back."

67 Gramm had a soft spot: Gary McWilliams, "The Quiet Man Who's Jolting Utilities," *Business Week*, June 9, 1997.

68 "Enron's business model": "Blind Faith: How Deregulation and Enron's Influence over Government Looted Billions from Americans," Public Citizen, December 2001, 3.

68 "As a single": Berke, "Tough Texan."

68 confidential e-mail: Eric Lipton, "Gramm and the 'Enron Loophole,'" *New York Times*, November 14, 2008.

69 "large sophisticated": "Blind Faith," 12.

69 two of the five: Ibid., 11.

69 "between $915,000": Ibid., 3.

69 inserted an amendment: Corn, "Foreclosure Phil."

69 Michael Greenberger: Ibid.

70 Gramm later claimed: Lipton, "Gramm and the 'Enron Loophole.'"

70 "Wholesale services" revenue: "Blind Faith," 20.

70 Other firms: Cathy Booth Thomas, "The Enron Effect," *Time*, May 28, 2006.

71 Gramm became vice president: Lisa Lerer, "McCain Guru Linked to Subprime Crisis," *Politico*, March 28, 2008.

71 The fault, he said: Lipton and Labaton, "A Deregulator Looks Back."

71 "a nation of whiners": Ibid.

5: No Child Left Behind

Interviews: David Anderson, Brenda Arredondo, Charles Barone, David Grissmer, Bill Hammond, Scott Hochberg, Sandy Kress, George Miller, Bill Ratliff, Paul Sadler, Barbara Wilson.

73 flyer: Gene B. Preuss, *To Get a Better School System* (College Station, TX: Texas A & M University Press, 1995), 28.

73 When World War Two began: Ibid., 69.

73 "We had the worst": Patrick Cox and Michael Phillips, *The House Will Come to Order* (Austin: University of Texas Press, 2010), 56.

74 "committing an act": *A Nation at Risk: The Imperative for Education Reform*, National Commission on Excellence in Education, 1983.

74 "It's important": Gail Collins, "Our Mister Bush," *New York Times*, March 21, 2000.

74 "Not about education": Ibid.

74 "We think we know": Vice presidential debate, October 5, 2000, available at: http://abcnews.go.com/Politics/story?id=122771&page=1.

75 Beginning public school teachers: McCall, *The Power of the Texas Governor*, 72.

75 Funding was wildly inequitable: *The Progress of Education in Texas*, Southwest Educational Development Laboratory, November 2000, 3.

75 "one of the first nerds": Ivins, *Molly Ivins Can't Say That*, 41.

75 "I've got pictures": McCall, *The Power of the Texas Governor*, 72.

76 Before his presidential adventures: Marty Primeau, "Ross Perot: He's the Dallas Billionaire Who Rescued His Men

in Iran, Fought Drug Abuse, Made Athletes Pass to Play and Gave Almost $100M to Charities Along the Way," *Dallas Morning News*, July 6, 1986.

76 spending an enormous amount: Ibid.

76 "H. Ross took off": Ivins, *Molly Ivins Can't Say That*, 25.

77 bumper sticker: Randy Galloway, "Perot Won't Break on Education Reforms," *Dallas Morning News*, March 7, 1985.

77 "In some respects": Bill Hobby, *How Things Really Work* (Austin: Dolph Briscoe Center for American History, 2010), 206.

77 "We have had three": "Texas : School Finance Bill Just Meets Deadline," *Los Angeles Times*, June 1, 1993.

78 "story on how our schools": Molly Ivins, "Who Deserves Credit for Texas?" Creators Syndicate, 2000.

79 "Testing is the cornerstone": Presidential Debate, October 3, 2000, available at: http://www.presidency.ucsb.edu/ws/index.php?pid=29418#axzz1bSIcUZfI.

79 "Write your governor": Collins, "Our Mister Bush."

79 "What's more important": *Good Morning America*, ABC, September 25, 2000.

79 "Regardless of where": "Study Shows Texas Schools Doing Well,"Associated Press, July 26, 2000, available at: http://lubbockonline.com/stories/072600/edu_072600015.shtml.

79 "I am proud": "Texas Cited as National Leader in Education," press release, July 25, 2000, available at: http://archive.newsmax.com/articles/?a=2000/7/26/14354.

79 "It's not a miracle": John Mintz, "Rand Study Suggests Texas' Test Score Claims Are Misleading," *Washington Post*, October 25, 2000.

80 "the opinion of a few": "Report Derides Education in Texas," Associated Press, October 24, 2000.

80 "All the emphasis": Jim Yardley, "Critics Say a Focus on Test Scores Is Overshadowing Education in Texas," *New York Times*, October 30, 2000.

80 During the 2000 Senate campaign: Gail Collins, "Those
    Who Can't, Test," *New York Times*, April 17, 2001.

80 teachers went into mourning: Ibid.

82 "Market discipline is": Louis V. Gerstner, *Reinventing Educa-
    tion* (New York: Dutton, 1994), p. 21. I first saw this quote in
    an article by Emily Pyle, "Te$t Market," *Texas Observer*, May
    14, 2005.

82 In 2011, the Texas Association: Morgan Smith, "Amid School
    Finance Shuffle, PreK Measure Returns," *Texas Tribune*, June
    9, 2011.

83 Karl Rove disagreed: "Karl Rove, The Architect," *Front-
    line*, PBS, April 12, 2005, available at: http://www.pbs.org/
    wgbh/pages/frontline/shows/architect/rove/cron.html.

87 In New York City: Sharon Otterman, "Protesting School
    Closings, in a Noisy Annual Ritual," *New York Times*, Febru-
    ary 3, 2011.

87 "the scholars presented": Diane Ravitch, *The Death and Life
    of the Great American School System* (New York: Basic Books,
    2010), 99.

88 "We go from 1,000": Diana Jean Shemo, "Questions on Data
    Cloud Luster on Houston Schools," *New York Times*, July 11,
    2003.

88 The state responded: Ibid.

89 "Some people think": Diana Jean Shemo, "Education Chief
    Defends Policy and Past," *New York Times*, January 28, 2004.

89 official in North Carolina: Sam Dillon, "Federal Research-
    ers Find Lower Standards," *New York Times*, October 30,
    2009.

89 In New York City: "Standards Raised, More Students Fail
    Tests," *New York Times*, July 28, 2010.

90 "This doesn't mean": Ibid.

90 In 2011, Secretary of Education: Sam Dillon, "Overriding a
    Key Education Law," *New York Times*, October 8, 2011.

91 the president invited: Lindsay Kastner, "No Child Left

Behind Waivers Offered; Texas Undecided," *San Antonio Express-News*, September 24, 2011.

91 Under the state's newest regimen: Texas Education Agency website, Student Assessment Division; and "STAAR, The Next Generation: State of Texas Assessments of Academic Readiness: A Parent's Guide to the Student Testing Program," Texas Education Agency, 2011, vol. 1, p. 1.

91 A survey: "More Teachers Forced into Extra Jobs," press release, Texas State Teachers Association, July 20, 2010.

92 Former First Lady: Barbara Bush, "We Can't Afford to Cut Education," *Houston Chronicle*, February 6, 2011.

92 "not a single person": Kimberly Hefling, "No Child Left Behind's Promise Falls Short after 10 Years," Associated Press, January 8, 2012.

92 George W. Bush gave: Andrew Rotherham, "'Let's Not Weaken It': An Exclusive Interview," *Time*, January 12, 2012.

93 "a federal takeover": Kate Alexander, "Texas Will Not Compete for Federal Education Grant," *Austin American-Statesman*, January 13, 2010.

93 "Texas was a model": "Gov. Perry's Education Plan Gains Federal Approval," Office of the Governor, July 26, 2002.

6: The Business of Schools

Interviews: David Anderson, Carolyn Boyle, Scott Hochberg, Sandy Kress, George Miller, Bill Ratliff, Diane Ravitch, Vernon Reaser, Paul Sadler, Michael Villarreal.

95 In Colorado: Mark Dinger, "Evaluation of NCLB Title I, Part I, Part A: Supplemental Educational Services," study submitted to the Colorado Department of Education, June 2010.

95 In Ohio: "White Hat Management: Ohio Charter School Giant," *StateImpact Ohio*, NPR, available at: http://stateimpact.npr.org/ohio/tag/white-hat-management/.

96 "When our hair is": Matt Dellinger, *Interstate 69*, 231.

96 "And that question": Ibid., 231–32.

97 At a protest march: Ibid., 274.

97 "We're talking about": Polly Ross Hughes, "Bidding to Begin on Call Centers," *Houston Chronicle*, June 8, 2004.

97 "It was like turning": "Accenture, R.I.P.," *Texas Observer*, March 23, 2007.

97 "Most infamously": Robert T. Garrett, "Exclusive: State Privatization Champion Gets Contract to Help Clear Up Welfare Mess," *Dallas Morning News*, March 13, 2010.

98 The Republicans held firm: Clay Robinson, "Texas GOP Leaders Censure Party Official," *Houston Chronicle*, October 5, 2003.

98 Forty percent: Morgan Smith and Nick Pandolfo, "For-Profit Teacher Certification Is Booming," *Texas Tribune*, as printed in *New York Times*, November 26, 2011.

99 "Ever since then": Gail Collins, "Reading, 'Riting and Revenues," *New York Times*, May 11, 2011.

99 At a hearing: Ibid.

99 Pearson, the London-based: John Egan, "Texas Education Agency Supports TAKS Operator Pearson in Wake of Florida Testing Debacle," examiner.com, July 6, 2010.

99 When a (doomed): Abby Rapoport, "The Pearson Graduate," *Texas Observer*, September 6, 2011.

100 The cost of those services: Based on the data reported by the fifty states, DC, and Puerto Rico, in SY 2009–2010, the federal Department of Education estimated that approximately $1 billion was spent on tutoring services under the No Child Left Behind law. The department does not collect information on how much was spent by for-profit versus non-profit providers.

100 In Columbus, Ohio: "Is the Cost of Private Tutoring Worth the Money?" *Education News*, November 11, 2011.

100 In Colorado: Dinger, "Evaluation of NCLB."

101 "I can afford to": "School Vouchers," *PBS Online Hour*, November 27, 1998, available at: http://www.pbs.org/news hour/bb/education/july-dec98/vouchers_11-27.html.

102 In 1998 Leininger provided: "Rick Perry Watch: Private

School Vouchers," Texas Freedom Network, available at: http://www.tfn.org/site/PageServer?pagename=issues_reli gious_right_watch_rick_perry.

102 beneficiary of Leininger's generosity: R. G. Ratcliff, "With Taxpayers' Help, Perry's a Long Way from the Cotton Farm," chron.com (*Houston Chronicle*, online edition), July 26, 2009; "Rick Perry Watch: Private School Vouchers," Texas Freedom Network.

102 In 1999, Perry blamed: "Bush Makes State Senate Visit as Voucher Bill Hits the Floor," Associated Press, as published in *LubbockOnline*, May 21, 1999.

103 "If you got to meet": April Castro, "Thousands Rally in Support of Vouchers," Associated Press, February 8, 2007.

104 "I tried to get": Gail Collins, "Education On Ice," *New York Times*, May 18, 2001.

104 A reporter visiting : Stuart Eskenazi, "Learning Curves," *Houston Press*, July 22, 1999.

104 A school in Dallas: Ibid.

104 In 2001, a Houston: Harvey Rice, "Three Plead Guilty to Fraud through Charter Schools," *Houston Chronicle*, April 19, 2005; Stella Chavez, "School Operators Rarely Face Criminal Charges in Fraud Cases," *Dallas Morning News*, April 5, 2008.

105 Over in Florida: Kathleen McGrory and Scott Hiaasen, "How Some States Rein in Charter School Abuses," *Miami Herald*, December 10, 2011.

105 By 2010 there were 5,000: "Charter Schools," *Education Week*, May 25, 2011.

106 By the No Child Left Behind: "Private Education Management Organizations Continue to Grow—but Results Are Mixed," National Education Policy Center, January 6, 2012.

106 Bennett resigned: "Bennett Under Fire for Remarks on Blacks, Crime," CNN, September 30, 2005, available at: http://articles.cnn.com/2005-09-30/politics/bennett.com ments_1_crime-rate-morally-reprehensible-thing-black-baby?_s=PM:POLITICS.

106 By 2011, there were an estimated: Jenny Anderson, "Students of Online Schools Are Lagging," *New York Times*, January 6, 2012.

107 In Tennessee, K^{12}: Gail Collins, "Virtually Educated," *New York Times*, December 2, 2011.

107 All in all, K^{12}: Stephanie Saul, "Profits and Questions at Online Charter Schools," *New York Times*, December 13, 2011.

107 In Pennsylvania: Ibid.

107 The prospects for: Ibid.

107 A study by the: Anderson, "Students of Online Schools are Lagging."

7: The Textbook Wars

Interviews: David Anderson, Keith Erekson, Julie McGee, Dan Quinn.

108 In 2009, the nation watched: Mariah Blake, "Revisionaires: How a Group of Texas Conservatives Is Rewriting Your Kids' Textbooks," *Washington Monthly*, January/February 2010.

108 In 2010, the subject was: Russell Shorto, "How Christian Were the Founders?" *New York Times Magazine*, February 11, 2010.

109 They brought their supporters: Blake, "Revisionaires."

109 Products of the Texas: Ibid.

110 Imagine the feelings: Eugenie C. Scott, "Texas Textbook Adoptions: Whither (Wither?) Evolution?" *National Center for Science Education*, Winter 1996.

111 Its most famous campaign: Karen Olsson, "Mr. Right," *Texas Monthly*, November 2002; Kathy Walt, "Religious Right Roaring into Race," *Houston Chronicle*, March 9, 1996.

111 Another organization Leininger has supported: Debbie Nathan, "Leininger Contributes to Conservative Causes with Money and Prayer, Wallet and Spirit," *Austin Chronicle* 18, issue 22, available at: http://www.austinchronicle.com/issues/vol18/issue22/pols.leininger.contr.html.

111 The chorus of objections: Patricia Kilday Hart, "Right Makes Right," *Texas Monthly*, May 2002.

112 Don McLeroy: Blake, "Revisionaires."

112 "this document that": "Talk of the Nation," NPR, March 16, 2010, available at: http://www.npr.org/templates/story/story.php?storyId=124737756.

112 In 2010, the board: Blake, "Revisionaires."

113 "only majorities can expand": Ibid.

113 "The way I evaluate": Ibid.

113 If the students were going: Brian Thevenot and Niran Babalola, "The Revision Thing," *Texas Tribune*, March 10, 2010.

113 "As a State Board": "The Texas State Board of Education: A Case of Abuse of Power," ACLU Texas, May 13, 2010, available at: http://www.aclutx.org/2010/05/13/the-texas-state-board-of-education-a-case-of-abuse-of-power/.

113 In 2010, the board tossed: Traci Shurley, "Name Confusion Gets Kids' Author Banned from Texas Curriculum," *Fort Worth Star Telegram*, January 25, 2010.

113 The final product: "Texas Education Agency Proposed Revisions to 19 TAC Chapter 113, Texas Essential Knowledge and Skills for Social Studies, Subchapter C, High School and 19 TAC Chapter 118, Texas Essential Knowledge and Skills for Economics with Emphasis on the Free Enterprise System and Its Benefits, Subchapter A, High School," 4–43.

115 When the discussions began: "What Does Dunbar Really Want to Teach?" *TFN Insider*, Texas Freedom Network, March 21, 2010.

115 a terrorist sympathizer: "Education Official Stands by Her Obama Terror Claim," *Houston Chronicle*, November 3, 2008.

115 After McLeroy himself: Nathan Bernier, "State Board of Education Chair's 'Christian' Remark Draws Fire," KUT News, November 5, 2011.

116 In 2011, the Thomas B. Fordham Institute: Sheldon Stern and Jeremy Stern, "The State of State U.S. History Standards 2011," Thomas B. Fordham Institute, February 16, 2011, 142.

116 "Maybe the most striking": Shorto, "How Christian Were the Founders?"

8: Speedy the Sperm and Friends

Interviews: Bob Deuell, Fran Hagerty, Susan Tortolero, Michael Villarreal.

118 "Is Jesus their": David Wiley and Kelly Wilson, "Just Say Don't Know: Sexuality Education in Texas Public Schools," Texas Freedom Network Education Fund, January 2009.

119 Carrie Williams: Reeve Hamilton, "Texas Forgoes Federal Funds for Comprehensive Sex Ed," *Texas Tribune*, October 4, 2010.

119 a herculean effort: Wiley and Wilson, "Just Say Don't Know."

122 Slightly over half: "Adolescent Sexual Behavior: Examining Data from Texas and the US," Christine Markham et al., *Journal of Applied Research on Children*, October 18, 2011, 5.

122 By the time they're seniors: Ibid.

122 third-highest rate: Ibid., 1.

122 Sixty-three out of: Ibid.

122 That compares to: "Adolescent Fertility Rate (Births per 1,000 Women Aged 15–19), 2000–2008," WHO World Health Statistics, 2011.

122 Back in 1992: S. K. Henshaw, "Teenage Abortion, Birth and Pregnancy Statistics by State, 1992," *Family Planning Perspectives*, May–June 1997, 115–22.

122 By 2008, when Texas's: Susan Tortolero and Paula Cuccaro, "A Tale of Two States: What We Learn from California and Texas," *Journal of Applied Research on Children*, October 18, 2011, 1.

123 "I'm in politics": "Prolife No Exceptions—Bryan Hughes and Bill Zedler," YouTube, uploaded February 10, 2011.

123 Governor Perry made an exception: Arlette Saenz, "After 'Transformation' Rick Perry Opposes Abortion in Cases of Rape and Incest," ABC News, December 27, 2011.

124 Texas has the second-highest: Centers for Disease Control and Prevention, National Center for Health Statistics, available at: http://www.cdc.gov/nchs/vitalstats.htm, accessed December 20, 2010.

124 $1 billion a year: Texas Health and Human Services Commission, "Impact on Texas If Medicaid Is Eliminated: A Joint Report Required by House Bill 497." Eighty-First Texas Legislature Regular Session, 2009. December 2010, available at: http://www.hhsc.state.tx.us/hb-497_122010 .pdf.

124 800,000 increase: "Enrollment in Texas Public Schools, 2010–11," Division of Research and Analysis, Texas Education Agency. October 11, 2011, ix.

125 Since the Texas Freedom Network: Renee C. Lee, "Abstinence-Plus Emerging in More Texas Schools," *Houston Chronicle*, December 27, 2011.

125 "Abstinence works": Evan Smith interview with Rick Perry, video posted October 29, 2011, http://www.texastribune .org/texas-people/rick-perry/perry-abstinence/.

9: Cooling to Global Warming

Interviews: Sherwood Boehlert, James Marston, Martin Melosi, Tom Smith, Daniel Weiss.

126 "In their eyes":"Text of Gov. Rick Perry's Remarks Regarding the EPA's Takeover of Texas' Air Permitting System," *Anahuac Progress*, June 2, 2010.

127 Marshall Kuykendall: Audrey Duff, "Cowboys & Critters," *Austin Chronicle*, January 28, 1996.

127 "Texans had spent": Haley, *Passionate Nation*, 542.

128 "First, . . . I will work": Jimmy Carter, Letter to Dolph Briscoe, October 19, 1976.

129 "a cocked gun": "Texas Demos, Once Jubilant, Now Feel Betrayed by Carter," New York Times News Service, printed in *El Paso Herald-Post*, October 20, 1977.

129 "potential war profiteering": "The Biggest Rip-Off," *Time*, October 24, 1977.

129 "If you can't get Bob": Robert Sherrill, "A Texan vs. Big Oil," *New York Times*, October 12, 1980.

130 "Instead of unleashing": Julie Connelly, "Energy: Oil for the Lamps of Reagan," *Time*, December 22, 1980.

130 took down the solar panels: Arthur Allen, "Prodigal Sun," *Mother Jones*, March/April 2000.

130 When H. W. ran: Byron W. Daynes and Glen Sussman, *White House Politics and the Environment: Franklin D. Roosevelt to George W. Bush* (College Station, TX: Texas A & M University Press, 2010), 157–58.

130 The first President Bush said: Ibid., 155, 157.

131 Its goal: "Bush Signs Major Revision of Anti-Pollution Law," Associated Press, printed in *New York Times*, November 16, 1990.

131 "The American way": Jack Beatty, "A Forecast of the 2000 Election Predicts Squalls and Continued Global Warming, *The Atlantic*, April 14, 1999.

131 "This guy is so": Ann Devroy, "Upbeat Bush Steps Up Rhetoric," *Washington Post*, October 30, 1992.

132 "If homosexuality was": Michael Crowley, "Barton Fink," *New Republic*, May 22, 2006.

132 "I do not want": Brian Montopoli, "Rep. Joe Barton Apologizes to BP's Tony Hayward for White House," CBS News, June 17, 2010.

132 A cement company paid: Alyssa Battistoni, "GOP Fights for Dirty Air," *Salon*, October 14, 2011.

132 "You've got to understand": Dubose and Reid, *The Hammer*, 96.

134 The 2000 Republican platform: Daynes and Sussman, *White House Politics*, 196.

134 Texas ranked first: John Mintz, "George W. Bush: The Texas Record; Evidence Contradicts Claims of Cleaner Air," *Washington Post*, October 15, 1999.

134 appointments: Ibid.

135 When the firm that had won: Ibid.

135 "Pat, we like wind": Thomas L. Friedman, "Whichever Way the Wind Blows," *New York Times*, December 15, 2006.

136 Bush decided to resolve: Thomas M. DeFrank, "Bush Bares Environment Plan but Foes Say He's Turned Texas Toxic," *New York Daily News*, June 2, 2000.

136 Under a law: Jim Yardley, "Bush Approach to Pollution: Preference for Self-Policing," *New York Times*, November 9, 1999.

136 "We have our limits": Mintz, "George W. Bush: The Texas Record."

136 Marquez was a former lobbyist: "Toxic Exposure: How Texas Chemical Council Members Pollute State Politics and the Environment," Texans for Public Justice, 1999.

136 He championed a Clear Skies: Daynes and Sussman, *White House Politics*, 195.

137 The environment in general: Ibid.

137 "Not since the rise": Howard Fineman and Michael Isikoff, "Big Energy at the Table," *Newsweek*, May 13, 2001.

137 "Conservation may be": Richard Benedetto, "Cheney's Energy Plan Focuses on Production," *USA Today*, May 1, 2001.

137 Ken Lay, who: John Nichols, "Ken Lay—Guilty, George Bush—Guilty," *Nation*, May 25, 2006.

138 In 2003, the General Accounting Office: "Energy Task Force: Process Used to Develop the National Energy Policy," United States General Accounting Office Report to Congressional Requesters, August 2003.

138 spending seven times as much: Lindsay Renick Mayer, "Big Oil, Big Influence," PBS, October 1, 2008, available at http://www.pbs.org/now/shows/347/oil-politics.html.

138 "We'll have a strong": "Bush Won't Ask Americans to Conserve," ABC News, May 8, 2001.

138 "That's a big no": Ibid.

138 "It is a darn": Carl Hulse and Michael Janofsky, "Congress, After Years of Effort, Is Set to Pass Broad Energy Bill," *New York Times*, July, 27, 2005.

138 A report by the Congressional: David Kocieniewski, "As Oil Industry Fights a Tax, It Reaps Subsidies," *New York Times*, July 3, 2010.

139 "It's the arrogance": Dubose and Reid, *The Hammer*, 111.

139 "It is quite pretentious": Paul Ford, "Weekly Review," *Harper's Magazine*, August 4, 2009.

139 humiliating for Whitman: Ron Suskind, *The Price of Loyalty* (New York: Simon & Schuster, 2004), 127.

140 "When I made": Tim Dickinson, "The Secret Campaign of President Bush's Administration to Deny Global Warming," *Rolling Stone*, June 20, 2007.

140 when the EPA issued: Katharine Q. Seelye, "President Distances Himself from Global Warming Report," *New York Times*, June 5, 2002.

140 when Bush held a press conference: Gail Collins, "The Fat Bush Theory," *New York Times*, October 19, 2008.

141 The Democratic minority: "The Most Anti-Environment House in the History of Commerce," Committee on Energy and Commerce Democrats, December 15, 2011.

142 Texan Ralph Hall: Coral Davenport, "Heads in the Sand," *National Journal*, December 4, 2011.

143 "destroying federalism": Rick Perry, *Fed Up* (New York: Little, Brown, 2010), 88.

143 Perry didn't put any stock: W. Gardner Selby and Asher Price, "Perry's Strong Views on Climate Change Can Be Muted at Home," *Austin American Statesman*, October 21, 2007.

143 "one contrived phony mess": Perry, *Fed Up*, 92.

143 Announcing the action: Asher Price, "Texas Sues to Stop EPA from Regulating Greenhouse Gases," *Austin American-Statesman*, February 16, 2010.

143 In response, climate scientists: "On Global Warming, the Science Is Solid," *Houston Chronicle*, March 7, 2010.

143 "I was just amazed": "Interview: Larry Soward," *Texas Climate News*, April 29, 2010.

144 "I like to tell people": Suzanne Goldenberg, "Rick Perry Officials Spark Revolt After Doctoring Environment Report," *Guardian*, October 14, 2011.

10: The Texas Miracle, Part II

Interviews: Don Baylor, Michael Brandl, Sara Collins, Leslie Helmcamp, Christopher King, Rick Levy, Richard Pena, Bill Ratliff, Mark Strama, Alex Winslow, Mine Yücel.

147 "For the last few weeks": Rick Wartzman, "Texas, the Jobs Engine," *Los Angeles Times*, July 3, 2011.

147 "Since June 2009": *Glenn Beck*, Fox News, June 14, 2011, available at: http://www.glennbeck.com/2011/06/14/rick-perry-makes-surprise-cameo-as-glenn-counts-down-to-june-30th/.

147 "Approximately 70 percent": "Gov. Perry: Texas Workforce and Economic Development are Key to Prosperity," press release, Office of Governor Rick Perry, January 15, 2009.

148 "In fact, if you throw out": "Recession Pounds Perry's Jobs Fund," Texans for Public Justice, January 27, 2010.

148 "There is still": The Perry quote was first reported by the *Texas Tribune*. You can hear the audio at DallasVoice.com.

148 "As the state of California": "Texas Governor Woos Vernon Businesses," *Los Angeles Times*, May 9, 2011.

148 when a trade association paid: "Making Connection: State Officials and Their Special-Interest Travel Agents," Texans for Public Justice, April 2007.

149 *Forbes*: Joel Kotkin, "The Next Big Boom Towns in the U.S.," *Forbes*, July 6, 2011.

149 CNBC chose Texas: "America's Top States for Business," CNBC, July 13, 2010.

149 *Site Selection*: Mark Arend, "Texas Soars," *Site Selection*, March 2011.

149 *Chief Executive* magazine: "Best/Worst States for Business," *Chief Executive*, May 3, 2011.

149 Andrew Puzder: Allison Wollam, "Will Carl's Jr. Really Move to Texas," *Houston Business Journal*, February 3, 2011.

150 However, Logue told: George Skelton, "Gavin Newsom Treks to Texas to Talk Jobs," *Los Angeles Times*, April 21, 2011.

150 The gang was trotted: "Missing Context: When Political Worlds Collide," chron.com (*Houston Chronicle* online edition), April 15, 2011.

150 "As well as Texas": Arend, "Texas Soars."

151 a Russian submarine invade Houston: McNeely and Henderson, *Bob Bullock*, 217.

152 "When we were faced": Hobby, *How Things Really Work*, 118.

152 A study by the Institute: "Census Data Reveal Fundamental Tax Mismatch in Texas," Institute on Taxation and Economic Policy, September 2010.

152 After the report came out: Robert Garrett, "Texas' Low Income Residents Paying a High Share of the Taxes," *Dallas Morning News*, November 19, 2009.

153 The Council on State Taxation: "Total State and Local Business Taxes," Council on State Taxation, FY 2010.

153 Those pilgrims: Laylin Copelin, "Should Perry Get Credit for Texas Economy?" *Austin American-Statesman*, July 17, 2011.

153 "a failed experiment": "The Texas Lesson on Business Taxes," Tax Foundation, August 17, 2011.

153 The lawmakers refused: "Letter from Comptroller Carole Keeton Strayhorn to Governor Rick Perry Regarding the Perry Tax Plan," May 15, 2006.

154 "the governor's slush fund": Paul Burka, "The Governor's 'Slush' Funds," *Texas Monthly*, May 13, 2009.

155 "Nationally, all we are doing": James Drew, "Report Says Texas Enterprise Fund Not Creating Jobs as Promised," *Dallas Morning News*, January 28, 2010.

155 Reporters discovered: Mark Maremont, "Behind Perry's Jobs

Success, Numbers Draw New Scrutiny," *Wall Street Journal*, October 11, 2011.

155 Texas Energy Center: Alec MacGillis, "The Permanent Candidate: What's Driving Rick Perry?" *New Republic*, October 20, 2011.

156 whopping local incentives: Dan McGraw, "What Free Parking?" *Fort Worth Weekly*, January 9, 2008.

156 "I know I speak": "Cabela's Opening Buda," press release, Office of Governor Rick Perry, June 29, 2005.

156 "But the property": McGraw, "What Free Parking?"

157 The lure, said Hilmar: "Recession Pounds Perry's Jobs Fund," Texans for Public Justice, January 27, 2010.

157 When people in the Hilmar: Jane Kay, "Bad Water? It's the Cheese," *Environmental Health News*, September 13, 2010.

157 Water quality enforcers: Chris Bowman, "The World's Biggest Cheese Factory Fouled Water and Air for Years," *Sacramento Bee*, December 12, 2004.

157 Then came the fine: "Recession Pounds Perry's Jobs Fund."

158 Three years later: Ibid.

158 "The most important": Rick Wartzman, "Texas, the Jobs Engine," *Los Angeles Times*, July 3, 2011.

158 "Here is what can happen": Mimi Swartz, "Hurt. Injured? Need a Lawyer? Too Bad!" *Texas Monthly*, November 2005.

160 McAllen: Atul Gawande, "The Cost Conundrum," *The New Yorker*, June 1, 2009.

160 In 2010, Texas families: C. Schoen, A. K. Fryer, S. R. Collins, and D. C. Radley, "State Trends in Premiums and Deductibles, 2003–2010: The Need for Action to Address Rising Costs," Commonwealth Fund, November, 2011.

161 "Where previously hundreds": Terry Carter, "Insult to Injury," *American Bar Association Journal*, October 1, 2011.

163 Texas's population is also young: Gary Maler and Harold D. Hunt, "The Changing Face of Texas." Texas A & M University Real Estate Center, July 2010, available at: http://recenter.tamu.edu/pdf/1938.pdf.

163 Juarez, Mexico, and El Paso: Andrew Rice, "Life on the Line," *New York Times Magazine*, July 28, 2011.

163 The state has only two: "LSG Analysis and Recommendations on State of Higher Education in Texas," Legislative Study Group, Texas House of Representatives, May 29, 2008.

163 All the four-year institutions: Laylin Copelin, "Should Perry Get Credit for Texas Economy?" *Austin American-Statesman*, July 17, 2011.

164 Counting in a different way: Ana Campoy and Sara Murray, "Public Sector Added to Texas Jobs Boom," *Wall Street Journal*, July 27, 2011.

164 In 2008, the Texas comptroller: "Fort Hood Impacts Texas Economy by $10.9 Billion," May 13, 2008.

164 6,000 more soldiers: Jeanna Smialek, "Ten Reasons Why the Texas Economy Is Growing That Have Nothing to Do with Rick Perry," *Texas on the Potomac* (blog), chron.com (*Houston Chronicle* online edition), July 31, 2011.

165 "Goverment doesn't create": Campoy and Murray, "Public Sector Added to Texas Jobs Boom."

165 "the key to prosperity": Ibid.

166 Nearly 10 percent: Lori Taylor and Heather Gregory, "Low Texas Wages Are Mostly Good News," *Austin American-Statesman*, July 16, 2011.

166 California, Florida, and Illinois: Ibid.

11: The Other Side of the Coin

Interviews: David Evans, David Lopez, Paige Phelps, Mark Strama.

167 Policy wonks: Copelin, "Should Perry Get Credit for Texas Economy?"

168 One of the high points: "Texas on the Brink: Fifth Edition," Texas House of Representatives, Legislative Study Group, February 2011.

169 "This report makes": April Castro, "Study Reveals Texas

Has Low Tax, Expenditures," Associated Press via *Lubbock-Online*, February 16, 2011.

170 "the Texas state climatologist": Neal Lane and Robert Harriss, "Climate Data Spark Battle in Congress," *Houston Chronicle*, July 17, 2011.

170 In 2011, reporters from: "Former St. Luke's Neurosurgeon Resigns from Texas Practice," *Duluth News Tribune*, October 1, 2011.

170 During their investigation: Brandon Stahl and Mark Stodghill, "In Texas, Former Duluth Surgeon May Be Sanction-Free," *Duluth News Tribune*, May 31, 2011.

170 If you're poor and mentally ill: Polly Ross Hughes, "Mental Health Reform Plans Meet Resistance," *Houston Chronicle*, July 5, 2004.

171 Senator John Cornyn: "Interview with Texas Senator John Cornyn," National Association of Wholesale Distributors, August, 2008.

171 In 2009, the Department: Andrea Ball, "Years After Mental Health Overhaul, New Picture of Needs Emerging," *Austin American-Statesman*, December 6, 2009.

171 Texans with mental illness: Patricia Kilday Hart, "Cop Drama," *Texas Monthly*, August 2010.

171 "The largest psychiatric": Ibid.

174 In Minnesota: The Henry J. Kaiser Family Foundation, *Health Insurance Coverage of the Total Population, States (2008–2009), U.S. (2009)*, available at: http://www.statehealthfacts.org/comparetable.jsp?ind=125&cat=3&sort=a&gsa=2.

175 a $1.2 billion budget: Mike Morris, "Harris County OKs Leanest Budget in Years," *Houston Chronicle*, March 8, 2011.

175 If you're a young doctor: Emily Ramshaw, "Conditions, Health Risks Sicken Colonias Residents," *Texas Tribune*, July 10, 2011.

12: We've Seen the Future, and It's Texas

Interviews: Joaquín Castro, Henry Cisneros, Shella Condino, Rodney Ellis, Bill Hobby, Dennis McEntire, Steve Murdock, Richard Murray, Robert Sanborn, Lionel Sosa, Teloa Swinnea.

179 "They used to take us there": Zev Chafets, "The Post-Hispanic Hispanic Politician," *New York Times Magazine*, May 9, 2010.

182 "Rosie Castro's son": Ibid.

183 The Texas legislature actually passed: Ibid.

183 Dick Armey ran into: Michael Sokolove, "Dick Armey Is Back on the Attack," *New York Times Magazine*, November 4, 2009.

183 During the 2011 state legislative session: Mariano Castillo, "Texas Immigration Bill Has Big Exception," CNN, March 1, 2011.

183 There was a bill: Tim Eaton, "Many Immigration Bills Not Likely to Make It Through Legislature," *Austin American-Statesman*, May 10, 2011.

184 "Illegal immigration is": Rick Casey, "A Suicidal Circular Firing Squad," *Houston Chronicle*, July 4, 2011.

184 "Voter fraud is a problem": Ibid.

187 Then he was indicted: Lauri Apple and Mike Clark-Madison, "Dumb and Dapper," *Austin Chronicle*, July 4, 2003; Guillermo Contreras, "Ex-Attorney General Morales at Halfway House," *Houston Chronicle*, December 22, 2006.

187 But the big, whopping: Guy Gugliotta, "Regarding Henry," *Washington Post*, October 12, 1994.

189 And all the trend lines: Stephen L. Klineberg, "Public Perception in Remarkable Times: Tracking Change Through 24 Years of Houston Surveys," Rice University Department of Sociology Center on Race, Religion, and Urban Life, 2005.

191 One was the legal limit: Ericka Mellon, "Class Sizes Grow Amid State Budget Cuts," *Houston Chronicle*, October 18, 2011.

191 A district north of Fort Worth: Morgan Smith, "Fees for Students Redefine 'Free' Public School," *Texas Tribune*, July 29, 2011.

191 Texas was already forty-seventh: "Texas on the Brink," Texas Legislative Study Group, February 2011, available at: http://texaslsg.org/texasonthebrink/?p=1. See Appendix.

Bibliography

Books

Ashman, Charles. *Connally: The Adventures of Big Bad John*, New York: William Morrow, 1974.

Bickerstaff, Steve. *Lines in the Sand: Congressional Redistricting in Texas and the Downfall of Tom DeLay*. Austin: University of Texas Press, 2007.

Black, William. *The Best Way to Rob a Bank Is to Own One: How Corporate Executives and Politicians Looted the S & L Industry*. Austin: University of Texas Press, 2005.

Brands, H.W. *Lone Star Nation: How a Ragged Army of Volunteers Won the Battle for Texas Independence—and Changed America*. New York: Anchor Books, 2004.

Burrough, Bryan. *The Big Rich: The Rise and Fall of the Greatest Texas Oil Fortunes*, New York: Penguin, 2009.

Bryce, Robert. *Cronies: Oil, the Bushes and the Rise of Texas, America's Superstate*. New York: PublicAffairs, 2004.

Cannon, Carl M., Lou Dubose, and Jan Reid. *Boy Genius: Karl Rove, the Architect of George W. Bush's Remarkable Political Triumphs*. New York: PublicAffairs, 2003.

Caro, Robert. *The Path to Power: The Years of Lyndon Johnson, Vol. 1.* New York: Knopf, 1982.

Cox, Patrick L., and Michael Phillips. *The House Will Come to Order: How the Texas Speaker Became a Power in State and National Politics.* Austin: University of Texas Press, 2010.

Daynes, Byron W., and Glen Sussman. *White House Politics and the Environment: Franklin D. Roosevelt to George W. Bush.* College Station, TX: Texas A & M University Press, 2010.

Dellinger, Matt. *Interstate 69: The Unfinished History of the Last Great American Highway.* New York: Simon and Schuster, 2010.

Dubose, Lou, and Jan Reid. *The Hammer: Tom DeLay: God, Money, and the Rise of the Republican Congress.* New York: Public-Affairs, 2004.

Gerstner, Louis V. *Reinventing Education: Entrepreneurship in America's Public Schools.* New York: Dutton, 1994.

Haley, James. *Passionate Nation: The Epic History of Texas.* New York: Free Press, 2006.

Harrigan, Stephen. *The Gates of the Alamo.* New York: Penguin, 2000.

Hobby, Bill. *How Things Really Work: Lessons From a Life in Politics.* Austin: Dolph Briscoe Center for American History, 2010.

Ivins, Molly. *Molly Ivins Can't Say That, Can She?* New York: Vintage, 1991.

Kirkland, Elithe Hamilton. *Love is a Wild Assault.* Fredericksburg, TX: Shearer Publishing, 1984.

Lind, Michael. *Made in Texas.* New York: New America, 2003.

Maxwell, William Earl, Ernest Crain and Adolfo Santos. *Texas Politics Today.* Boston: Wadsworth, 2009.

Mayer, Martin. *The Greatest Ever Bank Robbery: The Collapse of the Savings and Loan Industry.* New York: Collier, 1992.

McCall, Brian. *The Power of the Texas Governor: Connally to Bush.* Austin: University of Texas Press, 2009.

McNeely, Dave, and Jim Henderson. *Bob Bullock: God Bless Texas.* Austin: University of Texas Press, 2008.

O'Shea, James. *The Daisy Chain: How Borrowed Billions Sank a Texas S & L.* New York: Simon and Schuster, 1991.

Perry, Rick. *Fed Up!: Our Fight to Save America from Washington.* New York: Little, Brown, 2010.

Preuss, Gene. *To Get a Better School System: 100 Years of Education Reform in Texas.* College Station, TX: Texas A & M University Press, 2009.

Ravitch, Diane. *The Death and Life of the Great American School System: How Testing and Choice are Undermining Education.* New York: Basic Books, 2010.

Riccucci, Norma. *Unsung Heroes: Federal Execucrats Making a Difference.* Washington, DC: Georgetown University Press, 1995.

Richards, Ann. *Straight from the Heart: My Life in Politics and Other Places.* New York: Simon and Schuster, 1989.

Storey, John W., and Mary L. Kelley, eds. *Twentieth Century Texas: A Social and Cultural History.* Denton, TX: University of North Texas Press, 2008.

Suskind, Ron. *The Price of Loyalty.* New York: Simon and Schuster, 2004.

Texas Monthly, *Texas, Our Texas.* Austin: Texas Monthly Press, 1986.

Van Natta, Don. *First Off the Tee.* New York: PublicAffairs, 2003.

Zernike, Kate. *Boiling Mad: Inside Tea Party America.* New York: Times Books, 2010.

Reports and Articles

"America Goes to the Polls: A Report on Voter Turnout in the 2010 Election." Nonprofit Voter, 2010.

"Austin's Oldest Profession." Texans for Public Justice, 2010.

"Blind Faith: How Deregulation and Enron's Influence Over Government Looted Billions from Americans." Public Citizen, December 2001.

Ferguson, Chris. "The Progress of Education in Texas." Southwest Educational Development Laboratory, November 2000.

Markham, Christine, Melissa Peskin, Belinda Hernandez, Kimberly Johnson, and Richard Addy, "Adolescent Sexual Behavior: Examining Data from Texas and the US," *Journal of Applied Research on Children* 2, issue 2, article 3, available at: http://digitalcommons.library.tmc.edu/childrenatrisk/vol2/iss2/3.

"A Nation at Risk: The Imperative for Education Reform." National Commission on Excellence in Education, David P. Gardner, chairman, April 1983.

"The Progress of Education in Texas." Southwest Educational Development Laboratory, November 2000.

"Recession Pounds Perry's Jobs Fund." Texans for Public Justice, January 27, 2010.

Stern, Jeremy, and Sheldon Stern. "The State of the State U.S. History Standards 2011." Thomas B. Fordham Institute, February 16, 2011.

"The Texas State Board of Education: A Case of Abuse of Power." ACLU Texas, May 13, 2010.

"Toxic Exposure: How Texas Chemical Council Members Pollute State Politics and the Environment." Texans for Public Justice, 1999.

Wiley, David, and Kelly Wilson. "Just Say Don't Know: Sexuality Education in Texas Public Schools." Texas Freedom Network Education Fund, February 2009.

Appendix

Texas on the Brink
A Report from the Texas Legislative Study on the
State of Our State

"Texas on the Brink" is a measure of how the state stands up to the rest of the country, published at the beginning of every two-year session by the Legislative Study Group in the Texas House of Representatives.

When this 2011 version was produced, Representative Garnet Coleman was chair of the group. Its other officers were Representative Lon Burnam, vice chair, Representative Elliott Naishtat, treasurer, and Representative Rafael Anchia, secretary. The staff included Joe Madden, executive director, Phillip Martin, policy director, and policy analysts Jasie Boyd, Cappreese Crawley, David Kanewske, Lisa Mathews, Ashley Reeder, Kira Ruben, Mimi Tran, Rachel Watson, and Kimberly Willis.

Just spending money isn't a sign of progress. If your state came in at the bottom on student achievement, you probably wouldn't be comforted by the news that it had paid the most per capita on its students. And Texas does have a low cost of living. So the fact that it ranks forty-fourth in per pupil expenditures might not mean anything at all—if the high school graduate rate didn't clock in at forty-third.

If you check out only one thing, look at the numbers on the
environment—and then contemplate the fact that Texas members of Congress and Texas governors have spent the last couple
of decades bitterly denouncing the Environmental Protection
Administration for meddling in things that Texas can take care of
for itself.

                                                    —Gail Collins

Texas on the Brink

Since 1836, Texas has stood as an icon of the American dream.

Blessed with land, rivers, oil, and other abundant natural resources, early Texas welcomed everyone from cattle ranchers to *braceros*, from cotton farmers to Chinese railroad workers. These pioneers built a great state, and together we fulfilled a destiny.

From humble beginnings, we built a state with the firm belief that *every* Texan might rise as high and as far as their spirit, hard work, and talent might carry them. With education and determination every Texan might achieve great success—home ownership, reliable healthcare, safe neighborhoods, and financial prosperity.

In Texas today, the American dream is distant. Texas has the highest percentage of uninsured children in the nation. Texas is dead last in the percentage of residents with their high school diploma and near last in SAT scores. Texas has America's dirtiest air. If we do not change course, for the first time in our history, the Texas generation of tomorrow will be less prosperous than the generation of today.

Without the courage to invest in the minds of our children and steadfast support for great schools, we face a daunting prospect. Those who value tax cuts over children and budget cuts over college have put Texas at risk in her ability to compete and succeed.

Let us not forget that the business of Texas is Texans. To 'Close the Gap' in Texas, we must graduate more of our best and brightest with the skills to succeed in a world based on knowledge. If we invest in our greatest resource—our children—Texas will be the state of the future. If we do not, Texas will only fall further behind.

Texas is on the brink, but Texas can do better. The choice is ours.

State Rankings

State Taxes

(50th=Lowest, 1st=Highest)

- Tax Revenue Raised per Capita[1]   46th
- Tax Expenditures per Capita[2]   47th
- Sales Tax per Capita[3]   15th

Education

(50th=Lowest, 1st=Highest)

- Public School Enrollment[4]   2nd
- Average Salary of Public School Teachers[5]   33rd
- Average Teacher Salary as a Percentage of Average   34th
  Annual Pay[6]
- Current Expenditures per Student[7]   38th
- State & Local Expenditures per Pupil in Public   44th
  Schools[8]
- State Aid per Pupil in Average Daily Attendance[9]   47th
- Percent of Elementary/Secondary School Funding   37th
  from State Revenue[10]
- Scholastic Assessment Test (SAT) Scores[11]   45th
- Percent of Population 25 and Older with a High   50th
  School Diploma[12]
- High School Graduation Rate[13]   43rd
- Percent of Adults with at Least a Bachelor's Degree[14]   31st
- Percentage of Higher Education Enrollment[15]   9th
- Per Capita State Spending on State Arts Agencies[16]   43rd

State of the Child

(50th=Lowest, 1st=Highest)

- Birth Rate[17]   2nd
- Percent of Population Under 18[18]   2nd
- Percent of Uninsured Children[19]   1st
- Percent of Children Living in Poverty[20]   4th

- Percent of Children Fully Immunized[21]   34th
- Percent of Children Overweight[22]   19th

Health Care
(50th=Lowest, 1st=Highest)

- Percent of Population Uninsured[23]   1st
- Percent of Non-Elderly Uninsured[24]   1st
- Percent of Low Income Population Covered by   49th
  Medicaid[25]
- Percent of Population with Employer-Based Health   48th
  Insurance[26]
- Total State Government Health Expenditures as Per-   43rd
  cent of the Gross State Product[27]
- Per Capita State Spending on Mental Health[28]   50th
- Per Capita State Spending on Medicaid[29]   49th
- Percent of Population Physically Active[30]   36th
- Health Care Expenditures per Capita[31]   44th
- Hospital Beds per 1,000 Population[32]   27th
- Health Professionals per Capita:
- Physicians[33]   42nd
- Dentists[34]   39th
- Registered Nurses[35]   44th

Health and Well-Being
(50th=Lowest, 1st=Highest)

- Percent Living Below Federal Poverty Level[36]   4th
- Percent of Population with Food Insecurity[37]   2nd
- Average Monthly Women, Infants, and Children   47th
  (WIC) Benefits per Person[38]
- Prevalence of Obesity in Adults[39]   16th
- Rate of Death due to Heart Disease[40]   22nd
- Prevalence of Diagnosed Diabetes[41]   14th
- Diabetes Death Rate[42]   16th
- Percent of Population Who Visit the Dentist[43]   46th

Women's Issues

(50th=Lowest, 1st=Highest)

- Overall Birth Rate[44]   2nd
- Teenage Birth Rate[45]   7th
- Births to Unmarried Mothers[46]   17th
- Percent of Women with Pre-Term Birth[47]   9th
- Percent of Non-Elderly Women with Health   50th
  Insurance[48]
- Percent of Women Who Have Had a Dental Visit   45th
  within the Past Year[49]
- Rate of Women Aged 40+ Who Receive   40th
  Mammograms[50]
- Rate of Women Aged 18+ Who Receive Pap   37th
  Smears[51]
- Breast Cancer Rate[52]   42nd
- Cervical Cancer Rate[53]   11th
- Percent of Women with High Blood Pressure[54]   16th
- Family Planning[55]   37th
- Percent of Pregnant Women Receiving Prenatal   50th
  Care in First Trimester[56]
- Women's Voter Registration[57]   45th
- Women's Voter Turnout[58]   49th
- Percent of Women Living in Poverty[59]   6th
- Percentage of Women with Four or More Years of   30th
  College[60]
- Percent of Businesses Owned by Women[61]   17th
- Percent of Median Income for Full Time Work[62]   26th

Access to Capital

(50th=Lowest, 1st=Highest)

- Percent of Mortgage Loans that are Subprime[63]   9th
- Mortgage Debt as Percent of Home Value[64]   47th
- Foreclosure Rates[65]   10th
- Private Loans to Small Businesses[66]   30th

- Asset Poverty Rate[67]   36th
- Median Net Worth of Households[68]   47th
- Average Credit Score[69]   49th
- Retirement Plan Participation[70]   47th
- Median Credit Card Debt[71]   19th
- Average Credit Score[72]   49th

Environment
(50th=Lowest, 1st=Highest)

- Amount of Carbon Dioxide Emissions[73]   1st
- Amount of Volatile Organic Compounds Released   1st
  into Air[74]
- Amount of Toxic Chemicals Released into Water[75]   1st
- Amount of Recognized Cancer-Causing Carcino-   1st
  gens Released into Air[76]
- Amount of Hazardous Waste Generated[77]   1st
- Amount of Toxic Chemicals Released into Air[78]   5th
- Amount of Recognized Cancer-Causing Carcino-   7th
  gens Released into Water[79]
- Number of Hazardous Waste Sites on National Pri-   7th
  ority List[80]
- Consumption of Energy per Capita[81]   5th

Workforce
(50th=Lowest, 1st=Highest)

- Average Hourly Earnings of Production Workers on   38th
  Manufacturing Payrolls[82]
- Government Employee Wages and Salaries[83]   24th
- Percent of Workforce that are Members of a Union[84]   41st
- Workers' Compensation Coverage[85]   50th

Quality of Life
(50th=Lowest, 1st=Highest)
- Income Inequality Between the Rich and the Poor[86]   9th
- Income Inequality Between the Rich and the Middle Class[87]   5th
- Median Household Income[88]   34th
- Home Ownership Rate[89]   44th
- Homeowner's Insurance Affordability[90]   46th
- Auto Insurance Affordability[91]   24th
- Personal Bankruptcy Filings Rate, Per Capita[92]   39th
- Percent of Households with Internet Access[93]   42nd

Public Safety
(50th=Lowest, 1st=Highest)
- Number of Executions[94]   1st
- Rate of Incarceration[95]   9th
- Crime Rate[96]   35th
- Violent Crime Rate[97]   16th
- Murder Rate[98]   20th
- Percent of Murders Involving Firearms[99]   23rd
- Rape Rate[100]   21st
- Robbery Rate[101]   14th
- Property Crime Rate[102]   9th
- Larceny and Theft Rate[103]   6th
- Rate of Motor Vehicle Fatalities[104]   13th

Democracy
(50th=Lowest, 1st=Highest)
- Percent of Voting-Age Population that is Registered to Vote[105]   43rd
- Percent of Voting-Age Population that Votes[106]   45th

Key Facts and Figures

Children and Families:
- In Fiscal Year 2010, there were 78,718 confirmed cases of child abuse and neglect.[107]
- Over 280 children died due to abuse or neglect in 2009.[108]
- The rate of immunization in the 4:3:1 series (most basic vaccination series) for Texas children ages 19–35 months was 80.2 percent in 2009, below the national average of 81.5 percent.[109]
- 49 percent of children in Texas live in low-income families— families whose household income is twice the federal poverty level—as opposed to 42 percent nationwide.[110]
- 87 percent of children whose parents do not have a high school degree live in low-income families, compared to 30 percent of children whose parents have some college education.[111]
- In Texas, 66 percent of Latino children and 59 percent of black children live in low-income families, compared to 25 percent of white children.[112]
- 48 percent of children in urban areas and 55 percent of children in rural areas live in low-income families.[113]
- The maximum Temporary Assistance for Needy Families (TANF) grant for a family of three with no income is $250 per month in Texas, ranking 45th amongst the states.[114]
- In FY 2010, the average monthly benefit for Women, Infant, and Children (WIC) recipients in Texas was $26.86, the lowest in the nation. The national average was $41.52.[115]
- 24 percent of poor children in Texas are uninsured as compared to 17 percent nationwide.[116]

Education:
- In the 2008–2009 school year, Texas 4th graders who were proficient in reading fell 4 percent below the national level with reading levels of 28 percent proficiency.[117]

- In the 2008–2009 school year, Texas 8th graders who were proficient in reading fell 3 percent below the national level with reading levels of 27 percent proficiency.[118]
- 79 percent of 4th graders in families with low incomes were at a basic performance level in math in comparison to 95 percent of whites.[119]
- 69 percent of 8th graders in families with low incomes were at a basic performance level in math in comparison to 89 percent of whites.[120]
- One in three high school teachers serving the highest percentages of low-income students lack full certification in the subjects they are teaching.[121]
- Nearly 30 percent of the teachers in the highest-poverty schools are not fully certified in mathematics including algebra I, one of the most important courses in high school.[122]
- Almost half of English I teachers working in high schools with the highest proportion of African-American students lack certification in English.[123]

Achievement Gaps:

The National Assessment of Educational Progress (NAEP) is administered by the National Center for Education Statistics. It is a nationally recognized assessment of what America's students "know and can do in various academic subjects." According to the U.S. Department of Education website, "Achievement gaps are calculated by subtracting the scale scores of one subgroup from the scale scores of another subgroup. NAEP scores are based on a scale from 0 to 500. The scale scores are a measure of student performance on the NAEP."[124]

The following are the differences—or achievement gaps—between the average scale scores of the following groups of Texas students in the 2008–2009 school year:

Whites & Hispanic Students
- 4th grade math: 20
- 8th grade math: 24
- 4th grade reading: 22
- 8th grade reading: 22

White & Black Students
- 4th grade math: 23
- 8th grade math: 28
- 4th grade reading: 19
- 8th grade reading: 25

Higher Education:

- In Texas, only 30.7 percent of the population aged 25–35 has an associate's degree or higher, far less than the national average of 41.6 percent.[125]
- Texas is ranked 42nd in residents 25–35 with an associate's degree or higher.[126]
- Only 15.9 percent of Hispanics in Texas earned an associate's degree within a three-year time frame, compared to 43.8 percent for whites.[127]
- Undergraduate students in Texas borrowed on average $4,723 in student loans in 2007, up from $2,873 in 1995.[128]
- Texas currently ranks 42nd in the number of high school graduates going to college, with 55.4 percent.[129]
- In El Paso County, 18.8 percent of the population has a Bachelor's degree or higher, as opposed to 43.1 percent in Travis County.[130]
- The University of Texas at Austin and Texas A&M University at College Station are the only Texas public institutions of higher education ranked in the top 100 in U.S. News and World Report's Best Colleges in the U.S., with UT at #45 and Texas A&M at #63.[131]
- 50 percent of college freshman in Texas are enrolled in remedial

or developmental classes, compared with 28 percent across the U.S.[132]

- Texas funds only 32 percent of need-based financial aid, as opposed to 89 percent by the top-investing states.[133]
- The share of Texan family income needed to pay for college expenses at public four-year institutions increased from 18 percent to 26 percent between 2000 and 2008.[134]
- 36 percent of blacks and 38 percent of Hispanics graduate from a four-year institution within six years, compared with 56 percent of whites.[135]
- 50 percent of first-time, full-time college students earn a bachelor's degree within six years of entering college.[136]

The Elderly:
- In a 2009 report, Texas had an 18 percent poverty rate among the elderly population (ages 65 and older), compared to the U.S. that had a 14 percent national elderly poverty rate.[137]
- In 2009, there were 33.1 different prescriptions filled at retail drug stores by the elderly in Texas; in the United States, there were 31.2 prescriptions filled by retail drug stores for the elderly.[138]
- The population in Texas that is over 65 years of age will be expected to grow from 2.1 to 7.4 million, or 258 percent, by 2040.[139]
- The National Center on Elder Abuse reports that only one of every 14 elder abuse cases is reported. Only 1 of every 25 cases relating to financial abuse or exploitation—usually committed by family and trusted community members—is reported.[140]

The Uninsured:
- In 2009, about 50 million people in the United States, or 17 percent, of the non-elderly population were uninsured.[141]
- 28 percent or 6.1 million of the population of Texas is uninsured, the largest share of uninsured in the nation.[142]

- From 2000 to 2009, the annual family health insurance premiums in Texas rose from about $6,600 to $13,221, or about 50 percent. During the same time period, median earnings rose only 38 percent.[143]
- Less than 51 percent of Texas workers under age 65 had employer-based health coverage in 2008–09; which is down 9 percent from 2000–01.[144]
- 16.3 percent of children in Texas were uninsured in 2009, compared to 8.6 percent nationally.[145]
- In Texas, 63 percent of adults between the ages of 19 and 64 living in poverty do not have health insurance.[146]
- Of those uninsured, 59 percent or 3.6 million, are Hispanic.[147]
- 59 percent of Hispanics under age 65 had no health insurance compared with 11 percent of blacks and 26 percent of whites.[148]
- 1.3 million Texas children, or 21 percent of the population aged 18 and under, were without health insurance in 2009.[149]
- Texas does not provide Medicaid to parents making even poverty level incomes; therefore, a working parent of two does not qualify for coverage if he or she makes more than $4,943.70 in a year.[150]
- A working parent in Texas is eligible for Medicaid if his or her income does not exceed 27 percent of the federal poverty level (FPL). The FPL for a family of 3 is $18,310.[151]

Health Professionals:
- Texas will have over 27,000 nursing vacancies by 2010, and that number is expected to double by 2015.[152]
- By 2015, Texas would need more than 4,500 additional primary care doctors and other medical professionals in order to serve all of the state's medically disenfranchised population.[153]
- Harris County, which includes Houston, Texas, has 28,274 licensed Resident Nurses; 20,220 of whom are employed as full-time nurses while 2,921 are unemployed.[154]
- Travis County, which includes Austin, Texas, has 7,984 licensed

Resident Nurses; 5,118 of whom are employed as full-time nurses while 956 are unemployed.[155]

- Bexar County, which includes San Antonio, Texas, has 16,363 licensed Resident Nurses; 11,920 of whom are employed as full-time nurses while 1,582 are unemployed.[156]
- Dallas County, which includes Dallas, Texas, has 16,718 licensed Resident Nurses; 12,208 of whom are employed as full-time nurses while 1,521 are unemployed.[157]
- El Paso County, which includes El Paso, Texas, has 5,424 licensed Resident Nurses; 4,081 of whom are employed as full-time nurses while 517 are unemployed.[158]
- Lamar County, which includes Paris, Texas, has 650 licensed Resident Nurses; 491 of whom are employed as full-time nurses while 67 are unemployed.[159]
- Potter County, which includes Amarillo, Texas, has 1,228 licensed Resident Nurses; 858 of whom are employed as full-time nurses while 143 are unemployed.[160]

Income Disparity and Employment:
- The personal per capita income for Texans in 2009 was $36,484.[161]
- 4.26 million Texans live in poverty, representing 17.3 percent of the state's population.[162]
- Only 5.5 percent of Texas workers are members of a union.[163]
- 47 percent of Texas children live in low-income families.[164]
- Starr County led the state with 78.6 percent of the population considered low income.[165]
- The richest 20 percent of Texas families have average incomes 7.9 times larger than the poorest 20 percent of families, ranking as the 9th highest gap in the nation. This ratio was 7.0 in the late 1980s.[166]
- The richest 20 percent of Texas families have average incomes 2.8 times larger than the middle 20 percent of families, ranking as the 5th highest gap in the nation. This ratio was 2.3 in the late 1980s.[167]

- From the late 1980s to the mid-2000s, the average income of the poorest 20 percent of families increased $2,657, from $13,430 to $16,088.[168]
- From the late 1980s to the mid-2000s, the average income of the middle 20 percent of families increased $4,528, from $40,046 to $44,574.[169]
- From the late 1980s to the mid-2000s, the average income of the richest 20 percent of families increased $32,813, from $93,846 to $126,658.[170]

Taxation:

- A 2009 study named Texas' tax system as one of the ten most regressive states in the nation.[171]
- A 2009 study found that Texas requires families in the bottom 20 percent of the income scale to pay more than three-and-a-half times as great a share of their earnings in taxes as the top 1 percent.[172]
- The poor in Texas pay 12.2 percent of their income in taxes, the fifth highest percentage in the country.[173]
- According to Americans for Prosperity, local government debt in Texas is over $175 billion.[174]

Transportation:

- Dallas–Ft. Worth and Houston were ranked 5th and 6th respectively among the 15 largest metropolitan cities in the yearly number of hours delayed in traffic.[175]
- Over the next 25 years, road use in Texas will grow by 214 percent, much of it concentrated in the state's most congested metropolitan areas.[176]
- Texas has 50,189 bridges, about 40 percent more than any other state.[177]
- In 2009, there were 3,071 traffic fatalities.[178]

Sex Education:

- In 2008, the birth rate for ages 15–19 in Texas was 63.4 per every 1,000 people, compared to 41.5 in the U.S., giving Texas the third highest teen birth rate in the nation.[179]

- According to a 2009 study of sex education materials from 96 percent of all Texas schools, only 4 percent of schools in Texas teach about pregnancy and STD prevention in schools.[180]

- 3.7 million Texas students are not taught basic information in public schools about STD prevention and unplanned pregnancies, and 25 percent of Texas school districts have no formal policy regulating sex education.[181]

- 41 percent of sex education materials used in Texas school districts contains factual errors.[182]

- 53 percent of Texas students have had sexual intercourse, compared with 48 percent nationwide; 17 percent of Texas students have had sexual intercourse with four or more persons in their life, compared with 15 percent nationwide; and 43.6 percent of Texas students did not use a condom during their last instance of sexual intercourse, compared with 38.5 percent nationwide.[183]

---

1 The Henry J. Kaiser Family Foundation. State Government Tax Collections per Capita, 2009. Online. Available at: http://www.statehealthfacts.org/comparemaptable.jsp?ind=30&cat=1. Accessed January 17, 2011.

2 The Henry J. Kaiser Family Foundation. Total State Expenditures per Capita, SFY2008. Online. Available at: http://www.statehealthfacts.org/comparemaptable.jsp?ind=32&cat=1. Accessed January 17, 2011.

3 Tax Foundation. State General Sales Tax Collections Per Capita, Fiscal Year 2008. Online. Available at: http://www.taxfoundation.org/research/show/23255.html. Accessed January 17, 2011.

4 National Education Association, *Rankings & Estimates* (December 2009). Online. Available at: http://www.nea.org/assets/docs/010rankings.pdf. Accessed January 13, 2011.

5 *Id.*

6 *Id.*

7 *Id.*

8 Texas Legislative Budget Board, *2010 Texas Fact Book.* Online. Available at: http://www.lbb.state.tx.us/Fact_Book/Texas_FactBook_2010.pdf. Accessed January 14, 2011.

9 *Id.*

10 U.S. Census Bureau, *Public Education Finances 2008* (June 2010). Online. Available at: http://www2.census.gov/govs/school/08f33pub.pdf. Accessed January 21, 2011.

11 *College Board, College-Bound Seniors 2009.* Online. Available at: http://pro fessionals.collegeboard.com/profdownload/cbs-2009-Table-3_Mean-SAT-CR-MATH-and-Writing-Scores-by-State.pdf. Accessed: January 21, 2011.

12 Brookings Institution, *State of Metropolitan America.* (May 2010). Online. Available at: http://www.brookings.edu/~/media/Files/Programs/Met ro/state_of_metro_america/metro_america_report.pdf. Accessed January 19, 2011.

13 Texas Legislative Budget Board, *2010 Texas Fact Book.* Online. Available at: http://www.lbb.state.tx.us/Fact_Book/Texas_FactBook_2010.pdf. Accessed January 14, 2011.

14 *Id.*

15 *Id.*

16 ArtBistro, States Ranked by Funding for the Arts. Online Available at http://artbistro.monster.com/careers/articles/9960-states-ranked-by-funding-for-the-arts?print=true. Accessed January 31, 2011.

17 US Centers for Disease Control & Prevention, National Vital Statistics Report, 59(03). Online. Available at: http://www.cdc.gov/nchs/data/nvsr/nvsr59/nvsr59_03.pdf Accessed January 17, 2011.

18 The Henry J. Kaiser Family Foundation, *Population Distribution by Age, states (2008-2009), U.S. (2009).* Online. Available at: http://www.state healthfacts.org/comparebar.jsp?typ=2&ind=2&cat=1&sub=1&cha=1&o=a. Accessed January 31, 2011.

19 The Henry J. Kaiser Family Foundation, *Health Insurance Coverage of Children 0–18, states (2008–2009), U.S. (2009).* Online. Available at: http://www.statehealthfacts.org/comparetable.jsp?typ=2&ind=127&cat=3&sub=39&sortc=5&o=a. Accessed January 31, 2011.

20 The Henry J. Kaiser Family Foundation, *Poverty Rate by Age, states (2008–2009), U.S. (2009).* Online. Available at: http://www.statehealth facts.org/comparemaptable.jsp?ind=10&cat=1&sub=2&yr=199&typ=2 Accessed January 31, 2011.

21 The Henry J. Kaiser Family Foundation, *Percent of Children Age 19–35 Months Who Are Immunized, 2009.* Online. Available at: http://www .statehealthfacts.org/comparemaptable.jsp?typ=2&ind=54&cat=2&sub= 15&sortc=1&o=a. Accessed January 31, 2011.

22 The Henry J. Kaiser Family Foundation, *Percent of Children (10–17) who are Overweight or Obese, 2007.* Online. Available at: http://www.state healthfacts.org/comparemaptable.jsp?typ=2&ind=51&cat=2&sub=14&s ortc=1&o=a. Accessed January 31, 2011.

23 The Henry J. Kaiser Family Foundation, *State Health Facts Online, Health Insurance Coverage of the Total Population, states (2008–2009).* Online. Available at: http://www.statehealthfacts.org/comparetable.jsp?ind=125&cat =3. Accessed January 14, 2011.

24 The Henry J. Kaiser Family Foundation, *Health Insurance Coverage of Nonelderly 0–64, states (2008–2009), U.S. (2009).* Online. Available at: http://www .statehealthfacts.org/comparetable.jsp?ind=126&cat=3. Accessed January 14, 2011.

25 The Henry J. Kaiser Family Foundation, *State Health Facts Online, Health Insurance Coverage of Low Income Adults 19–64 (under 200% FPL), states (2008–2009), U.S. (2009).* Online. Available at: http://www.statehealth facts.org/comparetable.jsp?ind=878&cat=3. Accessed January 14, 2011.

26 The Henry J. Kaiser Family Foundation, *State Health Facts Online, Employer-Sponsored Coverage Rates for the Nonelderly by Age, states (2008– 2009), U.S. (2009).* Online. Available at: http://www.statehealthfacts .org/comparetable.jsp?ind=149&cat=3. Accessed January 16, 2011.

27 The Henry J. Kaiser Family Foundation, *State Health Facts Online, Total State Government Health Expenditures as Percent of the Gross State Product.* Online. Available at: http://www.statehealthfacts.org/comparemaptable .jsp?ind=263&cat=5. Accessed January 16, 2011.

28 The Henry J. Kaiser Family Foundation, *State Health Facts Online, State Mental Health Agency Per Capita Mental Health Services Expenditures, FY2005.* Online. Available at: http://www.statehealthfacts.org/compare maptable.jsp?ind=278&cat=5. Accessed January 16, 2011.

29 The Henry J. Kaiser Family Foundation, *State Health Facts Online, Total Medicaid Spending, FY2008.* Online. Available at: http://www.state healthfacts.org/comparetable.jsp?ind=177&cat=4&sub=47&yr=44&typ =4&sort=a. Accessed January 14, 2011.

30 The Henry J. Kaiser Family Foundation, *State Health Facts Online, Percents of Adults who Participated in Moderate or Vigorous Physical Activities, 2009.* Online. Available at: http://www.statehealthfacts.org/comparemaptable .jsp?ind=92&cat=2 Accessed January 14, 2011.

31 The Henry J. Kaiser Family Foundation, *State Health Facts Online, Health Care Expenditures per Capita by State of Residence, 2004.* Online. Available at: http://www.statehealthfacts.org/comparemaptable.jsp?ind=596&cat=5. Accessed January 14, 2011.

32 The Henry J. Kaiser Family Foundation, *State Health Facts Online, Hospital Beds per 1,000 Population, 2008.* Online. Available at: http://www .statehealthfacts.org/comparemaptable.jsp?ind=384&cat=8 Accessed January 14, 2011.

33 U.S. Department of Health and Human Services, *National Center for Health Workforce Analysis, 2000.* Online. Accessed January 17, 2011. http://bhpr .hrsa.gov/healthworkforce/reports/statesummaries/texas.html

34 *Id.*

35 *Id.*

36 The Henry J. Kaiser Family Foundation, *Distribution of Total Population by Federal Poverty Level, states (2008–2009), U.S. (2009).* Online. Available at: http://www.statehealthfacts.org/comparebar.jsp?typ=2&ind=9&cat= 1&sub=2&cha=1803&o=a. Accessed February 1, 2011.

37 U.S. Department of Agriculture, Economic Research Service, *Prevalence of Household-level food insecurity and very low food security by State, average 2006–08* (November 2007) at Table 7. Online. Available at http://www.ers .usda.gov/Publications/ERR83/ERR83.pdf. Accessed February 1, 2011.

38 U.S. Department of Agriculture, Food and Nutrition Services, *WIC Program: Average Monthly Benefit Per Person, FY 2009.* Online at: http://www .fns.usda.gov/pd/25wifyavgfd$.htm. Accessed February 1, 2011.

39 The Henry J. Kaiser Family Foundation, *Percent of Adults Who are Overweight or Obese, 2009.* Online. Available at: http://www.statehealthfacts. org/comparemaptable.jsp?typ=2&ind=89&cat=2&sub=26&sortc=1& o=a. Accessed February 1, 2011.

40 The Henry J. Kaiser Family Foundation, *Number of Deaths Due to Diseases of the Heart per 100,000 Population, 2007.* Online. Available at: http:// www.statehealthfacts.org/comparemaptable.jsp?typ=3&ind=77&cat=2& sub=23&sortc=1&o=a. Accessed February 1, 2011.

41 The Henry J. Kaiser Family Foundation, *Percent of Adults Who Have Ever Been Told by a Doctor that They Have Diabetes (2009).* Online. Available at: http://www.statehealthfacts.org/comparemaptable.jsp?typ=2&ind=70& cat=2&sub=22&sortc=1&o=a. Accessed February 1, 2011.

42 The Henry J. Kaiser Family Foundation, *Number of Diabetes Deaths per 100,000 Population, 2007.* Online. Available at: http://www.statehealth facts.org/comparemaptable.jsp?typ=3&ind=74&cat=2&sub=22&sortc=1 &o=a. Accessed February 1, 2011.

43 The Henry J. Kaiser Family Foundation, *Percentage of Adults Who Visited the Dentist or Dental Clinic with the Past Year, 2008.* Online. Available at: http://www.statehealthfacts.org/comparemaptable.jsp?typ=2&ind=108 &cat=2&sub=30&sortc=1&o=a. Accessed February 1, 2011.

44 US Centers for Disease Control & Prevention, National Vital Statistics Report, 59(03). Online. Available at: http://www.cdc.gov/nchs/data/ nvsr/nvsr59/nvsr59_03.pdf Accessed January 17, 2011.

45 *Id.*

46 *Id.*

47 *Id.*

48 The Henry J. Kaiser Family Foundation, Health Insurance Coverage of Women 0–64, states (2008–2009), U.S. (2009). Online. Available at: http://www.statehealthfacts.org/comparetable.jsp?typ=2&ind=132&cat =3&sub=178&sortc=5&o =a. Accessed January 15, 2011.

49 The Henry J. Kaiser Family Foundation, *State Health Facts Online, Percentage of Women who Visited the Dentist or Dental Clinic within the Past Year, 2006.* Online. Available at: http://www.statehealthfacts.org/compare maptable.jsp?ind=486&cat=10. Accessed January 12, 2011.

50 The Kaiser Family Foundation, Percent of Women Age 40 and Older Who Report Having a Mammogram Within the Last Two Years, 2008. Online. Available at: http://www.statehealthfacts.org/comparetable.jsp? ind=479&cat=10&sub=113&yr=63&typ=2&sort=a. Accessed January 17, 2011.

51 The Kaiser Family Foundation, Percent of Women Age 18 and Older Who Report Having a Pap Smear Within the Last Three Years, 2008. Online. Available at: http://www.statehealthfacts.org/comparetable.jsp? ind=482&cat=10&sub=113&yr=63&typ=2&sort=a. Accessed January 17, 2011.

52 The Kaiser Family Foundation, Breast Cancer Incidence Rate per 100,000 Women, 2006. Online. Available at: http://www.statehealth facts.org/comparetable.jsp?ind=469&cat=10&sub=112&yr=17&typ=3& sort=a. Accessed January 17, 2011.

53 The Kaiser Family Foundation, Cervical Cancer Incidence Rates per 100,000 Women, 2006. Online. Available at: http://www.statehealth facts.org/comparetable.jsp?ind=473&cat=10&sub=112&yr=17&typ=3& sort=a. Accessed January 17, 2011.

54 The Kaiser Family Foundation, Percent Women Who Report Ever Being Told by a Doctor they have High Blood Pressure, 2007. Online. Available at: http://www.statehealthfacts.org/comparetable.jsp?ind=477&cat= 10&sub=112&yr=18&typ=2&sort=a. Accessed January 17, 2011.

55 Guttmacher Institute, Contraceptive Needs and Services: National and State Date, 2008 Update. Online. Available at: http://www.guttmacher .org/pubs/win/contraceptive-needs-2008.pdf. Accessed January 17, 2011.

56 United Health Foundation: America's Health Rankings, Prenatal Care 2010. Online. Available at: http://www.americashealthrankings.org/ Measure/2010/Listpercent20All/Prenatalpercent20Care.aspx. Accessed January 17, 2011.

57 US Census Bureau: Voting and Registration, Table 4B: Reported Voting and Registration of the Voting Age Population, by Sex, Race and Hispanic Origin, for States: November 2008. Online. Available at: http:// www.census.gov/hhes/www/socdemo/voting/publications/p20/2008/ Tablepercent2004b.xls. Accessed January 17, 2011.

58 *Id*.

59 The Henry J. Kaiser Family Foundation, *Adult Poverty Rates by Gender, states (2008–2009), US (2009)*. Online. Available at: http://www .statehealthfacts.org/comparetable.jsp?ind=12&cat=1&sub=2&yr=199& typ=2 Accessed January 17, 2011.

60 Institute for Women's Policy Research, *The Status of Women in Texas, 2004*. Online. Available at: http://www.guttmacher.org/pubs/state_ data/states/texas.pdf. Accessed January 12, 2011. Figures based on the 2000 Census.

61 US Census Bureau, Survey of Business Owners, Women-Owned Businesses, 2007, Summary Statistics for Women-Owned Business by State: 2007. Online. Available at: http://www2.census.gov/econ/sbo/07/final/ tables/women_table2.xls. Accessed January 17, 2011.

62 US Census Bureau, Median Earnings for Female Full-Time, Year Round Workers, 2005–2009. Online. Available at: http://factfinder .census.gov/servlet/GCTTable?_bm=y&-context=gct&ds_name= ACS_2009_5YR_G00_&-mt_name=ACS_2009_5YR_G00_GCT 2002_US9F&-CONTEXT=gct&tree_id=5309&-geo_id=&-format =US-9F&-_lang=en. Accessed January 17, 2011.

63 IBM, *Visualizations: Subprime loans per 1000* Online. Available at: http:// www.958.ibm.com/software/data/cognos/manyeyes/visualizations/89 ade5ae1acac007011ad6a6255b0313/comments/3d7f0cf6ad9f11dd b3a3000255111976. Accessed January 17, 2011.

64 Corporation for Enterprise Development, *Assets and Opportunity Scorecard, 2009–2010, Median Debt as % of Home Value*. Online. Available at: http://scorecard.cfed.org/housing.php?page=mortgage_debt_percent age_home_value. Accessed January 17, 2011.

65 Corporation for Enterprise Development, *Assets and Opportunity Scorecard,*

2009–2010, Foreclosure Rate. Online. Available at: http://scorecard.cfed
.org/housing.php?page=foreclosure_rate. Accessed January 17, 2011.

66 Corporation for Enterprise Development, *Assets and Opportunity Scorecard, 2009–2010, Private Loans to Small Businesses.* Online. Available at:
http://scorecard.cfed.org/business.php?page=private_loans_small_busi
ness Accessed January 17, 2011.

67 Corporation for Enterprise Development, *Assets and Opportunity Scorecard, 2009–2010, Asset Poverty Rate.* Online. Available at: http://scorecard
.cfed.org/financial.php?page=asset_poverty_rate. Accessed January 17,
2011.

68 Corporation for Enterprise Development, *Assets and Opportunity Scorecard,
2009–2010, Net Worth.* Online. Available at: http://scorecard.cfed.org/
financial.php?page=net_worth. Accessed January 17, 2011.

69 Experian, *National Score Index.* Online. Available at http://www.national
scoreindex.com/. Accessed January 17, 2011.

70 Corporation for Enterprise Development, *Assets and Opportunity Scorecard, 2009–2010.* Online. Available at: http://scorecard.cfed.org/business
.php?page=retirement_plan_participation. Accessed January 17, 2011.

71 *Id.*

72 CreditReport.com, *Average Credit Scores by State.* Online. Available at:
http://www.creditreport.com/creditscores/creditratings/average-credit-
scores.aspx. Accessed January 17, 2011.

73 U.S. Environmental Protection Agency, *Energy CO2 Emissions by State,*
(2005). Online . Available at: http://www.epa.gov/climatechange/emis
sions/downloads/CO2FFC_2005.xls. Accessed January 12, 2011.

74 Scorecard: The Pollution Information Site, *Rankings of States by Air
Pollutants Emissions.* Online. Available at http://www.scorecard.org/
env-releases/cap/rank-states-emissions.tcl. Accessed January 14, 2011.

75 Scorecard: The Pollution Information Site, *States with Reported Releases of
Toxics Release Inventory: Water Releases.* Online. Available at: http://www
.scorecard.org/ranking/rankstates.tcl?how_many=100&drop_down_
name=Water+releases. Accessed January 14, 2011.

76 Scorecard: The Pollution Information Site, *States with Reported Releases of
Recognized Carcinogens to Air.* Online. Available at: http://www.scorecard
.org/ranking/rankstates.tcl?how_many=100&drop_down_name=Recog
nized+carcinogens+to+air. Accessed January 14, 2011.

77 U.S. Environmental Protection Agency, *National Biennial Resource Conservation and Recovery Act (RCRA) Hazardous Waste Report: Based on 2009 Data,*
(November 2010), Exhibit 1.2. Online. Available at: http://www.epa.gov/
osw/inforesources/data/br09/national09.pdf. Accessed January 31, 2011.

78 *Id.*

79 *Id.*

80 Texas Legislative Budget Board, *2010 Texas Fact Book.* Online. Available at: http://www.lbb.state.tx.us/Fact_Book/Texas_FactBook_2010.pdf. Accessed January 14, 2011.

81 U.S. Department of Energy, "Table R2. Energy Consumption by Source and Total Consumption per Capita, Ranked by State, 2008." Online. Available at: http://www.eia.gov/emeu/states/hf.jsp?incfile=sep_sum/plain_html/rank_use_per_cap.html. Accessed January 14, 2011.

82 Bureau of Labor Statistics. Average hours and earnings of production employees on manufacturing payrolls in States. Government Employment & Payroll. Online. Available at: http://www.bls.gov/sae/eetables/saetableb19.pdf. Accessed January 17, 2011.

83 US Census Bureau. Government Employment & Payroll. Online. Available at: http://www2.census.gov/govs/apes/09stlall.xls. Accessed January 17, 2011.

84 The Henry J. Kaiser Family Foundation. *Total Number of Workers Represented by Unions, 2010.* Online. Available at: http://www.statehealth facts.org/comparemaptable.jsp?yr=138&typ=2&ind=20&cat=1&sub=5. Accessed January 17, 2011.

85 Corporation for Enterprise Development, *Assets and Opportunity Scorecard, 2009–2010, Workers Compensation Coverage.* Online. Available at: http://scorecard.cfed.org/business.php?page=workers_comp_coverage. Accessed January 17, 2011.

86 PBS. *State-by-state income inequality.* Online. Available at: http://www.cbpp.org/states/4-9-08sfp-facttx.pdf. Accessed January 25, 2011.

87 *Id.*

88 The Henry J. Kaiser Family Foundation, *Median Annual Household Income, 2007–2009.* Online. Available at http://www.statehealthfacts.org/comparemaptable.jsp?ind=15&cat=1. Accessed January 17, 2011.

89 Assets and Opportunity Score Card, *Homeownership Rate.* Online. Available at http://scorecard.cfed.org/housing.php?page=homeownership_rate. Accessed January 17, 2011.

90 Suite 101, *Average Home Insurance Rates by State (November 2009).* Online. Available at http://www.suite101.com/content/average_home_insurance_rate_by_state_a168687 Accessed January 17, 2011.

91 Insure.com, *The Most and Least Expensive States for Car Insurance in 2010 (July 2010).* Online. Available at http://www.insure.com/car-insurance/most-and-least-expensive-states-2010.html Accessed January 17, 2011.

92 CreditCards.com, *Bankruptcy Filings, State by State, 2005–2010.* Online.

Available at http://www.creditcards.com/credit-card-news/state-bank ruptcy-filings-statistics-1276.php Accessed January 17, 2011.

93 Household Internet Usage by Type of Internet Connection and State: 2009 (October 2009). Online. Available at http://www.census.gov/ compendia/statab/2011/tables/11s1156.pdf Accessed January 17, 2011.

94 Death Penalty Information Center, Number of Executions by State and Region Since 1976. Online. Available at http://www.deathpenaltyinfo .org/number-executions-state-and-region-1976. Accessed January 14, 2011.

95 BURDEN OF INCARCERATION By John Bebow | Published: March 17, 2010. http://www.thecenterformichigan.net/burden-of-incarceration/. Accessed January 14, 2011.

96 2011, CQ Press, A Division of SAGE Publications. All Rights Reserved. Available online http://os.cqpress.com/rankings/2010/Crime_State_ Rankings_2010.pdf. Accessed January 14, 2011.

97 The Henry J. Kaiser Family Foundation, State Health Facts Online Violent Crime Offenses Rate per 100,000 Inhabitants, 2009 Online. Available at http://www.statehealthfacts.org/comparemaptable.jsp?ind=117&cat=2. Accessed January 14, 2011.

98 The Disaster Center.com United States: Uniform Crime Report —State Statistics from 1960—2009. Online. Available at http://www.disaster center.com/crime/txcrime.htm. Accessed January 14, 2011.

99 The Henry J. Kaiser Family Foundation, State Health Facts Online Number of Deaths Due to Injury by Firearms per 100,000 Population, 2007. Available at http://www.statehealthfacts.org/comparemaptable.jsp? ind=113&cat=2. Accessed January 14, 2011.

100 The Disaster Center.com United States: Uniform Crime Report —State Statistics from 1960–2009. Online. Available at: http://www.disaster center.com/crime/txcrime.htm. Accessed January 14, 2011.

101 Id.

102 Id.

103 Id.

104 Id.

105 U.S. Census Bureau, Voting and Registration in the Election of November 2008, Table 4b, Reported Voting and Registration of the Voting-Age Population, by Sex, Race and Hispanic Origin, for States: November 2008. Online. Available at: http://www.census.gov/hhes/www/ socdemo/voting/publications/p20/2008/tables.html. Accessed January 15, 2011.

106 Id.

107 Texas Department of Family Services. 2010. Online. Available at: http://www.dfps.state.tx.us/about/Data_Books_and_Annual_Reports/2010/cps_27-70.asp. Accessed January 31, 2011.

108 "Texas Dept. of Family & Protective Services Marks Go Blue Day Against Child Abuse." KBTX, April 6, 2010. http://www.kbtx.com/state/headlines/90021092.html Accessed January 31, 2011.

109 U.S. Centers for Disease Control and Prevention, National Information Services Survey, 2009. Online. Available at http://www.cdc.gov/vaccines/stats-surv/nis/data/tables_2009.htm Accessed January 31, 2011

110 National Center for Children in Poverty, Columbia University, Mailman School of Public Health, *Demographics of Low-Income Children: Texas* (January 2011). Online. Available at http://nccp.org/profiles/TX_profile_6.html. Accessed January 15, 2011.

111 *Id.*

112 *Id.*

113 *Id.*

114 Center on Budget and Policy Priorities, *TANF Payment Levels (June 2009)*. Online. Available at: http://www.isedsolutions.org/sites/default/files/TANFpercent20levelspercent20mappercent20(5)percent5B1percent5D_0.ppt. Accessed January 13, 2011.

115 U.S. Department of Agriculture, Food and Nutrition Service, *Average Monthly WIC Benefits per Person, 2010 (Preliminary)*. Online. Available at http://www.fns.usda.gov/pd/25wifyavgfd$.htm Accessed January 14, 2011.

116 The Henry J. Kaiser Family Foundation, *State Health Facts Online, Health Insurance Coverage of Children 0–18 Living in Poverty (under 100percent FPL), states (2008–2009), U.S. (2009)*. Online. Available at: http://www.statehealthfacts.org/comparebar.jsp?ind=128&cat=3. Accessed January 14, 2011.

117 U.S. Department of Education, *Texas State Detailed Snapshot, 2008*. Online. Available at: http://www.eddataexpress.ed.gov/state-report-detailed.cfm?state=TX . Accessed February 2, 2011.

118 *Id.*

119 *Id.*

120 *Id.*

121 Germeraad, Stephanie. *Educational Trust, Ed Trust Releases Their Fair Share Report and Web Tool Exposing Gaps in Teacher Quality in Texas, 2008*. Online. Available at: http://www.edtrust.org/dc/pressroom/press-release/ed-trust-releases-their-fair-share-report-and-web-tool-exposing-gaps-in-. Accessed on February 2, 2011.

122   *Id.*

123   *Id.*

124   U.S. Department of Education, *Texas State Detailed Snapshot, 2008.* Online. Available at: http://www.eddataexpress.ed.gov/state-report-detailed.cfm?state=TX . Accessed February 2, 2011.

125   The College Board, "The College Completion Agenda 2010 Progress Report". Online. Available at: http://completionagenda.collegeboard.org/sites/default/files/reports_pdf/Progress_Report_201 0.pdf. Accessed February 2, 2011.

126   *Id.*

127   *Id.*

128   *Id.*

129   The College Board, "The College Completion Agenda: Texas". Online. Available at: http://completionagenda.collegeboard.org/state-perfor mance/state/texas. Accessed February 2, 2011.

130   US Census Bureau, Fact Finder. "2005–2009 American Community Survey 5-Year Estimates". Online. Available at: http://factfinder.census. gov/home/saff/main.html?_lang=en Accessed February 2, 2011.

131   US News and World Report, "Best Colleges 2011". Online. Available at: http://colleges.usnews.rankingsandreviews.com/best-colleges/national-universities-rankings/state+TX. Accessed February 2, 2011.

132   Commission for a College Ready Texas, *The Report of the Commission for a College Ready Texas* (November 2007) at 18. Online. Available at: http://www.collegereadytexas.org/documents/CCRTpercent20Report-percent20FINAL.pdf. Accessed January 12, 2011.

133   The National Center for Public Policy and Higher Education, *Measuring Up 2008, The State Report Card on Higher Education* at 7. Online. Available at: http://measuringup2008.highereducation.org/print/state_reports/long/TX.pdf. Accessed January 12, 2011.

134   *Id.*

135   The National Center for Public Policy and Higher Education, *Measuring Up 2008, The State Report Card on Higher Education* at 9. Online. Available at: http://measuringup2008.highereducation.org/print/state_reports/long/TX.pdf. Accessed January 12, 2011.

136   *Id.*

137   The Henry J. Kaiser Family Foundation, *Poverty Rate by Age, states (2008–2009),* U.S. (2009). Online. Available at: http://www.statehealthfacts.org/comparebar.jsp?ind=10&cat=1. Accessed February 2, 2011.

138   The Henry J. Kaiser Family Foundation, *Retail Prescription Drugs Filled at Pharmacies (Annual per Capita by Age), 2009.* Online. Available at: http://www.

statehealthfacts.org/comparetable.jsp?ind=268&cat=5. Accessed February 2, 2011.

139 Texas Department of Aging and Disability Services, *Legislative Appropriations Request for Fiscal Year 2008–2009* (August 2006). Online. Available at http://cfoweb.dads.state.tx.us/lar/2008_09/VolumeI//Administrator Statement.pdf. Accessed January 12, 2011.

140 Texas Department of Family and Protective Services (October 2009). Online. Available at http://www.dfps.state.tx.us/About/News/2009/2009-10-02_exploitation.asp. Accessed February 02, 2011.

141 The Henry J. Kaiser Family Foundation, Medicaid and the Uninsured (September 2010). Online. Available at: http://www.kff.org/uninsured/upload/7806-03.pdf.Accessed February 2, 2011.

142 The Henry J. Kaiser Family Foundation, State Health Facts Online, Health Insurance Coverage of the Total Population, states (2008–2009), U.S. (2009). Online. Available at: http://www.statehealthfacts.org/compare table.jsp?typ=1&ind=125&cat=3&sub=39 Accessed February 2, 2011.

143 United States Department of Agriculture, Economic Research Service. County-Level Unemployment and Median Household Income for Texas. Online. Available at: http://www.statehealthfacts.org/comparetable.jsp?typ=4&ind=271&cat=5&sub=67. Accessed February 2, 2011.

144 Bailey, W. Scott.San Antonio Buiness Journal. Reach of employer-sponsored health coverage shrinking in Texas. Online. http://www.bizjournals.com/sanantonio/print-edition/2010/11/26/reach-of-employersponsored-health.html. Accessed on February 2, 2011.

145 The Henry J. Kaiser Family Foundation, State Health Facts Online, Uninsured Estimates of Children 0–17, American Community Survey (ACS), 2009. Online. Available at:http://www.statehealthfacts.org/com paremaptable.jsp?ind=883&cat=3. Accessed February 2, 2011.

146 The Henry J. Kaiser Family Foundation, State Health Facts Online, Texas: Health Insurance Coverage of Adults 19–64 Living in Poverty (under 100percent FPL), states (2008–2009), U.S. (2009). Online. Available at: http://www.statehealthfacts.org/profileind.jsp?ind=131&cat=3&rgn=45. Accessed on February 2, 2011.

147 The Henry J. Kaiser Family Foundation, State Health Facts Online, Texas: Distribution of the Nonelderly Uninsured by Race/Ethnicity, states (2008–2009), U.S. (2009). Online. Available at: http://www.state healthfacts.org/profileind.jsp?ind=138&cat=3&rgn=45. Accessed on February 2, 2011.

148 *Id.*

149 The Henry J. Kaiser Family Foundation, State Health Facts Online,

Texas: Nonelderly Uninsured. Online. Available at: http://www.state healthfacts.org/profileind.jsp?cat=3&sub=40&rgn=45. Accessed on February 2, 2011.

150   The Henry J. Kaiser Family Foundation, State Health Facts Online, Texas: Nonelderly Uninsured. Online. Available at: http://www.state healthfacts.org/profileind.jsp?cat=3&sub=40&rgn=45. Accessed on February 2, 2011.

151   Charles, Thomas. Medicaid Income Guidelines in Texas. Ehow. Online. Available at: http://www.ehow.com/list_6772571_medicaid-income-guidelines-texas.html. Accessed on February 2, 2011.

152   Texas Department of State Health Services, *The Supply of and Demand for Registered Nurses and Nurse Graduates in Texas.* Online. Available at: http://www.dshs.state.tx.us/chs/cnws/SB132rep.pdf. Accessed January 12, 2011.

153   National Association of Community Health Centers, *Access Transformed* (August 2008). Online. Available at: http://www.nachc.com/client/doc uments/ACCESSpercent20Transformedpercent20fullpercent20report. PDF Accessed January 12, 2011.

154   Texas Board of Nursing, *Texas Board of Nursing Currently Licensed Texas RN's by County of Residence-09/2010.* Online. Available at: http://www .bon.state.tx.us/about/stats/10-co-rn.pdf. Accessed February 2, 2011.

155   *Id.*

156   *Id.*

157   *Id.*

158   *Id.*

159   *Id.*

160   *Id*

161   U.S. Department of Commerce, Bureau of Economic Analysis. Online. Available at: http://www.bea.gov/newsreleases/regional/spi/2010/pdf/ spi0310.pdf. Accessed January 14, 2011.

162   *Fort Worth Star-Telegram,* "More Texans living in poverty, census figures show," September 16, 2010. Online. Available at: http://www .star-telegram.com/2010/09/16/2474711/more-texans-living-in-pov erty.html#ixzz1CqLP67Ys. Accessed January 16, 2011.

163   AFL-CIO, Union members by state. Online. Available at: http://www .aflcio.org/joinaunion/why/uniondifference/uniondiff16.cfm. Accessed February 1, 2011.

164   National Center for Children in Poverty, Columbia University, *Texas Family Economic Security Profile* (2007). Online. Available at: http://www .nccp.org/profiles/pdf/profile_fes_TX.pdf. Accessed January 12, 2011.

165   Texas Department of State Health Services, *Supply Trends Among Licensed*

Health Professionals, Texas 1980–2007, Third Edition (December 2007) at 2. Online. Available at: http://www.dshs.state.tx.us/CHS/hprc/07trends .pdf. Accessed January 12, 2011.

166 Center on Budget and Policy Priorities and Economic Policy Institute, *Pulling Apart: A State By State Analysis of Income Trends (April 2008).* Online. Available at: http://www.cbpp.org/states/4-9-08sfp-facttx.pdf. Accessed January 12, 2011.

167 *Id.*

168 *Id.*

169 Id

170 *Id.*

171 Institute on Taxation and Economic Policy, *"Who Pays? A Distributional Analysis of the Tax Systems of All 50 States."* (November 2009). Online. Available at: http://www.itepnet.org/whopays3.pdf Accessed January 31, 2011.

172 *Id.*

173 *Id.*

174 Americans for Prosperity, "Legacy of Local Government Debt." January 24, 2011. Online. Available at: https://americansforprosperity.org/ 012411-legacy-local-government-debt. Accessed January 29, 2011.

175 Texas Transportation Institute, *2010 Urban Mobility Report.* Online. Available at http://mobility.tamu.edu/ums/congestion_data/national_conges tion_tables.stm Accessed January 17, 2011.

176 Texas Department of Transportation, *Strategic Plan 2009-13* at 3. Online. Available at: ftp://ftp.dot.state.tx.us/pub/txdot-info/lao/public_strategic_ plan2009.pdf. Accessed January 12, 2011.

177 *Id.*

178 *Houston Chronicle*, "Texas road deaths fall to lowest level ever," September 17, 2010. Online. Available at: http://www.chron.com/disp/story.mpl/metro politan/7206674.html. Accessed January 20, 2011.

179 The Henry J. Kaiser Family Foundation, *State Health Facts Online, Teen Birth Rate per 1,000 Population Ages 15–19, 2005.* Online. Available at: http://www.statehealthfacts.org/comparemaptable.jsp?ind=37&cat=2. Accessed January 12, 2011.

180 Texas Freedom Network Education Fund, *Just Say Don't Know: Sexuality Education in Texas Public Schools.* January 2009. Online. Available at: http://www.tfn.org/site/PageServer?pagename=issues_public_schools_ sex_education_jsdk_report_index. Accessed January 17, 2011.

181 *Id.*

182 *Id.*

183 *Id.*

Index

About the Author

Gail Collins is an op-ed columnist for the *New York Times*. From 2001 to 2007 she was the editor of the *Times* editorial page, the first woman ever to hold that job. In her earlier incarnations she was a columnist for *New York Newsday* and the *Daily News*. She is the author of six books, including *When Everything Changed: The Amazing Journey of American Women from 1960 to the Present* and a recent biography of President William Henry Harrison.

Collins, who lives in Manhattan with her husband, Dan Collins, was born in Ohio, which produced way more presidents than Texas but still does not seem to have the same cachet.